Psychological Experts in Divorce Actions

Third Edition

By Marc J. Ackerman and Andrew W. Kane

Psychological Experts in Divorce Actions is the definitive guide to understanding the role of psychological evaluations in divorce and custody cases. Written with the practicing family lawyer in mind, the book explains how the tests are administered, how their results are commonly interpreted and reported, and how to use the findings to your clients' best advantage. Suggested questions are provided for the effective examination and cross-examination of psychological experts that can be used verbatim or with minor modifications. Helpful checklists and case law summaries are additional practice aids in handling the gamut of client-related psychological issues that arise in divorce and custody cases.

Highlights of the 2004 Cumulative Supplement

Some of the vital legal issues and developing scientific advances discussed in the 2004 Supplement include:

- The New American Psychological Association Code of Ethics
- Cases and studies on relocation issues
- Updates to the sections on The Stanford-Binet Intelligence Scale and the Wechsler Scales
- Discussion of the outcome of a new study entitled, *Experienced Custody Evaluators Views of Controversial Issues*
- Updates to the case digests for Chapters 1 and 4

The Table of Cases and Index have been completely updated for this supplement.

12/03

For questions concerning this shipment, billing, or other customer service matters, call our Customer Service Department at 1-800-234-1660.

For toll-free ordering, please call 1-800-638-8437.

A WoltersKluwer Company

PSYCHOLOGICAL EXPERTS IN DIVORCE ACTIONS
Third Edition

2004 Cumulative Supplement

This supplement supersedes all previous supplements

PSYCHOLOGICAL EXPERTS IN DIVORCE ACTIONS
Third Edition

2004 Cumulative Supplement

MARC J. ACKERMAN

ANDREW W. KANE

1185 Avenue of the Americas, New York, NY 10036
www.aspenpublishers.com

A Wolters Kluwer Company
www.aspenpublishers.com

Printed in the United States of America.

ISBN 0-7355-4335-6

About Aspen Publishers

Aspen Publishers, headquartered in New York City, is a leading information provider for attorneys, business professionals, and law students. Written by preeminent authorities, our products consist of analytical and practical information covering both U.S. and international topics. We publish in the full range of formats, including updated manuals, books, periodicals, CDs, and online products.

Our proprietary content is complemented by 2,500 legal databases, containing over 11 million documents, available through our Loislaw division. Aspen Publishers also offers a wide range of topical legal and business databases linked to Loislaw's primary material. Our mission is to provide accurate, timely, and authoritative content in easily accessible formats, supported by unmatched customer care.

To order any Aspen Publishers title, go to *www.aspenpublishers.com* or call 1-800-638-8437.

To reinstate your manual update service, call 1-800-638-8437.

For more information on Loislaw products, go to *www.loislaw.com* or call 1-800-364-2512.

For Customer Care issues, e-mail *CustomerCare@aspenpublishers.com*; call 1-800-234-1660; or fax 1-800-901-9075.

ASPEN PUBLISHERS
A Wolters Kluwer Company

SUBSCRIPTION NOTICE

This Aspen Publishers product is updated on a periodic basis with supplements to reflect important changes in the subject matter. If you purchased this product directly from Aspen Publishers, we have already recorded your subscription for the update service.

If, however, you purchased this product from a bookstore and wish to receive future updates and revised or related volumes billed separately with a 30-day examination review, please contact our Customer Service Department at 1-800-234-1660, or send your name, company name (if applicable), address, and the title of the product to:

ASPEN PUBLISHERS
7201 McKinney Circle
Frederick, MD 21704

ABOUT THE AUTHORS

Marc J. Ackerman, Ph.D., is a licensed psychologist in the state of Wisconsin and has been involved in over 1,500 family law and personal injury cases in Wisconsin and throughout the United States. He has testified in hundreds of family law, personal injury, and sexual abuse cases, and has been involved in these cases in over 20 states. Dr. Ackerman co-developed the Ackerman-Schoendorf Scale for Parent Evaluation of Custody (ASPECT), published in 1992 by Western Psychological Services, and authored *Clinician's Guide to Child Custody Evaluations* (John Wiley & Sons, 1995) and "*Does Wednesday Mean Mom's House or Dad's*" (John Wiley and Sons, 1997). He served as a founding faculty member and dean of the Wisconsin School of Professional Psychology from 1981 to 1987. Former director of clinical training at the Wisconsin School of Professional Psychology, he is currently a clinical full professor at the school. Dr. Ackerman served as president of both the Wisconsin Psychological Association and the Milwaukee Area Psychological Association, and was a member of the Board of Governors of the Wisconsin Society of Clinical and Consulting Psychologists. Current president of the Wisconsin Psychology Foundation, Dr. Ackerman has been appointed co-chair of the Interdisciplinary Committee, sponsored by the Wisconsin Psychological Association and the Wisconsin Bar Association, and as a member of the Expert Panel on Psychiatric and Psychological Evidence of the ABA Commission on Mental and Physical Disability Law.

As co-director of North Shore Psychotherapy Associates, Dr. Ackerman is a member of the National Register of Health Service Providers in Psychology, the American Psychological Association, the Wisconsin Psychological Association, and the Milwaukee Area Psychological Association. In addition, he is a diplomate of the American Board of Forensic Examiners and the American Board of Medical Psychotherapists. Dr. Ackerman has written dozens of professional publications and given dozens of professional seminars throughout the United States. In April 1997, he gave two presentations at the joint American Bar Association and American Psychological Association Conference. He recently received an award from the Wisconsin Psychological Association for outstanding contributions to the advancement of psychology as an applied profession.

ABOUT THE AUTHORS

Andrew W. Kane, Ph.D., is a licensed psychologist in private practice in Milwaukee, Wisconsin. He is a diplomate of the American Board of Forensic Examiners, the American Board of Assessment Psychologists, and the American Board of Medical Psychotherapists and Psychodiagnosticians. He is listed in the National Register of Health Service Providers in Psychology, and is a recipient of the Certificate of Professional Qualification in Psychology of the Association of State and Provincial Psychology Boards. Dr. Kane has been designated as an expert in more than 2,500 cases involving involuntary civil commitment, guardianship, family law, personal injury, children's court, criminal court, and other cases.

Dr. Kane is a professor at the Wisconsin School of Professional Psychology, a clinical professor in the Department of Psychology at the University of Wisconsin-Milwaukee, and an associate clinical professor in the Department of Psychiatry and Behavioral Medicine at the Medical College of Wisconsin. He is the author or co-author of four books and nearly four dozen professional papers and chapters.

Dr. Kane was a member of the Expert Panel on Psychiatric and Psychological Evidence of the American Bar Association's Commission on Mental and Physical Disability Law. Dr. Kane is a former president of the Wisconsin Psychological Association and of its Division of Forensic and Correctional Psychologists. He is also a former president of the Milwaukee Area Psychological Association. Dr. Kane also served as a member of the board of the Wisconsin Psychological Association's forensic division, and of the Board of Governors of the Wisconsin Society of Clinical and Consulting Psychologists. Dr. Kane is the Chair of the Professional Issues Committee, and a member of the Ethics Committee, of the Wisconsin Psychological Association.

Dr. Kane founded the Wisconsin Coalition on Sexual Misconduct by Psychotherapists and Counselors, a national model program in this problem area.

CONTENTS

CONTENTS

CHAPTER 1

THE EXPERT WITNESS

§ 1.1 Overview

Page 5, insert before ***Types of Expertise Required*** *subsection:*

Changes in the Federal Rules of Evidence[16.1]

Several changes have been made in the Federal Rules of Evidence regarding expert witnesses. The changes took effect December 1, 2000. The changes are designed to codify the *Daubert* and *Kumho* requirements that expert testimony be based on research that is scientifically and methodologically sound, as well as reliable.

Rule 701. Opinion Testimony by Lay Witnesses

> If the witness is not testifying as an expert, the witness' testimony in the form of opinions or inferences is limited to those opinions or inferences which are (a) rationally based on the perception of the witness, and (b) helpful to a clear understanding of the witness' testimony or the determination of a fact in issue, and (c) not based on scientific, technical, or other specialized knowledge within the scope of Rule 702. [revised portion is underlined]

According to forensic-evidence.com,[16.2] the change in Rule 701 (Opinion Testimony by Law Witnesses) was designed to prevent experts from testifying by labeling them lay witnesses whose opinions are rationally based on their perceptions. It is also designed to preclude experts from avoiding the disclosure requirements of Federal Rule of Civil Procedure (Rule 26) and the Federal Rules of Criminal Procedure (Rule 16) by offering opinion testimony as lay witnesses in areas in which they are experts.

The most significant changes are in Rule 702 (Testimony by Experts):

[16.1] The revised Federal Rules of Evidence may be downloaded from http://www.house.gov/judiciary/evid00.pdf.

[16.2] www.forensic-evidence.com. Andre A. Moenssens, editor, University of Missouri-Kansas City School of Law.

Rule 702. Testimony by Experts

> If scientific, technical, or other specialized knowledge will assist the trier of fact to understand the evidence or to determine a fact in issue, a witness qualified as an expert by knowledge, skill, experience, training or education may testify thereto in the form of an opinion or otherwise, if (1) the testimony is based upon sufficient facts or data, (2) the testimony is the product of reliable principles and methods, and (3) the witness has applied the principles and methods reliably to the facts of the case. [revised portion is underlined]

The revised Rule gives judges the basic criteria to use in fulfilling their role as gatekeepers. According to forensic-evidence.com, the Committee Note that accompanied the amended language of the draft revision emphasized that the checklist for judges is not restricted. Judges may use whatever criteria they feel are necessary to establish the *Daubert* requirement that expert testimony is reliable, has been subject to peer review (or has not, for a good reason), the error rate, the presence of standards and controls, and whether the technique or theory has been generally accepted in the scientific community. In *Kumho*, the Supreme Court made it clear that these are guidelines, and that courts should use whatever criteria are applicable in assessment of a specific case. The Court also indicated that the requirement applies not only to scientific evidence but also to "technical" and "other specialized knowledge."

Further, the revised Rule attempts to ensure not only that the testimony of the expert is based upon sufficient facts or data, and is the product of reliable principles and methods, but also that the expert has reliably applied the principles and methods to the facts that are at issue in the instant case.

Rule 703. Bases of Opinion Testimony by Experts

> The facts or data in the particular case upon which an expert bases an opinion or inference may be those perceived by or made known to the expert at or before the hearing. If of a type reasonably relied upon by experts in the particular field in forming opinions or inferences upon the subject, the facts or data need not be admissible in evidence in order for the opinion or inference to be admitted. Facts or data that are otherwise inadmissible shall not be disclosed to the jury by the proponent of the opinion or inference unless the court determines that their probative value in assisting the jury to evaluate the expert's opinion substantially outweighs their prejudicial effect. [revised portion is underlined]

The revision to Rule 703 (Bases of Opinion Testimony by Experts) clarifies that it is the reliability of the information on which the expert bases his or her opinion that is relevant, not whether that underlying information is admissible or has been admitted into evidence. Further, acceptance of an opinion based on inadmissible evidence does not make that evidence admissible.

With these changes to Rules 701, 702, and 703, the Supreme Court's decisions in *Daubert* and *Kumho* have been codified. Regardless of how qualified the expert is in general, the emphasis is now not on those qualifications but, instead, on the quality of the testimony as defined by the above criteria. These changes do not alter the ability of an attorney to call an expert to testify regarding general principles without directly tying those principles to the instant case. So long as the expert's testimony is relevant and reliable, he or she may testify.[16.3]

§ 1.3 Definition of Psychologist

Page 16, insert after last paragraph:

Karl and Kristen Kirkland surveyed the 61 member boards of the Association of State and Provincial Psychology Boards (ASPPB) with regard to complaints received related to child custody evaluations.[70.1] They also found that 11 percent of the ethics adjudications of the American Psychological Association relate to child custody matters.

The authors found that, in the early 1980s, it was not unusual to find a psychologist allied with a legal team in an adversarial child custody contest. By the 1990s, however, ethics committees and licensing boards increasingly found that the "best interests of the child" standard required that psychologists be objective, independent, and child-oriented.

Thirty-four of the 61 licensing boards (56 percent) responded to the survey. They identified 2,413 complaints related to child custody evaluations between 1990 and 1999, but only 27 of those (1 percent) were adjudicated with a finding of fault. Disciplinary actions ranged from continuing education to five years' probation. An unknown, but likely substantial, number of confidential letters admonishing psychologists about their practices had also been issued, but data are not available from most boards or the ASPPB Disciplinary Data Bank. Most boards reported a substantial increase in the number of complaints in recent years. The num-

[16.3] Steven R. Smith, *Politics, Disability, Sexual Predators and More: Recent Decisions of the U.S. Supreme Court*, 22 Bulletin of the American Academy of Forensic Psychology 1, 6-18 at 15 (2001).

[70.1] Kirkland, Karl & Kristen L. Kirkland, *Frequency of Child Custody Evaluation Complaints and Related Disciplinary Action: A Survey of the Association of State and Provincial Psychology Boards*, 32 Professional Psychology: Research and Practice 171-74 (2001).

bers suggest that psychologists who do child custody evaluations should expect a licensing complaint to be filed against them at some point.

One state has responded to the marked increase of complaints by passing a law that prohibits the Colorado licensure board from disciplining psychologists on the basis of a child custody evaluation. The statute[70.2] indicates that "[t]he provisions of this article shall not apply to custodial evaluations undertaken in domestic relations cases in the courts of this state or domestic and child abuse evaluations undertaken for purposes of legal proceedings in the courts of this state."

§ 1.7 Board Certification

*Page 21, insert at end of **Psychologists** subsection:*

While the **American Board of Assessment Psychology** continues to exist as an independent body, it has also been made a section of the Division of Clinical Psychology of the American Psychological Association. The purpose of this dual existence is to permit people who do not wish, or are not qualified, to pursue the Diplomate to have the opportunity to share membership with the diplomates of the Board. It also permits diplomates who are not members of the American Psychological Association to participate in the Assessment Section of the APA Division of Clinical Psychology.

A similar arrangement has been in effect for a number of years between the American Psychology-Law Society and the Division of Forensic Psychology of the American Psychological Association. Members of the APA division are automatically members of the Society, but one may be a member of the Society without becoming a member of the APA division.

§ 1.8 Other Professional Organizations

*Page 26, insert at end of the section on **Social Workers**:*

American Board of Examiners in Clinical Social Work. Founded in 1987, the ABECSW has credentialed more than 11,000 clinical social workers with the Board Certified Diplomate in Clinical Social Work (BCD). BCD status requires five years and 7,500 hours of direct clinical practice (of which at least 3,000 is under supervision), a master's degree

[70.2] Colorado Mental Health Statute Section 12-43-215(7) (1998).

in clinical social work from an accredited program, the highest license or certification in the jurisdiction in which the individual practices, and successful completion of the examination process. The Board verifies continued state licensure/certification of all diplomates on an annual basis. The Board has a code of ethics, available at www.abecsw.org/code_ethics.shtml.

§ 1.9 Skills Needed by Expert

Page 29, insert at the end of § 1.9:

California has added several requirements for evaluators under Chapter 2.6 of the Special Rules for Trial Courts:

Rule 1257.4. Education, experience, and training standards for court-appointed child custody investigators and evaluators.

(c)(1) A "child custody evaluator" is a court-appointed investigator as defined in Family Code section 3110.[127.1]

(2) A "child custody evaluation" is an expert investigation and analysis of the health, safety, welfare, and best interest of a child with regard to disputed custody and visitation issues.

(5) The terms "evaluation," "investigation," and "assessment" are synonymous.

(d) Requirements for evaluators' qualifications: education, experience, and training. Persons appointed as child custody evaluators must:

(1) Effective January 1, 2004, complete a total of 40 hours of initial training and education as described in subdivision (e). At least 20 of the 40 hours of education and training required by this rule must be completed by January 1, 2003. . . .

(e) Education and training requirements. Only education acquired after January 1, 2000 that meets the requirements for training and education providers described in subdivision (n) meets the requirements of this

[127.1] Family Code Section 3110 addresses requirements that a child custody evaluator has completed training in domestic violence and child abuse, including child sexual abuse. Evaluators must be psychiatrists, psychologists, licensed marriage and family therapists, or licensed clinical social workers, unless no such expert is available, in which case the court may appoint someone with other credentials. The complete text of the section may be found at http://www.leginfo.ca.gov/cgi-bin/displaycode?section=fam&group=03001-04000&file=3110-3118.

rule. . . . The hours required by this rule must include, but are not limited to, all of the following subjects:

(1) The psychological and developmental needs of children, especially as those needs relate to decisions about child custody and visitation;

(2) Family dynamics, including, but not limited to, parent-child relationships, blended families, and extended family relationships;

(3) The effects of separation, divorce, domestic violence, child sexual abuse, child physical or emotional abuse or neglect, substance abuse, and interparental conflict on the psychological and developmental needs of children and adults;

(4) The assessment of child sexual abuse issues required by Family Code Section 3110.5(b)(2)(A)-(F)[127.2] and Family Code Section 3118[127.3]; local procedures for handling child sexual abuse cases; and the effect that court procedures may have on the evaluation process when there are allegations of child sexual abuse;

(5) The significance of culture and religion in the lives of the parties;

(6) Safety issues that may arise during the evaluation process and their potential effects on all participants in the evaluation;

(7) When and how to interview or assess adults, infants, and children; gather information from collateral sources; collect and assess relevant data; and recognize the limits of data sources' reliability and validity;

(8) The importance of addressing issues such as general mental health, medication use, and learning or physical disabilities;

(9) The importance of staying current with relevant literature and research;

(10) How to apply comparable interview, assessment, and testing procedures that meet generally accepted clinical, forensic, scientific, diagnostic or medical standards to all parties;

(11) When to consult with or involve additional experts or other appropriate persons;

(12) How to inform each adult party of the purpose, nature, and method of the evaluation;

[127.2] Family Code Section 3118 indicates the obligations of an evaluator when there are allegations of child sexual abuse. The complete section may be found at http://www.leginfo.ca.gov/cgi-bin/displaycode?section=fam&group=03001-04000&file=3110-3118.

[127.3] *Id.*

(13) How to assess parenting capacity and construct effective parenting plans;

(14) Ethical requirements associated with the child custody evaluator's professional license and rule 1257.3;[127.4]

(15) The legal context within which child custody and visitation issues are decided and additional legal and ethical standards to consider when serving as a child custody evaluator;

(16) The importance of understanding relevant distinctions among the roles of evaluator, mediator, and therapist;

(17) How to write reports and recommendations, where appropriate;

(18) Mandatory reporting requirements and limitations on confidentiality;

(19) How to prepare for and give court testimony;

(20) How to maintain professional neutrality and objectivity when conducting child custody evaluations;

(21) The importance of assessing the health, safety, welfare and best interest of the child or children involved in the proceedings.

(f) Experience requirements. Persons appointed as child custody evaluators must satisfy initial experience requirements by:

(1) Completing or supervising three court-appointed partial or full child custody evaluations including a written or an oral report between January 1, 2000 and July 1, 2003; or

(2) Conducting six child custody evaluations in consultation with another professional who meets the education, experience, and training requirements of this rule.

(g) Continuing education and training. Effective January 1, 2004, persons appointed as child custody evaluators must annually attend 8 hours of update training covering subjects described in subdivision (e) after completing the initial 40 hours of training. This requirement is in addition to the annual update training described in rule 1257.7.

[127.4] Rule 1257.3 addresses definitions of terms, indicates that child custody evaluators shall consider the health, safety, welfare and best interest of the child(ren), minimize trauma to the child(ren), explain the evaluation process in an age-appropriate manner, and indicates the scope of the custody evaluations that are to be done of the family. It also notes requirements for evaluator qualifications, training, continuing education, and experience that are indicated in sections of the Family Code, and indicates ethical requirements of the evaluator. The complete rule may be found at http://www.courtinfo.ca.gov/rules/2002/titlefive/1180-1280.15.doc-68.htm#TopOfPage.

(k) Licensing requirements. On or after January 1, 2005, persons appointed as child custody evaluators must meet the criteria set forth in Family Code Section 3110.5(c)(1)-(5).[127.5]

Rule 1257.7. Domestic violence training standards for court-appointed child custody investigators and evaluators.

(d) Mandatory training. Persons appointed as child custody investigators . . . and persons who are professional staff or trainees in a child custody or visitation evaluation or investigation, must complete basic training in domestic violence issues . . . and in addition:

(1) Advanced training. Sixteen hours of advanced training shall be completed within a 12-month period. . . .

(2) Annual update training. Four hours of update training are required each year after the year in which the advanced training is completed. . . . [Subd (d) amended effective January 1, 2002]

§ 1.14 Preparing the Expert

*Page 41, insert after the **Daubert Requirements** subsection:*

State Expert Testimony Standards

The Commission on Mental and Physical Disability Law of the American Bar Association produced a *National Benchbook on Psychiatric and Psychological Evidence and Testimony* (Washington, D.C.: American Bar Association (1998)) in which there is a list of the standard followed by each of the states:

[127.5] *Supra* note 127.1.

Significant Decisions by Jurisdiction on Expert Testimony Standards*

States that Follow *Daubert* Analysis

Alabama *Turner v. Alabama*, No. 1952024 (Jan. 16, 1998).

Arkansas *Prater v. Arkansas*, 820 S.W.2d 429, 431 (1991).

Indiana *Harrison v. Indiana*, 644 N.E.2d 1243, 1252 (1995).

Iowa *Hutchison v. American Family Mut. Ins. Co.*, 514 N.W.2d 882, 885, 886 (1994).

Kentucky *Mitchell v. Kentucky*, 908 S.W.2d 100, 101 (1995).

Louisiana *Louisiana v. Foret*, 628 So. 2d 1116, 1122, 1123 (1993).

Maine *Maine v. Williams*, 388 A.2d 500, 504 (1978). *See also, Maine v. Taylor*, 694 A.2d 907, 910 (1997).

Massachusetts *Massachusetts v. Lanigan*, 641 N.E.2d 1342, 1349 (1994).

Montana *Montana v. Moore*, 885 P.2d 457, 471 (1994).

New Hampshire *New Hampshire v. Hungerford*, 697 A.2d 916, 922 (1997).

New Mexico *New Mexico v. Alberico*, 861 P.2d 192, 194, 203 (1993).

Connecticut *Connecticut v. Porter*, 698 A.2d 739, 742 (1997) *cert. denied*, *Porter v. Connecticut*, 118 S. Ct. 1384 (1998).

Delaware *Nelson v. Delaware*, 628 A.2d 69, 73 (1993).

North Carolina *North Carolina v. Goode*, 461 S.E.2d 631, 639, 640 (1995).

Ohio *Miller v. Bike Athletic Co.*, 687 N.E.2d 735, 741 (1998).

Oregon *Oregon v. Lyons*, 924 P.2d 802, 810 (1996). *See also, Oregon v. Brown*, 687 P.2d 751 (1984).

Rhode Island *Gallucci v. Humbyrd*, 709 A.2d 1059, 1064 (1998).

South Dakota *South Dakota v. Hofer*, 512 N.W.2d 482, 484 (1994).

Texas *E.I. DuPont de Nemours & Co. v. Robinson*, 923 S.W.2d 549, 556 (1995).

Utah *Utah v. Crosby*, 927 P.2d 638, 642 (1996). Utah applies a test similar to but more restrictive than *Daubert* following *Utah v. Rimmasch*, 775 P.2d 388 (1989).

Vermont *Vermont v. Brooks*, 643 A.2d 226, 229 (1993).

Virginia The Virginia Supreme Court rejected *Frye* in *Spencer v. Virginia*, 393 S.E.2d 609, 621 (1990), *cert. denied*, 498 U.S. 908 (1990).

West Virginia *Wilt v. Buracker*, 443 S.E.2d 196, 203 (1993), *cert denied*, 511 U.S. 1129 (1994).

Wyoming *Springfield v. Wyoming*, 860 P.2d 435, 442, 443 (1993).

* All cites are to a state's highest court unless otherwise noted.

States that Follow *Frye* Analysis

Arizona	*Arizona v. Johnson*, 922 P.2d 294, 296 (1996).
California	*California v. Leahy*, 882 P.2d 321, 331 (1994).
District of Columbia	*United States v. Porter*, 618 A.2d 629, 633 (1992).
Florida	*Hadden v. Florida*, 690 So. 2d 573, 574, 575 (1997).
Illinois	*Illinois v. Miller*, 670 N.E.2d 721, 731 (1996), *cert. denied, Miller v. Illinois*, 117 S. Ct. 1338 (1997).
Kansas	*Kansas v. Warden*, 891 P.2d 1074, 1085 (1995).
Maryland	*Reed v. Maryland*, 391 A.2d 364, 368 (1978). *See also, Armstead v. Maryland*, 673 A.2d 221, 228, 229 (1996).
Michigan	*Michigan v. Davis*, 72 N.W.2d 269 (1955). *See also, Michigan v. Berger*, 551 N.W.2d 421, 424 (Mich. Ct. App. 1996).
Mississippi	*Polk v. Mississippi*, 612 So. 2d 381, 390 (1992). *See also, Crawford v. Mississippi*, No. 94-DP-01016-SCT (Mar. 12, 1998).
Nebraska	*Nebraska v. Dean*, 523 N.W.2d 681, 692 (1994), *cert. denied, Dean v. Nebraska*, 515 U.S. 1123 (1995).
New Jersey	*New Jersey v. Harvey*, 699 A.2d 596, 620 (1997). Uses *Frye* in criminal cases.
New York	*New York v. Wesley*, 633 N.E.2d 451, 454 (1994).
Pennsylvania	*Pennsylvania v. Blasioli*, No Docket No., 1998 WL 313388 (1998).
Washington	*Washington v. Copeland*, 922 P.2d 1304, 1310 (1996).

Standard in State of Flux

Alaska	*Harmon v. Alaska*, 908 P.2d 434, 439 (Ak. Ct. App. 1995). "Given the supreme court's adherence to the *Frye* standard in *Contreras v. Alaska* 718 P.2d 129 (1986), the proper course of action is for us to follow the existing standard."

Standard in State of Flux, continued

Colorado	*Lindsey v. Colorado*, 892 P.2d 281, 288 (1995). "In *Fishback v. Colorado*, 851 P.2d 884 (1993), we affirmed our prior rulings that *Frye* sets forth the applicable standard for determining the admissibility of novel scientific evidence. We do not consider the relative merits of the *Frye* test or our corollary state rules of evidence for the simple reason the issue is not now before us, and has not been fully briefed or argued."
Georgia	*Smith v. Georgia*, 277 S.E.2d 678 (1981). *See also, Orkin Exterminating Co. v. McIntosh*, 452 S.E.2d 159, 165 (Ga. App. 1994). "We first note that *Daubert* involves the application of [Fed. R. Evid. 702], which has not been adopted in Georgia. The applicable law in Georgia is [Ga. Code Ann. §24-9-67], which provides: 'the opinions of experts on any question of science, skill or like questions shall always be admissible...'"
Hawaii	*Hawaii v. Maelega*, 907 P.2d 758, 768 (1995). *Frye* is highly probative but it should not be used as the exclusive threshold for admissibility determination.
Idaho	*Idaho v. Gleason*, 844 P.2d 691, 694 (1992). Uses *Frye* but reaffirms using Idaho R. Evid. 702 as the appropriate test for measuring the scientific reliability of evidence.
Minnesota	*Minnesota v. Klawitter*, 518 N.W.2d 577, 579 (1994). "We express no opinion on the continued validity of the *Frye* rule in Minnesota."
Missouri	*Callahan v. Cardinal Glennon Hosp.*, 863 S.W.2d 852, 860 (Mo. *en banc* 1993). Court did not decide whether Mo. Rev. Stat. §490.065 supersedes *Frye*. *See also, Missouri v. Love*, 963 S.W.2d 236, 242 (Mo. Ct. App. 1997). Missouri follows *Frye*.
Nevada	*Townsend v. Nevada*, 734 P.2d 705, 708 (1987). *See also, Yamaha Motor Co. U.S.A. v. Arnoult*, 955 P.2d 661, 667 (1998).
North Dakota	*North Dakota v. Brown*, 337 N.W.2d 138, 148 (1983). "Our court has never directly adopted the *Frye* rule."
Oklahoma	*Taylor v. Oklahoma*, 889 P.2d 319, 328-329 (Ok. Crim. App. 1995). Adopts *Daubert*.
South Carolina	*South Carolina v. Ford*, 392 S.E.2d 781, 783 (1990). Does not specifically follow *Frye*. *See also, South Carolina v. Morgan*, 485 S.E.2d 112, 115 (S.C. Ct. App. 1997).
Tennessee	*McDaniel v. CSX Transp., Inc.*, 955 S.W.2d 257, 265 (1997), *cert. denied*, 118 S. Ct. 2296 (1998). Tennessee's adoption of Rules 702 and 703 supersede *Frye*. However, the court does not expressly adopt *Daubert*.
Wisconsin	*Wisconsin v. Walstad*, 351 N.W.2d 469, 486 (1984). *See also, Wisconsin v. Peters*, 534 N.W.2d 867, 872 (Wis. Ct. App. 1995).

Page 46, insert after § 1.18:

§ 1.18A Expert Witness Liability and Immunity (New)

Psychologist Stuart Greenberg presented a detailed examination of the liability and immunity of the expert witness at the Annual Convention of the American Psychological Association on August 26, 2001.[197] According to Dr. Greenberg, courts consider two questions when determining whether to confer immunity on an expert: "to whom does the expert owe a legal duty" and "does the role or the activity of the expert confer immunity regardless of any legal duty that may exist?"

Experts potentially owe legal duties to the court, the retaining attorney, and third parties, with each involving a professional duty as well. The duty to the court involves the offering of testimony that is reliable, helpful, honest, and objective. The related professional (ethical) duty is to provide assistance to the finder of fact, and to perform that function in a way that is consistent with the highest standards of his or her profession.

The expert's duty to the retaining attorney includes providing services that are at or above the standard of practice while assisting the attorney in fulfilling his or her obligation to be a zealous advocate. The related professional (ethical) duty is to present information fairly and with sufficient foundation, and to resist any attempt to distort, misrepresent, or omit information that may be contrary to the position of the attorney.

Most courts have held that expert witnesses do not have a legal duty to third parties. In *Zamstein v. Marvasti,*[198] for example, a father sued a psychiatrist who withheld exculpatory evidence when the father was accused in the midst of a divorce proceeding of having sexually abused his children. The Connecticut Supreme Court ruled that, absent a special relationship between the expert and the father, there is no duty of care owed to the father. There is, however, a professional (ethical) duty of forensic psychologists to all parties in a case to present in a fair manner all evidence, findings, and conclusions. There also is a duty to behave in such a manner as to avoid diminishing or threatening the rights of any party.

Courts grant immunity to experts in order to ensure that the individual can freely express his or her information and opinions without fear of civil liability for statements made, or facing a potential civil lawsuit by an un-

---

[197] Greenberg, S. "Liability and Immunity of the Expert Witness." Symposium presented at the Annual Convention of the American Psychological Association, San Francisco, CA, August 2001.

[198] *Zamstein v. Marvasti*, 692 A.2d 781 (Conn. 1997).

happy party. Immunity fosters candor and the availability of expert witnesses facilitates the work of the trier of fact and increases judicial efficiency. The grant of immunity means that a civil suit against the expert would be dismissed even if the expert performed below the standard of care and harmed some person by so doing. Without such immunity, the expert could be sued and have to defend him- or herself, even though the expert could ultimately be vindicated at a trial. It is nearly always to the advantage of a retaining attorney to attempt to obtain a grant of immunity for his or her experts.

Immunity does not generally extend to protect the expert from criminal liability if he or she knowingly provides false testimony (perjury). The same is true if he or she commits criminal fraud (e.g., by stating he or she has a license that is, in fact, nonexistent), or engages in a criminal conspiracy (e.g., by agreeing to collude with someone to provide false testimony).

Courts cannot grant immunity to an expert with regard to licensing board or ethics committee complaints. An expert who violates the licensing laws of his or her state can be charged with that violation in an administrative proceeding and, if found guilty, may receive anything from a reprimand to the revocation of his or her license. Although neither state nor national ethics committees can directly affect an individual's license to practice, they can revoke the expert's membership in the professional association and can discreetly publicize that fact through mailings to members. They may also notify the relevant state licensing board of their action, opening the possibility that the licensing board will initiate an action *sua sponte*. It should be noted that in Washington, which is a state that grants broad immunity to experts, the state Supreme Court, in *Deatherage v. Examining Board of Psychology,*[199] a case involving allegations of malpractice while performing a custody evaluation, ruled that experts have immunity to civil liability but not to criminal or licensing actions.

Experts in court proceedings generally have one of two roles: as a forensic expert or as a "treating expert." The former role may result from a court appointment or from being retained by a private counsel. The expert may testify on the basis of examinations of one or more individuals (e.g., members of a family in a child custody contest), or on abstract or hypothetical matters germane to a case without having conducted any examinations (e.g., on the developmental needs of children at certain ages). The expert may assist one side in a case, or may be appointed by a court as a neutral expert to advise the court.

---

[199] *Deatherage v. Examining Board of Psychology*, 134 Wash. 2d 131, 948 P.2d 828 (Wash. 1997).

The latter role, that of a "treating expert," may also result from an appointment by a court or from being retained privately, and the expert may function either as a trial consultant or as a witness. The treating expert may not, however, function as an *independent* witness, because he or she owes a duty to the client as well as to the court and professional standards. The treating expert is ethically required to be primarily a fact witness, as discussed at length in § 2.7.

The expert who does not have a grant of immunity from the court opens him- or herself up to potential liability in several areas. One area is if an expert engages in activities that are not within the expert's role, but that are not otherwise negligent. An example would be the expert who was retained to conduct an examination, but who either performed psychotherapy instead of conducting the examination, or conducted the examination and then began a course of psychotherapy for one or more of the individuals examined. Another example is the expert who was appointed by the court to assist the court and/or both sides, but who assists one side only.

A second area of potential liability is if the expert engages in activities that are both outside of the expert's role *and* potentially negligent. Examples include committing fraud, perjury or conspiracy, physically harming an individual while conducting an examination, violating confidentiality or privilege, or altering or destroying evidence (spoliation).

A third area of potential liability is if the expert engages in activities that are both within the expert's role and potentially negligent. Examples include misdiagnosing someone, misusing tests, failing to acquire important records, failing to conduct essential interviews, or accepting appointment without understanding the relevant legal theory and criteria.

Although the immunity of expert witnesses has been addressed by many cases, two stand out: *Briscoe v. LaHue*[200] and *Bruce v. Byrne-Stevens.*[201] In *Briscoe v. LaHue*, the U.S. Supreme Court ruled that police officers and lay citizens are absolutely immune from civil liability (as well as 42 U.S.C.S. § 1983 liability) claims based on their testimony in judicial proceedings. In *Bruce v. Byrne-Stevens*, the Washington Supreme Court ruled that experts are entitled to absolute immunity not only for their testimony but also for actions in the course of preparation for testimony. Other cases in which courts found that expert witnesses are entitled to absolute judicial or quasi-judicial immunity include *Marrogi v. Howard*,[202] *Bird v. W.C.W.*,[203]

---

[200] *Briscoe v. LaHue*, 460 U.S. 325, 103 S.Ct. 1108 (1983).

[201] *Bruce v. Byrne-Stevens,* 113 Wash. 2d 123, 776 P.2d 666 (Wash. 1989).

[202] *Marrogi v. Howard,* 248 F.3d 382, 2001 U.S. App. LEXIS 6190 (5th Cir. La. 2001).

[203] *Bird v. W.C.W.*, 868 S.W.2d 767 (Tex. 1994).

Panitz v. Behrend,[204] *Laub v. Pesikoff,*[205] *Darragh v. Superior Court,*[206] *Aequitron Med. v. Dyro,*[207] *Parker v. Dodgion,*[208] and *Duff v. Lewis.*[209]

Note, however, that a few courts have permitted civil lawsuits against expert witnesses by the litigants who retained them. These claims are generally based on allegations of negligence, and are filed by clients who are disappointed that the expert was not able to adequately help them win their claims. In *Murphy v. A.A. Mathews,*[210] the court ruled that experts owe clients a duty of care, and that the fact that this professional service involved litigation rather than clinical care should not preclude the client from being protected against negligence. Immunity is reserved for independent experts, not the professional who agrees to help a party in return for a fee. In *LLMD of Mich. v. Jackson-Cross,*[211] the Pennsylvania Supreme Court found that immunity did not prevent a malpractice action against an expert when the alleged negligence was not premised on the substance of the expert's opinion.

In summary, experts face potential liability in some states when they provide services before litigation is filed, provide supportive services rather than acting as an expert witness, are retained by a party rather than court-appointed, practice below the standard of care, do not stay within the role associated with their appointment, and/or accept a role that does not involve exercising judicial or quasi-judicial authority.

§ 1.20 Case Digest

*Page 48, insert under **U.S. Supreme Court** heading:*

Kumho Tire Co. v. Carmichael, 119 S. Ct. 1167 (1999). On March 23, 1999, the U.S. Supreme Court ruled that an individual may be considered an expert if the individual has any type of specialized knowledge or experience that may contribute to the fact finder's understanding of a case. As indicated in *Daubert v. Merrell Dow Pharm.,* 509 U.S. 579 (1993),

[204] *Panitz v. Behrend*, 429 Pa. Super. 273, 632 A.2d 562 (Pa. Super. 1993).
[205] *Laub v. Pesikoff*, 979 S.W.2d 686 (Tex. Civ. App. 1998).
[206] *Darragh v. Superior Court*, 900 P.2d 1215 (Ariz. Ct. App. 1995).
[207] *Aequitron Med. v. Dyro,* 999 F. Supp. 294 (E.D.N.Y. 1998).
[208] *Parker v. Dodgion*, 971 P.2d 496 (Utah 1998).
[209] *Duff v. Lewis,* 958 P.2d 82 (Nev. 1998).
[210] *Murphy v. A.A. Mathews,* 841 S.W.2d 671 (Mo. 1992).
[211] *LLMD of Mich. v. Jackson-Cross*, 559 Pa. 297, 740 A.2d 186 (Penn. Supr. 1999).

expert testimony is subject to scrutiny for relevancy and reliability by the trial court. The Supreme Court wrote:

> In *Daubert v. Merrell Dow Pharmaceuticals, Inc.,* 509 U.S. 579 (1993), this Court focused upon the admissibility of scientific expert testimony. It pointed out that such testimony is admissible only if it is both relevant and reliable. And it held that the Federal Rules of Evidence "assign to the trial judge the task of ensuring that an expert's testimony both rests on a reliable foundation and is relevant to the task at hand." *Id.* at 597. . . . This case requires us to decide how *Daubert* applies to the testimony of engineers and other experts who are not scientists. We conclude that *Daubert's* general holding—setting forth the trial judge's general "gatekeeping" obligation—applies not only to testimony based on "scientific" knowledge, but also to testimony based on "technical" and "other specialized" knowledge. . . . We also conclude that a trial court *may* consider one or more of the more specific factors that *Daubert* mentioned when doing so will help determine that testimony's reliability. But, as the Court stated in *Daubert*, the test of reliability is "flexible," and *Daubert's* list of specific factors neither necessarily nor exclusively applies to all experts or in every case. Rather, the law grants a district court the same broad latitude when it decides *how* to determine reliability as it enjoys in respect to its ultimate reliability determination. See *General Electric Co. v. Joiner,* 522 U.S. 136, 143 (1997) (courts of appeals are to apply "abuse of discretion" standard when reviewing district court's reliability determination.)
>
> In *Daubert*, this Court held that Federal Rule of Evidence 702 imposes a special obligation upon a trial judge to "ensure that any and all scientific testimony . . . is not only relevant, but reliable." 509 U.S., at 589. The initial question before us is whether this basic gatekeeping obligation applies only to "scientific" testimony or to all expert testimony. We . . . believe that it applies to all expert testimony. . . . In *Daubert*, the Court specified that it is the Rule's word "knowledge," not the words (like "scientific") that modify that word, that "establishes a standard of evidentiary reliability." 509 U.S., at 589-90. . . .
>
> *Daubert* pointed out that Federal Rules 702 and 703 grant expert witnesses testimonial latitude unavailable to other witnesses on the "assumption that the expert's opinion will have a reliable basis in the knowledge and experience of his discipline." *Id.,* at 592 (pointing out that experts may testify to opinions, including those that are not based on firsthand knowledge or observation). The Rules grant that latitude to all experts, not just to "scientific" ones. . . .
>
> Experts of all kinds tie observations to conclusions through the use of what Judge Learned Hand called "general truths derived from specialized experience." [citation omitted] And whether the specific expert testimony focuses upon specialized observations, the specialized translation of those

> observations into theory, a specialized theory itself, or the application of such a theory in a particular case, the expert's testimony often will rest "upon an experience confessedly foreign in kind to [the jury's] own." *Ibid.* The trial judge's effort to assure that the specialized testimony is reliable and relevant can help the jury evaluate that foreign experience, whether the testimony reflects scientific, technical, or other specialized knowledge. . . .
>
> [W]e can neither rule out, nor rule in, for all cases and for all time the applicability of the factors mentioned in *Daubert*, nor can we now do so for subsets of cases categorized by category of expert or by kind of evidence. Too much depends upon the particular circumstances of the particular case at issue. *Daubert* itself is not to the contrary. It made clear that its list of factors was meant to be helpful, not definitive. Indeed, those factors do not all necessarily apply even in every instance in which the reliability of scientific testimony is challenged. It might not be surprising in a particular case, for example, that a claim made by a scientific witness has never been the subject of peer review, for the particular application at issue may never previously have interested any scientist. Nor, on the other hand, does the presence of *Daubert's* general acceptance factor help show that an expert's testimony is reliable where the discipline itself lacks reliability, as, for example, do theories grounded in any so-called generally accepted principles of astrology or necromancy. . . .
>
> The objective . . . is to make certain that an expert, whether basing testimony upon professional studies or personal experience, employs in the courtroom the same level of intellectual rigor that characterizes the practice of an expert in the relevant field. . . . The trial court must have the same kind of latitude in deciding *how* to test an expert's reliability, and to decide whether or when special briefing or other proceedings are needed to investigate reliability, as it enjoys when it decides *whether* that expert's relevant testimony is reliable. . . . Otherwise, the trial judge would lack the discretionary authority needed both to avoid unnecessary "reliability" proceedings in ordinary cases where the reliability of an expert's methods is properly taken for granted, and to require appropriate proceedings in the less usual or more complex cases where cause for questioning the expert's reliability arises.

It should be noted that the Supreme Court again makes it clear that judges have an obligation to exercise their gatekeeping function, rather than simply deferring to experts from any given profession. In addition, courts of appeal are to limit their reviews of admissibility decisions to whether the trial judge abused his or her discretion.[212]

---

[212] John W. Parry, *Admissibility of Expert Evidence*, 24 Mental and Physical Disability Law Reporter 10 (2000).

Forensic experts are advised to base their testimony or practice not only on the prevailing clinical standards of their communities but, also, on other, broader, bases of reliability such as research reported in peer-reviewed journals.[213]

It is essential that professionals are able to address either the *Daubert* criteria or other, equivalent, criteria if they are asked to defend the reliability of their testimony. If they cannot, the trial court could choose to exclude their testimony on the basis of the *Daubert* and *Kumho* criteria.[214]

The critical issue with regard to questions of "error rates" is the legal mandate to avoid false-positives. To the degree possible, psychological testimony should address the likelihood that a given result may be a false indictment of an individual.[215]

Finally, it must be noted that *Kumho* is applicable in federal courts, not state courts, unless a given state has taken a position on the issues through either a decision by its highest court or by legislative action.[216]

*Page 54, insert above **Federal District Courts**:*

Third Circuit

Hughes v. Long, 242 F.3d 121 (3d Cir. 2001). As part of an acrimonious child custody battle, Long, a licensed clinical social worker, was appointed to conduct an evaluation. While Long was court-appointed, she contracted privately with the parties, with each agreeing to pay 50 percent of the cost. Hughes, not liking the outcome, retained his own expert. Hughes alleges that Long, and two psychologists with whom she consulted, destroyed their raw data and manufactured new data that supported Long's recommendation. The court accepted Long's report in spite of the allegation, and awarded Hughes and his wife joint custody. Hughes appealed to the United States District Court for the Eastern District of Pennsylvania, alleging violations of his familial rights in violation of the Fourteenth Amendment and his civil rights under 42 U.S.C. §§ 1983 and 1985(3). He also alleged a number of state law violations. The appellees filed motions to dismiss. The District Court granted those motions under the Rooker-Feldman doctrine that a federal court does not have subject-matter jurisdiction to evaluate constitutional claims that are "inextricably intertwined" with a state

---

[213] Eric A. Youngstrom & Christine P. Busch, *Expert Testimony in Psychology: Ramifications of Supreme Court Decision in* Kumho Tire Co., Ltd. v. Carmichael, 10 Ethics & Behavior 185–193 (2000) at 189.

[214] Richard Wiener, *Extending Daubert Beyond Scientific Expert Testimony*, 30 APA Monitor 47 (1999).

[215] Youngstrom & Busch at 189.

[216] Youngstrom & Busch at 191.

court custody proceeding. It did not rule on the merits of appellees motions to dismiss.

The appellate court reversed the District Court regarding the Rooker-Feldman doctrine, and also refused to affirm the dismissal on the basis of an alternative argument that appellees are entitled to absolute prosecutorial immunity pursuant to *Ernst v. Child & Youth Servs.,* 108 F.3d 486 (3d Cir. 1997). The appellate court held that the trial record was not sufficiently developed regarding appellees precise functions and participation in the proceedings.

On remand, the District Court granted appellees motions for summary judgment on the basis of their being entitled to absolute prosecutorial immunity. Alternatively, the court held that they were entitled to witness immunity. It also ruled that Long and the psychologist were immune to state law claims. Hughes appealed.

The Third Circuit indicated that social workers and other child care workers may have absolute immunity for actions involving the initiation and prosecution of proceedings involving child custody or dependency. In the instant case, however, contrary to the District Court ruling, it is not prosecutorial immunity that is relevant. Instead, Long and the psychologist are entitled to judicial immunity on the basis of their acting under court appointment and having performed functions central to the court process. The District Court's grant of summary judgment was affirmed.

Page 55 insert above ***Alaska:***

Alabama

Mitchell v. Mitchell, 830 So. 2d 755 (Ala. Civ. App. 2002). The Alabama Court of Appeals reversed a trial court ruling that a psychologist who was not licensed in Alabama could not testify as an expert in a child visitation case. The appellate court indicated that the statute that defines the practice of psychology does not list testifying as a function of the practice of psychology. Therefore, while practicing psychology without a license is a crime in the state, the legislature did not intend to prevent psychologists licensed in another state from offering expert testimony. Source: 27 Mental and Physical Disability Law Reporter 214–15 (2003).

Page 56, insert under ***Arizona:***

In *Logerquist v. McVey*, 1 P.3d 113 (Ariz. 2000), the Arizona Supreme Court rejected the *Daubert* standard due to concern about judicial power, and ruled that Arizona would not reject the Frye standard. The concern of the court was that the U.S. Supreme Court had, in *Kumho v. Carmichael* (526 U.S. 19 (1999)), extended the gatekeeping function of the trial court judge to all expert testimony, not just scientific testimony. This, the court feared, would permit the trial judge to make decisions that were the proper province of the jury, for example, whether an expert witness was credible or whether the expert's credentials were adequate. The Arizona constitution, the court indicated, was not consistent with the *Kumho* extension of *Daubert*. The court indicated that judges should remain responsible for determining that testimony is relevant, but that the reliability of the expert is a matter for the jury to decide.

Page 57, insert under ***California:***

Laborde v. Aronson, 92 Cal. App. 4th 459, ___ Cal. Rptr. 2d ___ (September 21, 2001). A man sued a psychologist, Dr. Aronson, who had been retained to do a custody evaluation by the attorneys for the parties, and who was later appointed by the court as its expert. When the father learned the result of the evaluation, he threatened to sue the psychologist if she testified in the case, and refused to pay her bill. He also filed a complaint accusing the psychologist and his wife's attorney of conspiring against him. The psychologist and the attorney moved for and were granted summary judgment, with Dr. Aronson's based upon the litigation privilege. Both the psychologist and the attorney were awarded expenses on the bases that the action was frivolous, had no merit, and was filed in bad faith. The father appealed.

The appellate court affirmed. Although Dr. Aronson was initially retained by the parties, she was court-appointed prior to her testimony, and her report was accepted *nunc pro tunc* by the court at the trial. Citing *Gootee v. Lightner*, 224 Cal. App. 3d 587 (1990), the appellate court indicated that the suit against Dr. Aronson was barred by absolute privilege. The $24,000 award to Dr. Aronson was also affirmed.

Page 58, insert as the first case under ***Colorado:***

Ryder v. Mitchell, 00SC889 (Colo. Sup. Ct., Sept. 16, 2002). A mother sued her children's therapist, Gloria Ryder, for breach of fiduciary duty and negligence after Ryder formed an opinion that the mother was engaging in behavior designed to alienate her ex-husband from the children, with Ryder sending the ex-husband a copy of a letter to that effect. The trial court dismissed all of Mitchell's claims, indicating that the children were not parties to the action, and that the law created no duty from Ryder to Mitchell. The court of appeals reversed, holding that Ryder did owe Mitchell a duty of due care. The supreme court reversed, affirming the trial court's order of summary judgment and dismissing all claims.

> In examining the legal question of whether a duty exists, the court looks to the risk involved, the foreseeability and likelihood of injury as weighed

> against the social utility of the defendant's conduct, the magnitude of the burden of guarding against the harm and the consequences of placing the burden on the defendant. On balance, the court concludes that the duty the therapist owes the children themselves is primary and may, under certain circumstances, require disclosure to the parents or other involved parties. . . . [T]he possibility of liability to the children for breach serves as an adequate safeguard against negligent treatment by the therapist.

Dalton v. Miller, 984 P.2d 666 (Colo. App. Ct. Apr. 29, 1999). Patricia Dalton sued her insurance company for failure to renew her coverage, and alleged various emotional and other damages. The insurance company asked the court to order a psychiatric evaluation. The psychiatrist, Dr. Miller, evaluated Ms. Dalton, issued a report, and testified in a videotaped deposition. Ms. Dalton settled with the insurance company, but then sued Dr. Miller for "alleged discrepancies between his written report to the insurer and his videotaped deposition testimony," and "alleged numerous claims for relief, including: misrepresentation and deceit; intent to cause loss of improved chances for recovery and increased risk of harm . . . ; invasion of privacy by intrusion upon seclusion; abuse of process; intentional infliction of emotional distress and outrageous conduct; and civil conspiracy."[217] The trial court granted the defendant's motion to dismiss and for summary judgment. Ms. Dalton appealed.

The appeals court noted that, in *Awai v. Kotin,* a court-appointed psychologist was granted "absolute immunity because [his] activities were intimately related to the judicial process of finding facts and rendering decisions" and he was appointed by the trial court. "Such an appointee acts as an officer of the court."[218] Most courts recognize quasi-judicial immunity only when an examiner is appointed by and reports directly to the court, the appeals court indicated. An examiner retained by one of the parties does not normally receive such immunity. Therefore, "we hold that professionals conducting an independent medical or psychiatric examination pursuant to a [request of a party] are not entitled to absolute quasi-judicial immunity for their activities."

The defendant also contended that he was entitled to witness immunity for his actions in this case.

> The United States Supreme Court has held that trial witnesses are entitled to absolute immunity from subsequent civil liability for their trial testimony. *Briscoe v. LaHue,* 460 U.S. 325, 103 S. Ct. 1108, 75 L.Ed. 2d 96 (1983). . . . Witness immunity has been held to extend to statements and

---

[217] *Id.* at 667.

[218] *Id.* at 668.

> opinions offered in deposition testimony and advisory reports prepared in the course of litigation [by both federal and state courts]. . . . We find the rationale of these cases persuasive. If shadowed by the threat of liability, a witness might testify in a manner that would prevent a potential lawsuit, but would deprive the court of the benefit of candid, unbiased testimony. . . . [W]itness reliability is otherwise ensured by oath, cross-examination, and the threat of criminal prosecution for perjury. . . . Thus, we hold that defendant is entitled to absolute immunity from civil liability for any statements he made during the course of his videotaped trial preservation deposition testimony that would have been played at trial in lieu of actual testimony from the defendant. In addition, he is entitled to immunity for the contents of the report he prepared for counsel for insurer, which detailed his conclusions from his examination of plaintiff. *Dalton* at 669.

The appellate court indicated that it did not have sufficient information from the record regarding whether the psychiatrist may be liable for harm the plaintiff incurred during the psychiatric evaluation, on the basis that he violated a duty to the plaintiff. That question was remanded to the trial court for further proceedings.

Page 59, insert under ***Florida:***

Attorney Ad Litem for D.K. v. Parents of D.K., 780 So. 2d 301 (Fla. Dist. Ct. App. 2001). A psychologist appointed by the court to evaluate a family in a custody action requested D.K.'s medical and mental health records. Through the child's attorney *ad litem*, D.K. asserted the psychotherapist-patient privilege. The trial court denied the motion for a protective order, indicating that D.K.'s parents had waived such privilege. The District Court quashed the trial court's order, indicating that the statutory definition of "patient" includes "children." The child's privilege, therefore, was protected by statute. The court indicated that there was no Florida case law addressing who may waive privilege for a child. The weight of decisions in other jurisdictions is that, when the child's mental status may be relevant to litigation involving the parents, the parents are not permitted to either assert or waive the child's privilege. In the instant case the child, age 17, was considered old enough to assert the privilege on the child's own behalf.

Page 60, insert after end of carryover paragraph:

Iowa

In re Marriage of Peck, 2001 WL 194918 (Iowa Ct. App. Feb. 28, 2001). A former wife sought to modify the divorce decree that awarded her ex-husband physical placement of their two daughters. She called her ex-husband to testify at the trial and introduced mental health records of his that she had obtained from his previous wife with neither his knowledge or consent. On the basis of information from those records, the trial court transferred placement of the children to the wife. The appeals court ruled that his mental health records should not have been admitted. He had given the records to his previous wife for safekeeping, trusting that she would maintain their confidentiality. He testified about the information in the records only after they had erroneously been admitted. Neither factor constitutes a waiver of privilege, and the ex-husband therefore may assert the psychotherapist-patient privilege.

Page 60, insert above ***Maryland:***

Maine

Seider v. Board of Exam'rs of Psychologists, 762 A.2d 551 (Me. Sup. Jud. Ct. 2000). The Maine Board of Examiners of Psychologists was justified in sanctioning a psychologist who released records without the patient's consent or a court order.

A mother consulted a clinical psychologist, Dr. Seider, regarding the possibility her son was being sexually abused. After the mother terminated the relationship with Dr. Seider, Dr. Seider began a professional relationship with the mother's ex-husband and the couple's daughter. Dr. Seider disclosed that the son had been and was still being sexually abused, and disclosed her concerns about the daughter's risk of abuse. A custody dispute began. Dr. Seider also contacted the children's pediatrician to discuss the possibility the daughter was being sexually abused. She did not, however, immediately report her beliefs about the sexual abuse to the state Department of Human Services (DHS), as required by law. When DHS was made aware and investigated the allegations, Dr. Seider furnished all family treatment records and a 51-page report that contained a great deal of confidential information. The mother complained to the Board of Examiners of Psychologists.

The Board found 12 violations of the 1992 American Psychological Association's *Ethical Principles of Psychologists and Code of Conduct*, and violation of three rules of the Association of State and Provincial Psychology Boards' (ASPPB) *Code of Conduct*. Dr. Seider's 51-page report disclosed more information than necessary to comply with the DHS subpoena. Also, she did not obtain consent to release the information and did not do an adequate evaluation to justify some of her conclusions. She also disclosed information that should have remained confidential. The fact that the mother had disclosed much of the information to the father and the pediatrician did not lessen the violation, because the privilege belonged to the mother and could not be waived except by the mother or by a court order.

Page 60, insert under ***Maryland:***

In re Adoption/Guardianship No. CCJ14746, 759 A.2d 755 (Md. Ct. App. 2000). A mother in a termination of parental rights case asserted that a licensed clinical social worker was engaging in the practice of medicine by assigning her a diagnosis from the American Psychiatric Association's *Diagnostic and Statistical Manual of Mental Disorders, Fourth Edition* (DSM-IV). The appellate court ruled that social workers are, by statute, permitted to make "a diagnosis based on a recognized manual of mental and emotional disorders," and were not practicing medicine in so doing.

Laznovsky v. Laznovsky, 745 A.2d 1054 (Md. Ct. App. 2000). The Maryland Court of Appeals held that

> a person seeking an award of child custody that claims to be a fit parent, does not, without more, waive the confidential psychiatrist/psychologist-patient privilege in respect to his or her past mental health "diagnosis and treatment" communications and records. . . . An assertion that one is fit is merely an assertion that one meets the qualifications to be awarded custody. It does not serve to place their mental condition in issue. [745 A.2d at 1073]

The court noted that the states are divided regarding whether a party seeking sole custody automatically permits disclosing privileged mental health records. The Indiana Supreme Court has held that the mere filing of a custody suit places a parent's mental health at issue, thereby waiving the privilege. Florida courts, in contrast, have held that merely filing for custody does not place one's mental health at issue.

If a trial court determines that the mental health of a parent is of concern, the court may order evaluations of the parties. Release of confidential psychiatric/psychological records is not essential when adequate information can be obtained through the evaluation process.

Page 63, insert above ***New Jersey:***

Nevada

Duff v. Lewis, 958 P.2d 82 (Nev. 1998). The Nevada Supreme Court held that a court-appointed psychologist in a child custody action was entitled to absolute quasi-judicial immunity.

Dr. Lewis was appointed by the court to evaluate a family as part of a post-judgment action. He recommended that the children permanently remain in the custody of their mother and her new husband. The father reported Dr. Lewis to the Nevada Board of Psychological Examiners, which concluded that Dr. Lewis's evaluation had been deficient in three areas: (1) he had not given an opinion regarding the affect of the father's medications on his psychological test performance; (2) he had selectively reported his findings, giving an impression that the father was of below-average intelligence; and (3) he misled the court by failing to indicate that the father's IQ was in the average range. A private letter of reprimand was issued to Dr. Lewis.

The father then sued Dr. Lewis for negligence. The district court dismissed the suit on the basis that the doctor had quasi-judicial immunity. The father appealed, and the state Supreme Court affirmed. On this issue of first impression, the Supreme Court indicated that the common law doctrine of absolute immunity extends to anyone who is an central part of a judicial proceeding. This preserves the independence of the witness and fosters truthfulness by eliminating any fear that the witness may be threatened with personal liability. It also increases the pool of experts willing to accept court appointments and prevents experts from shading their feedback to the court in order to limit liability. Safeguards that hold experts accountable include cross-examination and the ability of a litigant to appeal a trial court verdict.

*Page 63, insert under **New Jersey**:*

Runyon v. Smith, 730 A.2d 881 (N.J. Super. Ct. App. Div. 1999). A woman received a temporary restraining order (TRO) against her husband. The husband sought an immediate hearing to contest the TRO. He called his wife's treating psychologist to testify. The psychologist testified that the wife had an obsessive-compulsive personality disorder and abused her children. The psychologist also submitted a written report to the court. A friend of the wife also testified that she was abusive toward the children. The court granted temporary custody of the children to the father. The wife sued the psychologist and her employer, alleging violation of the psychologist-patient privilege. The trial court granted summary judgment to the defendants. The appeals court reversed. The trial court, it indicated, had not applied *In re Kozlov*, 298 A.2d 882 (N.J. 1979), which established that

> a party may avoid the privilege if (1) there is a legitimate need for the evidence, (2) the evidence is relevant and materials to the issue to be decided, and (3) the information sought cannot be secured from any less intrusive source.

23 Mental and Physical Disability Law Reporter 483.

The appellate court indicated that had the trial court applied the third prong, it would have found that the testimony of the husband and friend were far less intrusive than the testimony and records of the psychologist, as well as sufficient to deny giving her custody. There was also other evidence that could have been considered as an alternative to the psychologist's testimony. In addition, the appeals court indicated that the wife had a cause of action against the psychologist for revealing confidential information without her consent or a court order.

Page 63, insert as the first case under ***New York:***

Ochs v. Ochs, 749 N.Y.S.2d 650 (N.Y. Sup. Ct. 2002). In a custody dispute between Mitchell and Stacy Ochs, a forensic psychologist appointed by the court recommended that custody be awarded to Mitchell. Stacy made a request for the psychologist's notes and raw test data prior to cross-examination. The court denied the request.

The "court found that court-appointed neutral psychologists differ from experts retained by litigants in other matters in that their reports are not used to advocate a party's position. Instead, these psychologists provide the court with an unbiased professional opinion." While the conclusions of an expert are subject to cross-examination, and the expert's notes and raw data are subject to discovery, "courts must discard or limit procedures for litigating custody disputes if they are not likely to improve the result sufficiently to justify their financial and emotional costs. . . . Before allowing discovery in custody cases, New York courts require a showing of some specific need for disclosure. . . . Here . . . the psychologist's raw data and notes may add to the relevant information before the court, but at a significant cost. Because the parties will continue to interact after the litigation, disclosure may make their future relationship more difficult. . . ." Disclosure would permit a party to attempt to discredit the testimony of the psychologist by criticizing the psychologist's methodology, while failing to test the psychologist's conclusions. This process would be of limited value, while increasing the emotional and financial costs to the parties, including the children. In addition, if psychologists expect litigants to review their data and notes they may be less willing to state impressions they form during the interviews they conduct. Only a showing of bias or another basis for questioning the credibility of the report would be sufficient to cause disclosure. 27 Mental and Physical Disability Law Reporter 55 at 55 (2003).

Page 63, insert as the first case under ***Ohio:***

In re Jones, 2001 WL 1607732 (Ohio Ct. App. Dec. 18, 2001). The Ohio Court of Appeals ruled that a trial court did not err when it admitted a psychological assessment of the mother in a child dependency case. Because the psychological assessment was for forensic rather than treatment purposes, the psychologist-patient privilege does not apply. 26 Mental and Physical Disability Law Reporter 193 (2002).

Page 64, insert above ***Tennessee:***

Pennsylvania

Althaus v. Cohen, 756 A.2d 1166 (Pa. 2000). A teenager alleged that she was sexually abused by her father, and she was removed from the family home. She underwent more than a year of psychotherapy with a psychiatrist, Dr. Cohen. Dr. Cohen attended, but did not testify at, several proceedings. As the allegations became increasingly fanciful, she indicated that the teenager could not distinguish fact from fiction, and the charges against the parents were later dropped. The parents sued Dr. Cohen and her employer, alleging negligent diagnosis and treatment. A jury and an appeals court found for the plaintiffs. The supreme court reversed.

> To determine whether a duty exists, several factors must be weighed: the relationship between the parties; the social utility of the actor's conduct; the nature of the risk imposed and the foreseeability of the harm incurred; the consequences of imposing a duty on the actor; and the overall public interest in the proposed solution. . . . Applying those factors . . . , the relationship between Cohen and [the parents] does not weigh in favor of imposing a duty of care. Cohen had minimal contact with the parents and did not participate in the original criminal investigation, which gave rise to the criminal charges, or testify against the parents at any court proceeding related to those charges.
>
> Second, the social utility of effective therapeutic treatment of child victims of alleged sexual abuse by parents, when weighed against the nature and foreseeability of harm of a false accusation of sexual abuse, also does not support imposing a duty of care. Cohen did not create the harm suffered by the parents, did not participate in the original criminal investigation, played no legal role in the child's initial accusations against the parents, and was not called as a witness against the parents in the criminal proceedings. . . .
>
> Third, imposing a duty of care would alter the important therapeutic relationship between victims and professionals, and perhaps, cause such professionals to avoid providing treatment in sexual abuse cases. Finally, society's interest in encouraging treatment of child abuse victims and maintaining the trust and confidentiality within the therapist-patient relationship weighed against imposing a duty. Victims may become reluctant to seek treatment if confidentiality of treatment is not guaranteed and conflicting duties arose.

24 Mental and Physical Disability Law Reporter 983–84 (2000).

Page 65, insert above ***Vermont:***

Texas

Macurak v. Doyle, 2002 WL 1263900 (Tex. Ct. App. June 7, 2002). Randal Macurak brought claims on his own behalf and that of his son against a psychologist and psychiatrist who had treated his son. The trial court granted summary judgment for both defendants, indicating that they owed no duty of care to Macurak, a third-party non-patient.

During their bitter 1993 divorce, Macurak's wife alleged that their four-year-old son had seen a pornographic movie while with his father. The trial court ordered a psychological evaluation. The clinical assessment indicated that the child had been sexually traumatized, but that the father's involvement could neither be confirmed nor refuted. The trial court ordered that the child's treatment by a team that included psychologist Doyle and psychiatrist Lewis continue. The parents were also ordered to obey instructions by the treatment team, unless modified by order of the court or agreed upon in writing by the parties. The father was initially given supervised one-hour-per-week visitation, with expansion of visitation left to the discretion of the treatment team.

In October 1994, the child's condition deteriorated. The treatment team temporarily suspended the father's visitation. There was little contact between father and son for the next two and a half years. In 1997 the family court ordered limited visitation resumed. A jury trial in family court in 1998 led to the father being appointed "joint managing conservator" with unsupervised visitation involving up to 45 percent of the child's time. In 1999, Macurak sued the members of the treatment team and their hospital, alleging negligence, gross negligence, deceptive trade practices, civil conspiracy, breach of a duty of good faith and fair dealing, breach of fiduciary duty, and loss of consortium.

The appellate court, citing *Bird v. W.C.W.*, 868 S.W.2d 767 (Tex. 1994), affirmed the decision of the trial court that Doyle and Lewis "owed no duty to Macurak, a third-party non-patient, to provide competent medical health care to his son."

Abrams v. Jones, 35 S.W.3d 620, 2000 WL 890385 (Tex. July 6, 2000). The Texas Supreme Court ruled that a divorced father did not have a right to detailed notes regarding his daughter's sessions with her psychologist, because release of the notes would have been harmful to his daughter's emotional health. The court indicated that (1) a mental health professional need not provide confidential records to a parent who is not acting "on behalf of" the child, according to Texas law, and (2) even if a parent *is* acting on the child's behalf, the records may be refused if the professional believes that releasing them would be harmful to the patient's physical, mental, or emotional health. It was noted that professionals may limit the release of records to a patient when such release is believed to be harmful to the patient's physical, mental, or emotional health, and that a parent who is standing in the patient's stead has no greater right to the records than does the patient. [Cited in 24 Mental and Physical Disability Law Reporter 729 at 729–30.]

*Page 65, insert under **Vermont:***

A Vermont case underscores the recommendation that experts get a court appointment to conduct a custody evaluation rather than be directly retained by the parties for that purpose.

Politi v. Tyler, 751 A.2d 788 (Vt. 2000). The parents divorced in 1990. A custody and placement dispute came to a head in 1993. The family court issued an order for an evaluation in a custody action and directed the parties to recommend the psychologist who would do the evaluation. The parents contracted with Dr. Janet Tyler, a psychologist, and split her fees evenly. The psychologist wrote a report, which she gave to the parents and about which she testified in court. The parents stipulated to a modified custody agreement in 1994. In 1997, the mother sued Dr. Tyler for slander, malpractice, and intentional infliction of emotional distress. Dr. Tyler moved dismissal on the grounds that she had absolute judicial immunity as a court-appointed expert or, in the alternative, that she had immunity as a witness in a judicial proceedings. She also asserted that the suit was barred by the statute of limitations, and that she did not owe a duty to the plaintiff that would justify a malpractice claim. The trial court held that Dr. Tyler was not entitled to a judicial immunity defense, that she did owe a duty of care, and that the statute of limitations for this duty was six years. The other two claims were dismissed.

Dr. Tyler appealed. The Vermont Supreme Court affirmed the trial court. It concluded that Dr. Tyler was not a court-appointed expert because she contracted directly with the parties rather than having received an appointment by the family court. The court's order that a forensic evaluation be done was not sufficient to permit Dr. Tyler to claim to be a court-appointed expert. Further, Dr. Tyler's contract with the parents contained no language suggesting that she was acting as an arm of the family court. The contract also specified that the evaluation and testimony was predicated upon payment by the parties rather than upon authority granted by a court order.

The Vermont Supreme Court agreed that Dr. Tyler was entitled to witness immunity for statements made during her actual court testimony. She was, however, not entitled to such immunity for the acts of conducting a forensic evaluation or preparing a report. The court further held that Dr. Tyler owed a duty of care predicated upon her contract with the parties.

*Page 66, insert above **Wisconsin**:*

Washington

Gustafson v. Mazer, 54 P.3d 743, 113 Wash. App. 770 (Wash. Ct. App. 2002). A mother in a child custody dispute sued a psychologist and her employer, claiming that the psychologist negligently and defamatorily reported to the Guardian ad Litem that the mother may suffer from Munchausen Syndrome by Proxy (MSBP).

At the request of the GAL, Dr. Mazer had been retained by the parents to conduct an evaluation of the parents and child. She prepared a memorandum giving the basis for her suspicions. The GAL brought an *ex parte* motion seeking a transfer of custody. She attached Dr. Mazer's memorandum to the motion. The court commissioner granted the motion immediately transferring custody to the father. Three days later, Dr. Mazer testified in support of her memorandum at an emergency hearing to vacate the transfer of custody. The motion was denied. However, a superior court judge returned the child to the mother's custody 17 days later. Seven months later, Dr. Mazer submitted a report indicating that her allegations of MSBP were not substantiated.

Dr. Mazer moved for summary judgment in the mother's malpractice suit, and the superior court granted it based on witness immunity. Gustafson appealed. The appellate court found that Dr. Mazer had no professional relationship with Gustafson because she assisted the GAL and she functioned much like an expert appointed by the court. Further, Dr. Mazer was entitled to witness immunity for her report to the GAL, in part because she had prepared it in anticipation of testimony. The appellate court affirmed the decision of the superior court.

CHAPTER 2

ETHICAL ISSUES

Insert on page 70 as § 2.1A. Delete everything between the space after the third line at the top of the page and the space after "Standard 2.05" on that page.

§ 2.1A New American Psychological Association Code of Ethics (New)

A major revision of the *Ethical Principles of Psychologists and Code of Conduct* (hereinafter, "Ethics Code") went into effect on June 1, 2003. There are a number of changes that directly affect the forensic work of psychologists. The complete revision of the Code of Ethics will be found in Appendix C.

The most significant changes include:

1. There is no longer a section of the Code labeled "Forensic Activities." Forensic ethics standards are now interspersed among the other standards. According to the Chair of the Ethics Code Task Force, this change was made because of evidence that many psychologists with little or no forensic training have entered the forensic arena as either expert or fact witnesses. By interspersing the forensic ethics standards with other areas addressing professional practice, it is hoped that these psychologists will become aware of the ethical issues they must bear in mind before they become involved in a legal case or some aspect of the legal system.

2. The change that may be of greatest interest to attorneys is with regard to the release of raw test data. As discussed in § 2.24, raw test data has generally been considered to include both the test questions or other test-related material *and* the individual's responses to the questions/material. That is no longer the case: test data and test materials are now clearly differentiated:

> Ethical Standard 9.04 Release of Test Data
>
> (a) The term *test data* refers to raw and scaled scores, client/patient responses to test questions or stimuli, and psychologists' notes and recordings concerning client/patient statements and behavior during an examination. Those portions of test materials that include client/patient

> responses are included in the definition of *test data*. Pursuant to a client/patient release, psychologists provide test data to the client/patient or other persons identified in the release. Psychologists may refrain from releasing test data to protect a client/patient or others from substantial harm or misuse or misrepresentation of the data or the test, recognizing that in many instances release of confidential information under these circumstances is regulated by law.
>
> (b) In the absence of a client/patient release, psychologists provide test data only as required by law or court order.[9]

This Ethical Standard must be considered along with Ethical Standard 9.11, Maintaining Test Security:

> The term *test materials* refers to manuals, instruments, protocols, and test questions or stimuli, which do not include *test data* as defined in Standard 9.04, Release of Test Data. Psychologists make reasonable efforts to maintain the integrity and security of test materials and other assessment techniques consistent with law and contractual obligations, and in a manner that permits adherence to this Ethics Code.[9.1]

Thus, *test data* refer to a specific client/patient and to the responses of that particular individual, while *test materials* refer to the instrument or test to which the client/patient was responding. Test material, therefore, contains nothing that is unique to a given individual.[9.2] Taken together, these two Ethical Standards indicate that:

> (1) psychologists *may* provide test data, as defined, to attorneys, provided that the client/patient has given informed consent, in writing, to that release.
>
> (2) However, the psychologist may withhold test data from the client/patient, from the attorney, and/or from others if the psychologist believes that release of the test data may cause substantial harm to the client/patient or others, or if the psychologist believes that the test data that are released may be misused or misrepresented.

---

[9] American Psychological Association, *Ethical Principles of Psychologists and Code of Conduct,* 57 American Psychologist 1060–73 (2002) at 1071–72 (hereinafter "Ethics Code").

[9.1] *Id.* at 1072.

[9.2] Stephen Behnke, "Release of Test Data and APA's New Ethics Code." 34 *Monitor on Psychology* 70–72 (2003).

(3) Psychologists are required to follow statutory law related to release of information. Thus, if a state law prohibits release under conditions or circumstances that exist in a given case, the law would take precedence, and the psychologist would not release the test data. The same would be true if release of the test data was believed by the psychologist to violate the federal Health Insurance Portability and Accountability Act (HIPAA). It is also important to note that "HIPAA does not require release of records to clients/patients when information is compiled in reasonable anticipation of, or for use in, civil, criminal, or administrative actions or proceedings."[9.3]

(4) If the client/patient has not provided a written, informed consent for release, the psychologist is not permitted to release the test data without specific statutory authority or a court order. A subpoena from an attorney is not a sufficient basis for the release of test data.[9.4] Attorneys are not trained to understand or evaluate most of the raw obtained data from an evaluation. Therefore, intentional or not, it is likely that they will be unable to validly use or present the data without the assistance of a psychologist retained for that purpose.[9.5] A psychologist who releases test data with neither a signed, informed consent from the client/patient nor a court order is likely to be in violation of Standard 9.04.[9.6]

(5) "Test materials" are defined as the test instruments themselves. If the client/patient responds by writing on the test materials, or if the psychologist writes the individual's responses on the test materials, the test materials *become* test data, because of the presence of those client /patient responses. If, however, the responses are recorded on a separate document or paper, it is only the responses, not the test questions or stimuli, that may be released.

(6) If the psychologist has been retained by an attorney, appointed by a court, or otherwise retained by an organization rather than by the individual who is being evaluated, the test data do not have to be released to that individual because he or she is not the client.

[9.3] Celia B. Fisher, Decoding the Ethics Code: A Practical Guide for Psychologists. Thousand Oaks, CA: Sage (2003) at 29.

[9.4] Behnke at 72.

[9.5] Solomon Fulero, personal communication, May 4, 2003; Jeanne J. Johnson & Jeffrey L. Helms, "Test Security in the Twenty-First Century," 21 *American Journal of Forensic Psychology* 19–32 at 25–26 (2003).

[9.6] Behnke at 72.

(7) Whenever possible, psychologists have a responsibility to avoid releasing test materials, due to the need to maintain the integrity and security of those test materials, the contractual agreements between the psychologist and the test publisher, and the need to minimize entry of the test materials into the public domain.[9.7]

(8) Ethical Standard 9.04 specifies that "test data" includes "psychologists' notes and recordings concerning client/patient statements and behavior *during an examination*." [Emphasis added.] "The term 'notes' in this standard is limited to the assessment or test and does not include psychotherapy notes documenting or analyzing the contents of conversation during a private counseling session."[9.8]

3. The revised Code modified the Standard related to "multiple relationships (Ethical Standard 1.17 in the 1992 Code). Ethical Standard 3.05(a) reads, in part, that

> A psychologist refrains from entering into a multiple relationship if the multiple relationship could reasonably be expected to impair the psychologist's objectivity, competence, or effectiveness in performing his or her functions as a psychologist, or otherwise risks exploitation or harm to the person with whom the professional relationship exists.[9.9]

This strongly reinforces the prohibition, discussed in § 2.7 of this book, against a psychologist acting as an evaluator or expert witness (rather than solely as a fact witness) when his or her psychotherapy patient/client is a participant in the legal process.

4. Ethical Standard 3.10, Informed Consent, has been expanded to make it clear that the autonomy of the patient/client is to be maximized. If the patient/client is permitted to either accept or refuse the psychological services, he or she must receive an explanation sufficient to permit a knowing and voluntary choice to be made, "using language that is reasonably understandable to that person. . . ."[9.10]

According to Ethical Standard 3.10(b),

[9.7] Jeanne J. Johnson & Jeffrey L. Helms, "Test Security in the Twenty-First Century," 21 *American Journal of Forensic Psychology* 19–32 at 24 and 27–28 (2003).

[9.8] Fisher at 192.

[9.9] Ethics Code at 1065.

[9.10] *Id.*

> For persons who are legally incapable of giving informed consent, psychologists nevertheless (1) provide an appropriate explanation, (2) seek the individual's assent, (3) consider such persons' preferences and best interests, and (4) obtain appropriate permission from a legally authorized person, if such substitute consent is permitted or required by law. When consent by a legally authorized person is not permitted or required by law, psychologists take reasonable steps to protect the individual's rights and welfare.[9.11]

Further, according to Ethical Standard 3.10(c),

> When psychological services are court ordered or otherwise mandated, psychologists inform the individual of the nature of the anticipated services, including whether the services are court ordered or mandated and any limits of confidentiality, before proceeding.[9.12]

According to Cecilia Fisher, Ph.D., the Chair of the Ethics Code Task Force,

> Psychologists conducting a court-ordered forensic assessment must inform the individual tested: why the assessment is being conducted; that the findings may be entered into evidence in court; and if known to the psychologist, the extent to which the individual and his or her attorney will have access to the information. The psychologist should not assume the role of legal advisor, but can advise the individual to speak with his or her attorney when asked about potential legal consequences of noncooperation.[9.13]

When the psychological service is an assessment, Ethical Standard 9.03(a) reinforces the above requirements by indicating that informed consent "includes an explanation of the nature and purpose of the assessment, fees, involvement of third parties, and limits of confidentiality, and sufficient opportunity for the client/patient to ask questions and receive answers."[9.14] Finally, for individuals who are court-ordered to be evaluated, or who are not legally competent to give informed consent, which would include children in child custody matters, psychologists are required by Ethical Standard 9.03(b), which is new, to inform them "about the nature and purpose of the proposed assessment services, using language that is

---

[9.11] *Id.*

[9.12] *Id.*

[9.13] Fisher at 80.

[9.14] Ethics Code at 1071.

reasonably understandable to the person being assessed,"[9.15] as well as telling them who is expected to receive copies of the psychologist's report.

Ethical Standard 6.04(d) indicates that "if limitations to services can be anticipated because of limitations in financing, this is discussed with the recipient of services as early as is feasible."[9.16] That is, if the psychologist does not believe that he or she can reasonably perform the requested service due to limitations on finances, this must be discussed with the retaining attorney, the Court, or another party as early in the process as possible. If the limitations due to finances will prevent the psychologist from doing everything necessary to provide an adequate assessment, the psychologist should generally withdraw from the case. If the psychologist only becomes aware that the actual cost of an assessment or other services will be greater than the amount agreed upon when well into the process, the psychologist must discuss any limitations with the party(ies) with whom he or she contracted as soon as possible, and try to work out limitations on the services provided or another equitable solution.

The present authors recommend that the informed consent statements be given both orally and in writing, and that the signature of the person being evaluated (or his/her guardian, if relevant) be obtained whenever possible. The limits of confidentiality and the foreseeable ways in which the information will be used should be repeated at subsequent assessment sessions, or expanded if circumstances change over time.

5. While a court-ordered evaluation is not confidential, *per se,* since it is done in anticipation of a court proceeding and a number of people, including the parties themselves, the attorneys, a Guardian ad Litem, and a judge, at minimum, would be expected to review the report, psychologists still "have a primary obligation and take reasonable precautions to protect confidential information obtained through or stored in any medium, recognizing that the extent and limits of confidentiality may be regulated by law. . . ."[9.17] This includes ensuring that the computer on which test data or a report are stored is adequately protected from access by unauthorized individuals, including encryption, password protection, and use of an effective firewall. The same holds true for confidential information sent via e-mail, because e-mail that is not encrypted is accessible to knowledgeable individuals ("hackers"). Further, the psychologist has an obligation to ensure that the recipient of confidential information by e-mail, fax, or other electronic transmission has an adequate confidentiality policy and that in-

---

[9.15] *Id.* at 1071.
[9.16] *Id.* at 1068.
[9.17] Ethical Standard 4.01 Maintaining Confidentiality, *id.* at 1066.

dividuals who are not authorized to view the confidential information do not have access to it.[9.18]

6. While psychologists do not often make audio or video records of assessments, a psychologist who does so is required by Ethical Standard 4.03, Recording, to get permission from each individual who is recorded, or from his or her legal representative, or a court order. "[U]nder Standard 4.03, no . . . exceptions are permissible for service providers."[9.19]

7. Ethical Standard 6.01, Documentation of Professional and Scientific Work and Maintenance of Records, indicates that psychologists must "maintain, disseminate, store, retain, and dispose of records and data relating to their professional . . . work"[9.20] in ways that facilitate provision of services and ensure compliance with the law. "Creating or maintaining records that are illegible to others would be a violation of this standard."[9.21]

8. While Ethical Standard 6.04(a), Fees and Financial Arrangements, is not significantly different from 1992 Ethical Standard 1.25(a), Dr. Fisher's commentary indicates that forensic psychologists must make a financial arrangement as early in the professional relationship as is feasible.

> In specifying compensation, psychologists must include a description of all reasonably anticipated costs. For forensic . . . services this might include charges for telephone conversations; client, employee or participant interviews; library or computer research; statistical analysis; court preparation time; travel; postage; or duplication. Psychologists arranging compensation for assessment services should provide information about fees for test administration, scoring, interpretation, and report writing.[9.22]

9. Ethical Standard 9.01, Bases for Assessment, addresses the requirements for an assessment to be considered adequate. Ethical Standard 9.01(a) indicates that psychologists must provide opinions that are adequately substantiated by the information reviewed and/or the methods used, a slight modification of 1992 Ethical Standard 2.01(b). A more significant change is Ethical Standard 9.01(b), which indicates that

> Except as noted in 9.01(c), psychologists provide opinions of the psychological characteristics of individuals only after they have conducted an examination of the individuals adequate to support their statements or conclusions. When, despite reasonable efforts, such an examination is not

---

[9.18] Fisher at 86.

[9.19] *Id.* at 93.

[9.20] Ethics Code at 1067.

[9.21] Fisher at 115.

[9.22] *Id.* at 124.

practical, psychologists document the efforts they made and the result of those efforts, clarify the probable impact of their limited information on the reliability and validity of their opinions, and appropriately limit the nature and extent of their conclusions or recommendations.[9.23]

Ethical Standard 9.01(c) is new:

When psychologists conduct a record review or provide consultation or supervision and an individual examination is not warranted or necessary for the opinion, psychologists explain this and the sources of information on which they based their conclusions and recommendations.[9.24]

Dr. Fisher's commentary specifies that

Standard 9.01(b) specifically addresses the importance of in-person evaluations of individuals about whom psychologists will offer a professional opinion. Under this standard, with few exceptions psychologists must conduct individual examinations sufficient to obtain personal verification of information on which to base their professional opinions and refrain from providing opinions about the psychological characteristics of an individual if they themselves have not conducted an examination of the individual adequate to support their statement or conclusions.[9.25]

The recommended meaning of "reasonable efforts" is tied to the standard of practice, i.e., the prevailing professional practice and judgment of psychologists engaged in similar activities regarding the minimum effort necessary if the psychologist is to be able to state an opinion to a reasonable degree of psychological/scientific certainty. If a psychologist, despite reasonable efforts, is unable to conduct a personal interview, the psychologist is obligated to state in both written and oral opinions the limitations that that lack of a personal interview has on the validity and reliability of his or her opinions. The psychologist must also limit any conclusions or recommendations to those that are based upon information that the psychologist has personally verified, and to specify the source and nature of that information.

This does not, in our opinion, preclude an attorney from asking a psychologist a hypothetical question that involves the specific allegations in a case, and to ask for an opinion based upon the assumption that those allegations are true. The court, of course, may limit or exclude such testimony.

[9.23] Ethics Code at 1071.

[9.24] *Id.* at 1071.

[9.25] Fisher at 181.

Dr. Fisher also notes that some forensic opinions only require that records be reviewed. Examples include determination as to whether an assessment that was conducted was both appropriate and sufficient, recommendations in disability or professional liability cases in which there is a sufficient record available, or other cases in which a personal interview is not generally considered essential. As indicated above, the psychologist must still specify any limitations and identify why an interview is not essential to the opinion being offered.[9.26]

10. Ethical Standard 9.02, Use of Assessments, has been expanded beyond what was in the 1992 Code. Ethical Standard 9.02(a) indicates that

> Psychologists administer, adapt, score, interpret, or use assessment techniques, interviews, tests, or instruments in a manner and for purposes that are appropriate in light of the research on or evidence of the usefulness and proper application of the techniques.[9.27]

Ethical Standard 9.02(b) is new:

> Psychologists use assessment instruments whose validity and reliability have been established for use with members of the population tested. When such validity or reliability has not been established, psychologists describe the strengths and limitations of test results and interpretation.[9.28]

Thus, a psychologist should ensure that a test or other instrument has been validated for use with individuals the age, ethnicity, language, gender, and/or disability or other characteristics of the client/patient. Some of this information will come from the test/instrument manual. The psychologist also needs to be sufficiently familiar with the research literature on the test/instrument to be able to assess whether new research supports or questions particular uses of the test or instrument or specific interpretations of the results. If a test or other instrument is used despite the lack of research-based support for the particular use, the psychologist is required to specify why it was used, the advantages of using it, and any limitations on interpretations and recommendations as a result of its use.[9.29]

A psychologist who violates the Ethical Standards of the American Psychological Association faces sanctions ranging from educational advisories regarding errors at minimum, to expulsion from the Association (if he or she is a member) at maximum. A California appellate court has upheld the

---

[9.26] *Id.* at 183.

[9.27] Ethics Code at 1071.

[9.28] *Id.* at 1071.

[9.29] Fisher at 186.

right of the American Psychological Association to censure a member who provided false testimony in a child custody proceeding.[9.30] More significant, because most of the statutes licensing psychologists make reference to the APA Code, the psychologist could be sanctioned by his or her licensing board, including the potential for having his or her license revoked if the misconduct is especially egregious.

While the Ethical Principles of Psychologists and Code of Conduct were substantially revised, there have been no changes made in either the *Guidelines for Child Custody Evaluations in Divorce Proceedings*[9.31] or the *Specialty Guidelines for Forensic Psychologists*.[9.32] The *Specialty Guidelines for Forensic Psychologists* is undergoing review at the present time, and a revision is expected to be published in 2005.

HIPAA and the new APA Code of Ethics

There is no reason to believe that the provisions of the Health Insurance Portability and Accountability Act (HIPAA) controls any aspect of a forensic psychological evaluation, with one exception. HIPAA explicitly excludes "release of records to clients/patients when information is compiled in reasonable anticipation of, or for use in, civil, criminal, or administrative actions or proceedings."[9.33] Furthermore, the forensic services are provided in order to respond to a legal question or issue, not a psychotherapeutic question or issue. The forensic psychological services are also provided at the behest of a third party, not the client/patient him/herself, and the services are not provided within the health care system. Finally, the services fall outside of the health care system, so they are not covered by health insurance.[9.34]

The exception is that a forensic psychological evaluation may involve the psychologist receiving Protected Health Information (PHI), including medical and/or psychological records. A request for records is often a part of a custody evaluation, and if there is an allegation of abuse or neglect the records take on particular importance. Thus, the forensic psychologist must maintain the security of any PHI he or she receives. The psychologist

---

[9.30] *Budwin v. American Psychological Assoc.*, 24 Cal. App. 4th 875, 29 Cal. Rptr. 2d 453 (Cal. App. 3d Dist. 1994).

[9.31] American Psychological Association, 1994; see § 3.11–3.14.

[9.32] Committee on Ethical Guidelines for Forensic Psychologists, 1991. See Appendix F.

[9.33] Fisher at 29.

[9.34] Mary Connell and Gerald P. Koocher, "Expert Opinion: HIPAA and Forensic Practice," 23 *American Psychology-Law Society News* 16-19 at 18-19 (2003).

may also get the informed consent of the patient/client to a waiver of any expectation that he or she will have access to the PHI.

Standards under *Daubert*, *Joiner* and *Kumho*

Several Ethical Standards have particular relevance to the requirements set down by the Supreme Court in *Daubert v. Merrell Dow Pharmaceuticals, Inc.*,[9.35] *General Electric Co. v. Joiner*,[9.36] and *Kumho Tire Co. v. Carmichael*[9.37] (see Chapter 1 for an extensive discussion of these cases):

> Ethical Standard 2.04 Psychologists' work is based upon established scientific and professional knowledge of the discipline.[9.38]

> Ethical Standard 9.01(a) Psychologists base the opinions contained in their recommendations, reports, and diagnostic or evaluative statements, including forensic testimony, on information and techniques sufficient to substantiate their findings.
>
> (b) Except as noted in 9.01(c), psychologists provide opinions of the psychological characteristics of individuals only after they have conducted an examination of the individuals adequate to support their statements or conclusions. When, despite reasonable efforts, such an examination is not practical, psychologists . . . clarify the probable impact of their limited information on the reliability and validity of their opinions, and appropriately limit the nature and extent of their conclusions or recommendations.
>
> (c) When psychologists conduct a record review or provide consultation . . . and an individual examination is not warranted or necessary for the opinion, psychologists explain this and the sources of information on which they based their conclusions and recommendations.[9.39]

> Ethical Standard 9.02(a) Psychologists administer, adapt, score, interpret, or use assessment techniques, interviews, tests, or instruments in a manner and for purposes that are appropriate in light of the research on or evidence of the usefulness and proper application of the techniques.
>
> (b) Psychologists use assessment instruments whose validity and reliability have been established for use with members of the population

---

[9.35] 509 U.S. 579, 113 S. Ct. 2786, 125 L. Ed. 2d 469 (1993). *See also Daubert v. Merrell Dow Pharmaceuticals, Inc.*, 43 F.3d 1311 (9th Cir. 1995).

[9.36] 522 U.S. 136 (1997).

[9.37] 119 S. Ct. 1167 (1999).

[9.38] Ethics Code at 1064.

[9.39] *Id.* at 1071.

tested. When such validity or reliability has not been established, psychologists describe the strengths and limitations of test results.[9.40]

Ethical Standard 9.06 When interpreting assessment results . . . , psychologists take into account the purpose of the assessment as well as the various test factors, test-taking abilities, and other characteristics of the person being assessed, such as situational, personal, linguistic, and cultural differences, that might affect psychologists' judgments or reduce the accuracy of their interpretation. They indicate any significant limitations of their interpretations.[9.41]

Ethical Standard 9.08(a) Psychologists do not base their assessment or intervention decisions or recommendations on data or test results that are outdated for the current purpose.

(b) Psychologists do not base such decisions or recommendations on tests and measures that are obsolete and not useful for the current purpose.[9.42]

Page 76, insert after § 2.4:

§ 2.4A Rights and Responsibilities of Test Takers (New)

The Joint Committee on Testing Practices of the American Educational Research Association, the American Psychological Association, and the National Council on Measurement in Education has published a set of "guidelines and expectations" on "the rights and responsibilities of test takers," "the rights of test takers: guidelines for testing professionals," and "the responsibilities of test takers: guidelines for the testing professionals."

Rights and Responsibilities of Test Takers: GUIDELINES AND EXPECTATIONS

1. **Test Takers:**
   A. You Have Rights
   B. You Have Responsibilities
   C. You have rights and responsibilities
   D. All of the above

[9.40] *Id.*
[9.41] *Id.* at 1072.
[9.42] *Id.*

§ 2.1A NEW APA CODE OF ETHICS

The Rights and Responsibilities of Test Takers: Guidelines and Expectations was developed by the Joint Committee on Testing Practices (JCTP), a cooperative effort of several professional organizations, that has as its aim the advancement, in the public interest, of the quality of testing practices. The joint committee was initiated by the American Educational Research Association, the American Psychological Association, and the National Council on Measurement in Education. In addition to these three groups, the American Counseling Association, American Speech-Language-Hearing Association, and the National Association of School Psychologists are now also sponsors of the joint committee.

The Rights and Responsibilities of Test Takers: Guidelines and Expectations has been endorsed by the American Counseling Association, the American Psychological Association, and the National Association of School Psychologists.

This is not copyrighted material. Reproduction and dissemination are encouraged. For other JCTP products and information, as well as electronic copies of the *Rights and Responsibilities of Test Takers: Guidelines and Expectations* document, please go to the JCTP Web site: http://www.apa.org/science/jctpweb.html.

PREAMBLE

The intent of this statement is to enumerate and clarify the expectations that test takers may reasonably have about the testing process, and the expectations that those who develop, administer, and use tests may have of test takers. Tests are defined broadly here as psychological and educational instruments developed and used by testing professionals in organizations such as schools, industries, clinical practice, counseling settings, and human service and other agencies, including those assessment procedures and devices that are used for making inferences about people in the above-named settings. The purpose of the statement is to inform and to help educate not only test takers, but also others involved in the testing enterprise so that measurements may be most validly and appropriately used. This document is intended as an effort to inspire improvements in the testing process and does not have the force of law. Its orientation is to encourage positive and high quality interactions between testing professionals and test takers.

The rights and responsibilities listed in this document are neither legally based nor inalienable rights and responsibilities such as those listed in the United States of America's Bill of Rights. Rather, they represent the best judgments of testing professionals about the reasonable expectations that those involved in the testing enterprise (test producers, test users, and test takers) should have of each other. Testing professionals include developers of assessment products and services, those who market and sell them, persons who select them, test administrators and scorers, those who interpret test results, and trained users of the information. Persons who engage in each of these activities have significant responsibilities that are described elsewhere, in documents such as those that follow (American Association for Counseling and Development, 1988; American Speech-Language-Hearing Association, 1994; Joint Committee on Testing Practices, 1988; National Association of School Psychologists, 1992; National Council on Measurement in Education, 1995).

In some circumstances, the test developer and the test user may not be the same person, group of persons, or organization. In such situations, the professionals involved in the testing should clarify, for the test taker as well as for themselves, who is responsible for each aspect of the testing process. For example, when an individual chooses to take a college admissions test, at least three parties are involved in addition to the test taker: the test developer and publisher, the individuals who administer the test to the test taker, and the institutions of higher education who will eventually use the information. In such cases test takers may need to request clarifications about their rights and responsibilities. When test takers are young children (e.g., those taking standardized tests in the schools) or are persons who spend some or all of their time in institutions or are incapacitated, parents or guardians may be granted some of the rights and responsibilities, rather than, or in addition to, the individual.

Perhaps the most fundamental right test takers have is to be able to take tests that meet high professional standards, such as those described in Standards for Educational and Psychological Testing (American Educational Research Association, American Psychological Association, & National Council on Measurement in Education, 1999) as well as those of other appropriate professional associations. This statement should be used as an adjunct, or supplement, to those standards. State and federal laws, of course, supersede any rights and responsibilities that are stated here.

REFERENCES

American Association for Counseling and Development (now American Counseling Association) & Association for Measurement and Evaluation in Counseling and Development (now Association for Assessment in Counseling). (1989). *Responsibilities of users of standardized tests: RUST statement revised.* Alexandria, VA: Author.

American Educational Research Association, American Psychological Association, & National Council on Measurement in Education. (1999). *Standards for educational and psychological testing.* Washington, DC: American Educational Research Association.

American Speech-Language-Hearing Association. (1994). *Protection of rights of people receiving audiology or speech-language pathology services.* ASHA (36), 60-63.

Joint Committee on Testing Practices. (1988). *Code of fair testing practices in education.* Washington, DC: American Psychological Association.
National Association of School Psychologists. (1992). *Standards for the provision of school psychological services.* Author: Silver Spring, MD.
National Council on Measurement in Education. (1995). *Code of professional responsibilities in educational measurement.* Washington, DC: Author.

THE RIGHTS AND RESPONSIBILITIES OF TEST TAKERS: GUIDELINES AND EXPECTATIONS

As a test taker, you have the right to:

1. **Be informed of your rights and responsibilities as a test taker.**
2. **Be treated with courtesy, respect, and impartiality, regardless of your age, disability, ethnicity, gender, national origin, religion, sexual orientation, or other personal characteristics.**
3. **Be tested with measures that meet professional standards and that are appropriate, given the manner in which the test results will be used.**
4. **Receive a brief oral or written explanation prior to testing about the purpose(s) for testing, the kind(s) of tests to be used, if the results will be reported to you or to others, and the planned use(s) of the results. If you have a disability, you have the right to inquire and receive information about testing accommodations. If you have difficulty in comprehending the language of the test, you have a right to know in advance of testing whether any accommodations may be available to you.**
5. **Know in advance of testing when the test will be administered, if and when test results will be available to you, and if there is a fee for testing services that you are expected to pay.**
6. **Have your test administered and your test results interpreted by appropriately trained individuals who follow professional codes of ethics.**
7. **Know if a test is optional and learn of the consequences of taking or not taking the test, fully completing the test, or canceling the scores. You may need to ask questions to learn these consequences.**
8. **Receive a written or oral explanation of your test results within a reasonable amount of time after testing and in commonly understood terms.**
9. **Have your test results kept confidential to the extent allowed by law.**

10. Present concerns about the testing process or your results and receive information about procedures that will be used to address such concerns.

As a test taker, you have the responsibility to:

1. **Read and/or listen to your rights and responsibilities as a test taker.**
2. **Treat others with courtesy and respect during the testing process.**
3. **Ask questions prior to testing if you are uncertain about why the test is being given, how it will be given, what you will be asked to do, and what will be done with the results.**
4. **Read or listen to descriptive information in advance of testing and listen carefully to all test instructions. You should inform an examiner in advance of testing if you wish to receive a testing accommodation or if you have a physical condition or illness that may interfere with your performance on the test. If you have difficulty comprehending the language of the test, it is your responsibility to inform an examiner.**
5. **Know when and where the test will be given, pay for the test if required, appear on time with any required materials, and be ready to be tested.**
6. **Follow the test instructions you are given and represent yourself honestly during the testing.**
7. **Be familiar with and accept the consequences of not taking the test, should you choose to not take the test.**
8. **Inform appropriate person(s), as specified to you by the organization responsible for testing, if you believe that testing conditions affected your results.**
9. **Ask about the confidentiality of your test results, if this aspect concerns you.**
10. **Present concerns about the testing process or results in a timely, respectful way, if you have any.**

THE RIGHTS OF TEST TAKERS: GUIDELINES FOR TESTING PROFESSIONALS

Test takers have the rights described below. It is the responsibility of the professionals involved in the testing process to ensure that test takers receive these rights.

1. **Because test takers have the right to be informed of their rights and responsibilities as test takers, it is normally the responsibility of the individual who administers a test (or the organization that prepared the test) to inform test takers of these rights and responsibilities.**
2. **Because test takers have the right to be treated with courtesy, respect, and impartiality, regardless of their age, disability, ethnicity, gender, national origin, race, religion, sexual orientation, or other personal characteristics, testing professionals should:**

   a. Make test takers aware of any materials that are available to assist them in test preparation. These materials should be clearly described in test registration and/or test familiarization materials.

   b. See that test takers are provided with reasonable access to testing services.
3. **Because test takers have the right to be tested with measures that meet professional standards that are appropriate for the test use and the test taker, given the manner in which the results will be used, testing professionals should:**

   a. Take steps to utilize measures that meet professional standards and are reliable, relevant, useful (given the intended purpose), and fair for test takers from varying societal groups.

   b. Advise test takers that they are entitled to request reasonable accommodations in test administration that are likely to increase the validity of their test scores if they have a disability recognized under the Americans With Disabilities Act or other relevant legislation.
4. **Because test takers have the right to be informed, prior to testing, about the tests purposes, the nature of the test, whether test results will be reported to the test takers, and the planned use of the results (when not in conflict with the testing purposes), testing professionals should:**

   a. Give or provide test takers with access to a brief description about the test purpose (e.g., diagnosis, placement, selection, etc.) and the kind(s) of tests and formats that will be used (e.g., individual/group, multiple-choice/free response/performance, timed/untimed, etc.), unless such information might be detrimental to the objectives of the test.

   b. Tell test takers, prior to testing, about the planned use(s) of the test results. Upon request, the test taker should be given information about how long such test scores are typically kept on file and remain available.

c. Provide test takers, if requested, with information about any preventative measures that have been instituted to safeguard the accuracy of test scores. Such information would include any quality control procedures that are employed and some of the steps taken to prevent dishonesty in test performance.

d. Inform test takers, in advance of the testing, about required materials that must be brought to the test site (e.g., pencil, paper) and about any rules that allow or prohibit use of other materials (e.g., calculators).

e. Provide test takers, upon request, with general information about the appropriateness of the test for its intended purpose, to the extent that such information does not involve the release of proprietary information. (For example, the test taker might be told, "Scores on this test are useful in predicting how successful people will be in this kind of work" or "Scores on this test, along with other information, help us to determine if students are likely to benefit from this program.")

f. Provide test takers, upon request, with information about re-testing, including if it is possible to re-take the test or another version of it, and if so, how often, how soon, and under what conditions.

g. Provide test takers, upon request, with information about how the test will be scored and in what detail. On multiple-choice tests, this information might include suggestions for test taking and about the use of a correction for guessing. On tests scored using professional judgment (e.g., essay tests or projective techniques), a general description of the scoring procedures might be provided except when such information is proprietary or would tend to influence test performance inappropriately.

h. Inform test takers about the type of feedback and interpretation that is routinely provided, as well as what is available for a fee. Test takers have the right to request and receive information regarding whether or not they can obtain copies of their test answer sheets or their test materials, if they can have their scores verified, and if they may cancel their test results.

i. Provide test takers, prior to testing, either in the written instructions, in other written documents, or orally, with answers to questions that test takers may have about basic test administration procedures.

j. Inform test takers, prior to testing, if questions from test takers will not be permitted during the testing process.

k. Provide test takers with information about the use of computers, calculators, or other equipment, if any, used in the testing and give them an opportunity to practice using such equipment, unless its unpracticed use is part of the test purpose, or practice would compromise the validity of the results, and to provide a testing accommodation for the use of such equipment, if needed.

l. Inform test takers that, if they have a disability; they have the right to request and receive accommodations or modifications in accordance with the provisions of the Americans With Disabilities Act and other relevant legislation.

m. Provide test takers with information that will be of use in making decisions if test takers have options regarding which tests, test forms, or test formats to take.

5. Because test takers have a right to be informed in advance when the test will be administered, if and when test results will be available, and if there is a fee for testing services that the test takers are expected to pay, test professionals should:

a. Notify test takers of the alteration in a timely manner if a previously announced testing schedule changes, provide a reasonable explanation for the change, and inform test takers of the new schedule. If there is a change, reasonable alternatives to the original schedule should be provided.

b. Inform test takers prior to testing about any anticipated fee for the testing process, as well as the fees associated with each component of the process, if the components can be separated.

6. Because test takers have the right to have their tests administered and interpreted by appropriately trained individuals, testing professionals should:

a. Know how to select the appropriate test for the intended purposes.

b. When testing persons with documented disabilities and other special characteristics that require special testing conditions and/or interpretation of results, have the skills and knowledge for such testing and interpretation.

c. Provide reasonable information regarding their qualifications, upon request.

d. Ensure that test conditions, especially if unusual, do not unduly interfere with test performance. Test conditions will normally be similar to those used to standardize the test.

e. Provide candidates with a reasonable amount of time to complete the test, unless a test has a time limit.

f. Take reasonable actions to safeguard against fraudulent actions (e.g., cheating) that could place honest test takers at a disadvantage.

7. **Because test takers have the right to be informed about why they are being asked to take particular tests, if a test is optional, and what the consequences are should they choose not to complete the test, testing professionals should:**

   a. Normally only engage in testing activities with test takers after the test takers have provided their informed consent to take a test, except when testing without consent has been mandated by law or governmental regulation, or when consent is implied by an action the test takers have already taken (e.g., such as when applying for employment and a personnel examination is mandated).

   b. Explain to test takers why they should consider taking voluntary tests.

   c. Explain if a test taker refuses to take or complete a voluntary test, either orally or in writing, what the negative consequences may be to them for their decision to do so.

   d. Promptly inform the test taker if a testing professional decides that there is a need to deviate from the testing services to which the test taker initially agreed (e.g., should the testing professional believe it would be wise to administer an additional test or an alternative test), and provide an explanation for the change.

8. **Because test takers have a right to receive a written or oral explanation of their test results within a reasonable amount of time after testing and in commonly understood terms, testing professionals should:**

   a. Interpret test results in light of one or more additional considerations (e.g., disability; language proficiency), if those considerations are relevant to the purposes of the test and performance on the test and are in accordance with current laws.

   b. Provide, upon request, information to test takers about the sources used in interpreting their test results, including technical manuals, technical reports, norms, and a description of the comparison group, or additional information about the test taker(s).

   c. Provide, upon request, recommendations to test takers about how they could improve their performance on the test, should they choose or be required to take the test again.

d. Provide, upon request, information to test takers about their options for obtaining a second interpretation of their results. Test takers may select an appropriately trained professional to provide this second opinion.

e. Provide test takers with the criteria used to determine a passing score, when individual test scores are reported and related to a pass-fail standard.

f. Inform test takers, upon request, how much their scores might change, should they elect to take the test again. Such information would include variation in test performance due to measurement error (e.g., the appropriate standard errors of measurement) and changes in performance over time with or without intervention (e.g., additional training or treatment).

g. Communicate test results to test takers in an appropriate and sensitive manner, without use of negative labels or comments likely to inflame or stigmatize the test taker.

h. Provide corrected test scores to test takers as rapidly as possible, should an error occur in the processing or reporting of scores. The length of time is often dictated by individuals responsible for processing or reporting the scores, rather than the individuals responsible for testing, should the two parties indeed differ.

i. Correct any errors as rapidly as possible if there are errors in the process of developing scores.

9. **Because test takers have the right to have the results of tests kept confidential to the extent allowed by law, testing professionals should:**

a. Ensure that records of test results (in paper or electronic form) are safeguarded and maintained so that only individuals who have a legitimate right to access them will be able to do so.

b. Provide test takers, upon request, with information regarding who has a legitimate right to access their test results (when individually identified) and in what form. Testing professionals should respond appropriately to questions regarding the reasons why such individuals may have access to test results and how they may use the results.

c. Advise test takers that they are entitled to limit access to their results (when individually identified) to those persons or institutions, and for those purposes, revealed to them prior to testing. Exceptions may occur when test takers, or their guardians, consent to release the test results to others or when testing professionals are authorized by law to release test results.

   d. Keep confidential any requests for testing accommodations and the documentation supporting the request.

10. **Because test takers have the right to present concerns about the testing process and to receive information about procedures that will be used to address such concerns, testing professionals should:**

   a. Inform test takers how they can question the results of the testing if they do not believe that the test was administered properly or scored correctly, or other such concerns.
   b. Inform test takers of the procedures for appealing decisions that they believe are based in whole or in part on erroneous test results.
   c. Inform test takers, if their test results are under investigation and may be canceled, invalidated, or not released for normal use. In such an event, that investigation should be performed in a timely manner. The investigation should use all available information that addresses the reason(s) for the investigation, and the test taker should also be informed of the information that he/she may need to provide to assist with the investigation.
   d. Inform the test taker, if that test taker's test results are canceled or not released for normal use, why that action was taken. The test taker is entitled to request and receive information on the types of evidence and procedures that have been used to make that determination.

THE RESPONSIBILITIES OF TEST TAKERS: GUIDELINES FOR THE TESTING PROFESSIONALS

Testing Professionals should take steps to ensure that test takers know that they have specific responsibilities in addition to their rights described above.

1. **Testing professionals need to inform test takers that they should listen to and/or read their rights and responsibilities as a test taker and ask questions about issues they do not understand.**
2. **Testing professionals should take steps, as appropriate, to ensure that test takers know that they:**

   a. Are responsible for their behavior throughout the entire testing process.

b. Should not interfere with the rights of others involved in the testing process.

c. Should not compromise the integrity of the test and its interpretation in any manner.

3. **Testing professionals should remind test takers that it is their responsibility to ask questions prior to testing if they are uncertain about why the test is being given, how it will be given, what they will be asked to do, and what will be done with the results. Testing professionals should:**

   a. Advise test takers that it is their responsibility to review materials supplied by test publishers and others as part of the testing process and to ask questions about areas that they feel they should understand better prior to the start of testing.

   b. Inform test takers that it is their responsibility to request more information if they are not satisfied with what they know about how their test results will be used and what will be done with them.

4. **Testing professionals should inform test takers that it is their responsibility to read descriptive material they receive in advance of a test and to listen carefully to test instructions. Testing professionals should inform test takers that it is their responsibility to inform an examiner in advance of testing if they wish to receive a testing accommodation or if they have a physical condition or illness that may interfere with their performance. Testing professionals should inform test takers that it is their responsibility to inform an examiner if they have difficulty comprehending the language in which the test is given. Testing professionals should:**

   a. Inform test takers that, if they need special testing arrangements, it is their responsibility to request appropriate accommodations and to provide any requested documentation as far in advance of the testing date as possible. Testing professionals should inform test takers about the documentation needed to receive a requested testing accommodation.

   b. Inform test takers that, if they request but do not receive a testing accommodation, they could request information about why their request was denied.

5. **Testing professionals should inform test takers when and where the test will be given, and whether or not payment for the testing is required. Having been so informed, it is the responsibility of the test taker to appear on time with any required materials, pay for testing services, and be ready to be tested. Testing professionals should:**

- **a.** Inform test takers that they are responsible for familiarizing themselves with the appropriate materials needed for testing and for requesting information about these materials, if needed.
- **b.** Inform the test takers if the testing situation requires that test takers bring materials (e.g., personal identification, pencils, calculators, etc.) to the testing site if the testing situation requires that test takers do so.

6. Testing professionals should advise test takers, prior to testing, that it is their responsibility to:

- **a.** Listen to and/or read the directions given to them.
- **b.** Follow instructions given by testing professionals.
- **c.** Complete the test as directed.
- **d.** Perform to the best of their ability if they want their score to be a reflection of their best effort.
- **e.** Behave honestly (e.g., not cheating or assisting others who cheat).

7. Testing professionals should inform test takers about the consequences of not taking a test, should they choose to not take the test. Once so informed, it is the responsibility of the test taker to accept such consequences, and the testing professional should so inform the test takers. If test takers have questions regarding these consequences, it is their responsibility to ask questions of the testing professional, and the testing professional should so inform the test takers.

8. Testing professionals should inform test takers that it is their responsibility to notify appropriate persons, as specified by the testing organization, if they do not understand their results, or if they believe that testing conditions affected the results. Testing professionals should:

- **a.** Provide information to test takers, upon request, about appropriate procedures for questioning or canceling their test scores or results, if relevant to the purposes of testing.
- **b.** Provide to test takers, upon request, the procedures for reviewing. retesting, or canceling their scores or test results, if they believe that testing conditions affected their results and if relevant to the purposes of testing.
- **c.** Provide documentation to the test taker about known testing conditions that might have affected the results of the testing, if relevant to the purposes of testing.

9. Testing professionals should advise test takers that it is their responsibility to ask questions about the confidentiality of their test results, if this aspect concerns them.

10. **Testing professionals should advise test takers that it is their responsibility to present concerns about the testing process in a timely, respectful manner.**

Page 86, insert after § 2.8:

§ 2.8A Utilization of Psychologists Licensed in Jurisdictions Outside the State in Which the Custody Contest Is being Waged ("Foreign" Jurisdictions) (New)

Although every state restricts the practice of psychology to those individually licensed in that state, it is possible in many jurisdictions for a psychologist to temporarily practice for a specific purpose such as doing an evaluation for a court proceeding and testifying in court about that evaluation.

According to psychiatrist Robert Simon and law professor Daniel Shuman,[52.1] many states preclude psychologists and psychiatrists from practicing without a license from that specific state. If a forensic expert were to conduct an evaluation and/or testify in a state in which he or she is not licensed, the expert "may not be permitted to testify, may incur civil and criminal liability, or may face professional disciplinary action."[52.2] Experts may also find that their professional liability insurance does not cover actions brought while practicing without a license. Although there are only a small number of reports of problems for experts practicing across state lines, experts need to be aware of the potential for very serious problems when they practice outside the state(s) in which they are licensed. Violations are reported to the National Practitioner Data Bank and a disciplinary action could be brought against an expert in his or her home state. It is also possible that a malpractice suit could be filed against a psychiatrist or psychologist who is found to be practicing without a license in the jurisdiction in which a case is being tried.

Every state considers diagnosis and treatment to be components of the practice of medicine, the authors indicate. A non-state-licensed forensic psychiatrist is very likely to be required to diagnose, placing him or her in violation of state law.

[52.1] Robert I. Simon & Daniel W. Shuman, *Conducting Forensic Examinations on the Road: Are You Practicing Your Profession Without a License?* 27 Journal of the American Academy of Psychiatry & Law 75–82 (1999).

[52.2] *Id.* at 75.

Many states have exceptions for physicians or psychologists from contiguous states, generally based on reciprocity. Some laws require that the guest physician be in consultation with or be supervised by a resident physician.

There are, generally, two lines of case law. One indicates that state licensure is a minimum requirement for expert testimony in that state. A lack of the required licensed means a lack of competency or qualification to testify. The other line of case law treats licensure as only one of several factors relevant to whether the individual is qualified as an expert, and considers local licensure to relate to the weight given the testimony rather than to its admissibility. The authors cite Maryland and Illinois as states that, by statute, limit or exclude testimony by psychologists not licensed in those states. In contrast, Wisconsin permits out-of-state psychologists to practice in the state for up to 60 "working days" per year, though the psychologist must report the nature and extent of his or her practice in the state if the practice exceeds 20 working days in a single year.[52.3]

Experts who limit their activities to jury consultation or consultation with an attorney generally do not have to worry about licensing, because they are not diagnosing or treating anyone. If an expert is reviewing medical, psychological, or other health-related records, it is not clear whether the expert needs a license, because such review generally includes making conclusions regarding diagnoses.

A psychologist or psychiatrist who considers accepting a case in another state must ascertain whether he or she needs a license from that state in order to avoid a possible licensing, civil, or criminal action against him or her. The psychologist or psychiatrist should ask the attorney requesting the consultation to identify the relevant statute(s) and administrative code, *and* to send a copy of all relevant sections to the psychologist or psychiatrist. The expert should not take the chance that the attorney will not accurately interpret the provisions, and a claim to that effect will not mitigate a licensing complaint. Given the relative ease with which state statutes and administrative code can be accessed via the Internet, the expert is also advised to do his or her own search for relevant sections.[52.4] The authors also advise that it is not sufficient to have the out-of-state client consent to an evaluation and sign a statement that a doctor-patient relationship is not being created, because that will not protect an expert from laws designed to protect citizens from unqualified or incompetent professionals.

[52.3] Section 455.03, Wisconsin Statutes.

[52.4] A frequently-used web site is www.findlaw.com. Most states' web sites are also accessible at www.[enter name of state].gov.

§ 2.8A TEMPORARY LICENSURE

If the request for consultation comes from a court, the authors recommend that the expert inform the court of the licensing question and get a ruling regarding the relevance of licensing. The expert should still obtain a copy of the relevant statutes and administrative code and do the review him- or herself.

To obtain a temporary license from a state that allows temporary practice, the psychologist or physician should contact the licensing board in the state in which he or she wishes to consult. Current addresses for all state and provincial licensing boards are available at *www.asppb.org*.

The following table[52.5] indicates the requirements of each state regarding the performance of forensic evaluations by psychologists not licensed in that state. Those designated "a" in the "temporary license or exemption" column have the easiest task, since the evaluation may be done without any formal notification to the psychology licensing board, let alone needing consent of that board. Second easiest are those designated "b," since they must only notify the state licensing board of the temporary professional practice. The other options are generally more complicated.

As indicated in **Table 2–2,** most states grant temporary licensure for purposes such as conducting a forensic evaluation. Some will also provide formal licensure without requiring that a national or local examination be passed. Certification by the American Board of Professional Psychology (ABPP, see **§ 1.7**) eases the process in 29 jurisdictions. Listing in the National Register of Health Service Providers in Psychology (see **§ 1.3**) eases the process in one state, Missouri.

The Certificate of Professional Qualification in Psychology (CPQ) is a relatively new certification. Initiated in August of 1998 by the Association of State and Provincial Psychology Boards (ASPPB), the CPQ is designed to facilitate psychologists' ability to practice in more than the jurisdiction of original licensure, whether on a temporary or permanent basis. As of August, 2002, 27 jurisdictions in North America accept the CPQ: Alberta, British Columbia, California, Connecticut, District of Columbia, Idaho, Kentucky, Louisiana, Manitoba, Maryland, Michigan, Mississippi, Missouri, Nevada, New Hampshire, New Mexico, Nova Scotia, Ohio, Oklahoma, Ontario, Pennsylvania, Quebec, Rhode Island, Vermont, Virginia, Wisconsin, and Wyoming. In addition, 13 jurisdictions have voted to accept the CPQ and are in the process of making administrative and/or legislative changes necessary to implement the CPQ: Alabama, Alaska,

[52.5] Table 1 is from Eric Y. Drogin, *Prophets in Another Land: Utilizing Psychological Expertise from Foreign Jurisdictions*, 23 Mental and Physical Disability Law Reporter 767–771 at 768 (1999).

Table 2: Methods and Requisite Factors for Performing Forensic Psychological Evaluations in State Jurisdictions and the District of Columbia

Jurisdiction	Temporary License or Exemption	National Exam Waiver	Local Exam Waiver
AL	—	f, g, h, i, m	f, g, h, i, m
AS	—	f, i	f, i
AZ	a	f, i	—
AK	—	f, g, m	f, g, m
CA	a	f, g, i, l	g, i, l
CO	—	g	g
CT	—	f, i	—
DE	a	i	i
DC	b, d, n	e, f	e, f
FL	c, f	f, i	—
GA	a, f	f	f
HI	—	f, i, l	f, i
ID	—	f	f
IL	—	f, g, l	f, g, l
IN	—	f, l	—
IA	c, f	f, i	f, i
KS	a	f	f
KY	b	e, f, l, j	—
LA	a, n	—	—
ME	—	f	f
MD	g	f, g	f, g
MA	b, f, n	f, h	f, h
MI	—	—	—
MN	a	g, i, l	—
MS	a	f, e, i	f, e, i
MO	a, k	e, f, i, k	—
MT	a	f	f
NE	c, f	f, i, l	f, i, l
NV	a, f, n	f, i, l	f, i, l
NH	—	f	f
NJ	c, f, g	f, h	f, h
NM	—	f, i	f
NY	b	—	—
NC	a	e, i, f, l	e, i, f, l
ND	a	f	f
OH	c	f, i	f, i
OK	b	e, i, j	e, i, j
OR	c, f	f, i	—
PA	—	f	f
RI	c, f	f, i	f, i
SC	c	f, g, i, m	f, g, i, m
SD	a	f, i, l	f, i, l
TN	—	f, g, i, m	f, g, i, m
TX	—	e, f, i	—
UT	—	f, i, l	—
VT	b, f	f, i	f, i
VA	a, n	f, g, i	—
WA	—	f, i, l	f, i, l
WVA	c, f	f, i	f, i
WI	a	g, l	—
WY	m	f	f

Key for Requisite Factors

a: no board notification necessary
b: must notify board
c: must secure board permission
d: various home jurisdictions acceptable
e: home jurisdiction with reciprocity acceptable
f: home jurisdiction standards equivalent and/or higher
g: psychologist meets and/or exceeds visiting jurisdiction standards
h: various national certifications acceptable
i: ABPP diplomate acceptable
j: CPQ acceptable
k: National Register acceptable
l: length of practice requirement
m: public interest weighed as factor
n: collaboration required

Arizona, Georgia, Nebraska, New Brunswick, New Jersey, Newfoundland (MRA),[52.6] Oregon, Prince Edward Island (MRA), Saskatchewan (MRA), South Dakota, and Washington. A psychology licensing board that accepts the CPQ has agreed to accept the psychologist's educational training, supervised experience, and performance on the national examination or equivalent. CPQ holders may also be required to pass special requirements

[52.6] Provinces that are parties to the Mutual Recognition Agreement (MRA) will honor the CPQ as of July, 2003. However, this may apply only to residents of Canada.

of a given board, such as a test on mental health laws or on ethics, or to be personally interviewed by the board.[52.7]

A newly published article by Jill Tucillo, Nick DeFilippis, Robert Denney and John Dsurney[52.8] updates information regarding the laws and administrative codes governing temporary practice in the U.S.A. and Canada. The data was gathered between July, 1999 and May, 2000. Since both laws and administrative code continually change, *the chart should be considered as suggestive rather than definitive*. Practicing one's profession in a state in which one is not licensed may have very serious consequences, including being unable to testify, civil (fines from $100 to $50,000 per day) or criminal liability (a felony in five states), and/or a disciplinary action by the licensing board (with report to the National Practitioner Data Bank). Failing to comply may also be an ethics violation, as psychologists are required to comply with laws related to the practice of psychology. Licensing boards also require widely varying amounts of information about the visiting psychologist, ranging from a statement of intended practice to graduate school transcripts plus letters of reference plus a curriculum vitae and more. Some boards also charge a "processing fee." Contact information for all of the state and provincial licensing boards may be obtained from the Association of State and Provincial Psychology Boards at *www.asppb.org*.

State	Temporary Practice	Time Limits
Alabama	Only when court ordered	
Alaska	No[52.12]	
Arizona	Yes	20 days/year
Arkansas	No standard policy	
California	Yes	30 days/year
Colorado	No[52.12]	
Connecticut	No[52.12]	
Delaware	Yes	6 days/year
District of Columbia	No standard policy	(no information)[52.10]
Florida	Yes	5 days/month but maximum of 15 days/year
Georgia	Yes	30 days/year

52.7 Report from the Association of State and Provincial Psychology Boards, Aug., 2002.

52.8 Jill A. Tucillo, Nick A. DeFilippis, Robert L. Denney & John Dsurney, *Licensure Requirements for Interjurisdictional Forensic Evaluations*, 33 Professional Psychology: Research and Practice 377-383 (2002).

State	Temporary Practice	Time Limits
Hawaii	Yes	90 days/year[52.9]
Idaho	No[52.12]	
Illinois	No[52.12]	
Indiana	No[52.12]	
Iowa	Yes	10 consecutive days or 15 business days in Any 90 day period
Kansas	Yes	90 days/year
Kentucky	Yes	30 days every two years
Louisiana	Yes	30 days/year[52.10]
Maine	Yes	1 year and 1 time only[52.9]
Maryland	Yes	Unspecified; 1 time only
Massachusetts	Yes	1 days/month
Michigan	No[52.12]	
Minnesota	Yes	30 days/year
Mississippi	Yes	10 days
Missouri	Yes	Maximum of 10 consecutive days in a 90-day period or 15 total in a 9-month period.
Montana	Yes	60 days/year
Nebraska	Yes	30 days/year
Nevada	Yes	30 days/year[52.10,52.11]
New Hampshire	No[52.12]	
New Jersey	Yes	10 days in 90-day period; one time only.
New Mexico	No, but in process of revising Rules	
New York	Yes	15 intermittent or 10 consecutive days every 90 days
North Carolina	Yes	30 days/year[52.9]
North Dakota	Yes	30 days/year

§ 2.8A TEMPORARY LICENSURE

State	Temporary Practice	Time Limits
Ohio	Yes	30 days/year
Oklahoma	Yes	5 days/year
Oregon	Yes	120 days/24 months
Pennsylvania	Yes	6 months; once only
Rhode Island	Yes	None[52.10,52.11]
South Carolina	No[52.12]	
South Dakota	Yes	20 days/year
Tennessee	Yes	30 days/year
Texas	Yes	30 days/year
Utah	Only for providing expert testimony; no exemption for doing an evaluation	
Vermont	Yes	10 days or 80 hours/ year
Virginia	Yes	(no information)[52.9]
Washington	Yes	90 days/year
West Virginia	Yes	90 days, one time only
Wisconsin	Yes	60 days/year; Must report nature & extent of practice if over 20 days in a year
Wyoming	Only for providing expert testimony; no exemption for doing an evaluation	
U.S. Territories		
Guam	No[52.12]	
U.S. Virgin Islands	Yes	30 days
Provinces		
Alberta	Yes	1 year
British Columbia	No, but draft is pending[52.12]	

State	Temporary Practice	Time Limits
Manitoba	No[52.12]	
New Brunswick	Yes	Always time-limited, but no standard policy
Newfoundland	Yes	6 months
Nova Scotia	Yes	None
Ontario	No[52.12]	
Quebec	Yes	12 months, with option to renew
Saskatchewan	No, but under consideration[52.12]	

[52.9] Licensing boards in Hawaii, Maine, North Carolina Tennessee and Virginia permit temporary practice for the purpose of doing an assessment, but require that the visiting psychologist be supervised by a local psychologist.

[52.10] Visiting psychologists must "usually" be supervised by or associated with a local psychologist in the District of Columbia, Louisiana, Nevada and Rhode Island.

[52.11] Nevada and Rhode Island require that a visiting psychologist have been invited by a local psychologist to serve as a consultant. In Nevada, the visiting psychologist must give a "sworn statement" that one is solely practicing as a consultant.

[52.12] Interjurisdictional practice was expressly forbidden in Alaska, British Columbia, Colorado, Connecticut, Guam, Idaho, Illinois, Indiana, Manitoba, Michigan, New Hampshire, Ontario, Saskatchewan, and South Carolina at the time of the survey.

§ 2.12 Requirements That Tests and Interviews Be Correctly Administered

Page 94, replace the first full paragraph with:

The Joint Committee on the Standards for Educational and Psychological Testing, consisting of representatives of the American Psychological Association, the American Educational Research Association, and the National Council on Measurement in Education, has revised the *Standards for Educational and Psychological Testing*, last published in 1985. They invited more than 700 organizations to appoint advisors to the Joint Committee.[78] The revision was completed, and endorsed by the three organi-

[78] Jo-Ida Hansen, *Practitioner Concerns Regarding the Standards for Educational and Psychological Testing*, Paper presented at the Annual Convention of the American Psychological Association, Chicago (Aug. 16, 1997).

zations, in 1999. It is the intent of the sponsoring organizations to offer guidelines that are based upon the most up-to-date studies of test construction, validation, and administration.[79]

A major change in the *Standards* is the elimination of labeling some standards as "primary" and some as "secondary" or "conditional." It was the intent of the authors of the 1985 *Standards* to emphasize that some standards are considered mandatory (primary), while others are considered applicable to specific situations but not to others (secondary or conditional). The authors of the current *Standards* caution that "the absence of designations such as 'primary' or 'conditional' should not be taken to imply that all standards are equally significant in any given situation. Depending on the context and purpose of test development or use, some standards will be more salient than others. . . . Further, the current *Standards* does not include standards considered secondary or 'desirable. . . .' [E]ach standard should be carefully considered to determine its applicability to the testing context under consideration. In a given case there may be sound professional reason why adherence to the standard is unnecessary." However, they indicate, test developers or users are not expected to have documentation of their decision making regarding each standard routinely available.[79.1]

The *Standards* define "test" as "an evaluative device or procedure in which a sample of an examinee's behavior in a specified domain is obtained and subsequently evaluated and scored using a standardized process. While the label *test* is ordinarily reserved for instruments on which responses are evaluated for their correctness or quality and the terms *scale* or *inventory* are used for measures of attitudes, interest, and dispositions, the *Standards* uses the single term *test* to refer to all such evaluative devices." They also note that there is a distinction between the terms "test" and "assessment," with the latter "referring to a process that integrates test information with information from other sources (e.g., information from the individual's social, educational, employment, or psychological history). The applicability of the *Standards* to an evaluation device or method is not altered by the label applied to it (e.g., test, assessment, scale, inventory)." Finally, they note that the field of test development continues to evolve, and that it is not the intent of the *Standards* to prescribe the use of any particular technical methodology.[79.2]

---

[79] Beth Azar, *Changes Will Improve Quality of Tests*, 30 APA Monitor 30 (1999).

[79.1] Joint Committee on Standards for Educational and Psychological Testing of the American Educational Research Association, the American Psychological Association, and the National Council on Measurement in Education (hereinafter, Joint Committee), *Standards for Educational and Psychological Testing*. Washington, D.C.: American Educational Research Association, 1999, at 2–3.

[79.2] *Id.* at 4.

Page 94, insert after the quotation at the bottom of the page:

Thus, while a test may have criterion, content and construct validity, the test developer or user also has an obligation to try to ensure that there are not unintended consequences of the use of the test. A test that accurately measures variables directly related to, e.g., job or school performance or qualities of parenting, and does not also measure extraneous variables that do not directly relate to job or school performance or qualities of parenting, would have consequential validity as well. If, however, the test measured characteristics of the individual not directly related to the stated goal, potentially causing the individual to get a higher or lower score than is justified, the consequential validity would be in question.[80.1] A test of parenting on which every item related to some aspect of parenting demonstrated by the professional literature to be relevant to good parenting would likely have substantial consequential validity. Any items that were extraneous to that goal, e.g., questions that measure socioeconomic status, political viewpoints, gender roles, or other extraneous variables would have questionable consequential validity.

Page 95, insert at the end of § 2.12:

Examples of standards that may be particularly relevant to child custody matters include:

Standard 1.3: If validity for some common or likely interpretation has not been investigated, or if the interpretation is inconsistent with available evidence, that fact should be made clear and potential users should be cautioned about making unsupported interpretations.

Standard 1.4: If a test is used in a way that has not been validated, it is incumbent on the user to justify the new use, collecting new evidence if necessary.

Standard 5.1: Test administrators should follow carefully the standardized procedures for administration and scoring specified by the test developer, unless the situation or a test taker's disability dictates that an exception should be made.

Standard 5.2: Modifications or disruptions of standardized administration procedures or scoring should be documented.

Standard 5.4: The testing environment should furnish reasonable comfort with minimal distractions.

[80.1] Joint Committee at 16.

Standard 5.6: Reasonable efforts should be made to assure the integrity of test scores by eliminating opportunities for test takers to attain scores by fraudulent means.

Standard 5.7: Test users have the responsibility of protecting the security of test materials at all times.

Standard 8.2: Where appropriate, test takers should be provided, in advance, as much information about the test, the testing process, the intended test use, test scoring criteria, testing policy, and confidentiality protection as is consistent with obtaining valid responses.

Standard 8.4: Informed consent should be obtained from test takers, or their legal representatives when appropriate, before testing is done except (a) when testing without consent is mandated by law or governmental regulation, (b) when testing is conducted as a regular part of school activities, or (c) when consent is clearly implied.

Standard 8.6: Test data maintained in data files should be adequately protected from improper disclosure. . . .

Standard 8.9: When test scores are used to make decisions about a test taker or to make recommendations to a test taker or a third party, the test taker or the legal representative is entitled to obtain a copy of any report of test scores or test interpretation, unless that right has been waived or is prohibited by law or court order.

Standard 9.1: Testing practices should be designed to reduce threats to the reliability and validity of test score inferences that may arise from language differences.

Standard 10.1: In testing individuals with disabilities, test developers, test administrators, and test users should take steps to ensure that the test score inferences accurately reflect the intended construct rather than any disabilities and their associated characteristics extraneous to the intent of the measurement.

Standard 11.2: When a test is to be used for a purpose for which little or no documentation is available, the user is responsible for obtaining evidence of the test's validity and reliability for this purpose.

Standard 11.3: Responsibility for test use should be assumed by or delegated only to those individuals who have the training, professional credentials, and experience necessary to handle this responsibility. Any special qualifications for test administration or interpretation specified in the test manual should be met.

Standard 11.4: The test user should have a clear rationale for the intended uses of a test or evaluation procedure in terms of its validity and contribution to the assessment and decision-making process.

Standard 11.6: Unless the circumstances clearly require that the test results be withheld, the test user is obligated to provide a timely report of the results that is understandable to the test taker and others entitled to receive this information.

Standard 11.7: Test users have the responsibility to protect the security of tests, to the extent that developers enjoin users to do so.

- When tests are involved in litigation, inspection of the instruments should be restricted—to the extent permitted by law—to those who are legally or ethically obligated to safeguard test security.

Standard 11.8: Test users have the responsibility to respect test copyrights.

Standard 11.15: Test users should be alert to potential misinterpretations of test scores and to possible unintended consequences of test use; users should take steps to minimize or avoid foreseeable misinterpretations and unintended negative consequences.

Standard 11.20: In educational, clinical and counseling settings, a test taker's score should not be interpreted in isolation; collateral information that may lead to alternative explanations for the examinee's test performance should be considered.

Standard 12.1: Those who use psychological tests should confine their testing and related assessment activities to their areas of competence, as demonstrated through education, supervised training, experience, and appropriate credentialing.

Standard 12.5: The selection of a combination of tests to address a complex diagnosis should be appropriate for the purposes of the assessment as determined by available evidence of validity. The professional's educational training and supervised experience also should be commensurate with the test user qualifications required to administer and interpret the selected tests.

Standard 12.8: Professionals should ensure that persons under their supervision, who administer and score tests, are adequately trained in the settings in which the testing occurs and with the populations served.

Standard 12.11: Professionals and others who have access to test materials and test results should ensure the confidentiality of the test results and testing materials consistent with legal and professional ethics requirements.

Standard 12.13: Those who select tests and draw inferences from test scores should be familiar with the relevant evidence of validity and reliability for tests and inventories used and should be prepared to articulate a logical analysis that supports all facets of the assessment and the inferences made from the assessment.

Standard 12.14: The interpretation of test results in the assessment process should be informed when possible by an analysis of stylistic and other qualitative features of test-taking behavior that are inferred from observations during interviews and testing and from historical information.

Standard 12.15: Those who use computer-generated interpretations of test data should evaluate the quality of the interpretations and, when possible, the relevance and appropriateness of the norms upon which the interpretations are based.

Standard 12.16: Test interpretation should not imply that empirical evidence exists for a relationship among particular test results, prescribed interventions, and desired outcomes, unless empirical evidence is available for populations similar to those representative of the examinee.

Standard 12.18: The interpretation of test or test battery results generally should be based upon multiple sources of convergent test and collateral data and an understanding of the normative, empirical, and theoretical foundations as well as the limitations of such tests.

Standard 12.19: The interpretation of test scores or patterns of test battery results should take cognizance of the many factors that may influence a particular testing outcome. Where appropriate, a description and analysis of the alternative hypotheses or explanations that may have contributed to the pattern of results should be included in the report.

Finally, the *Standards*' authors address "testing for judicial and governmental decisions." It is noted that participation in the assessment may not be voluntary, and admonishes the clinician to "clarify the purpose of the evaluation, who will have access to the test results and reports, and any rights that the client may have to refuse to participate in court-ordered evaluations."[83.1] Further, the professional is responsible for accurately relating the assessment results to the legal criteria by which the fact finder will make decisions. It is also "important to assess the examinee's test-taking orientation including response bias to ensure that the legal proceedings have not affected the responses given."[83.2]

It is noted that "[s]ome tests are intended to provide information about a client's functioning that helps clarify a given legal issue (e.g., parental functioning in a child custody case . . .). However, many tests measure constructs that are generally relevant to the legal issues even though norms specific to the judicial or governmental context may not be available. Pro-

[83.1] Joint Committee at 128.

[83.2] Joint Committee at 129.

fessionals are expected to make every effort to be aware of evidence of validity and reliability that supports or does not support their inferences and to place appropriate limits on the opinions rendered. Test users who practice in judicial and government settings are expected to be aware of conflicts of interest that may lead to bias in the interpretation of test results." Finally, "the test taker does have a right to expect that test results will be communicated only to persons who are legally authorized to receive them and that other information from the testing session that is not relevant to the evaluation will not be reported. It is important for the professional to be apprised of possible threats to confidentiality and test security (e.g., releasing the test questions, the examinee's responses, and raw and scaled scores on tests to another qualified professional) and to seek, if necessary, appropriate legal and professional remedies."

Paul Sackett, Ph.D., of the University of Minnesota, indicated that the joint committee tried to word the standards to make it clear that the Standards are not meant be a checklist that a psychologist should follow to the letter. Rather, "[d]epending on the context and purpose of test development or use, some standards will be more salient than others."[83.3]

Sackett also indicated that the definition of "validity" has been changed by the committee that drafted the Standards. While it used to be said that a test itself was valid or invalid, or that the test possessed construct and/or content and/or criterion-based validity, one now addresses whether the test is valid for the specific purpose for which it is being used. The presence or absence of construct, content and/or criterion-based validity is now considered evidence regarding whether the test is valid for its intended purpose. "Test developers and users need to start with the question: What are the inferences we wish to draw from the test score. . . . Then they accumulate evidence to support that." Thus, there are no valid tests, there are valid uses of tests. The psychologist's task is to provide evidence to support the validity of the inference made rather than the test itself, according to Sackett.[83.4]

Page 126, insert after § 2.28:

§ 2.28A Interplay between the Guardian-ad-Litem and Psychological Expert

The role of the guardian-ad-litem in a divorce case cannot be underestimated or ignored. However, states define guardians-ad-litem in different

[83.3] Quoted in Beth Azar, *Changes Will Improve Quality of Tests*, 30 APA Monitor 30 (1999) at 30.

[83.4] *Id.*

ways. Some states allow only attorneys to be guardians-ad-litem, while other states allow non-attorneys such as psychologists or social workers to be guardians-ad-litem. If an attorney is used as a guardian-ad-litem, some states define the guardian-ad-litem as an individual who is to represent the best interest of the child(ren), while other states will indicate that the attorney represents the child in court.

As in other types of legal representation, when a child is represented by the guardian-ad-litem, individuals are not allowed to communicate with the child about the case without the permission of the guardian-ad-litem. In particular, this extends to the psychologist acting as a therapist or evaluator of a child, when an attorney guardian-ad-litem is involved in a case as the child's attorney. If a psychologist sees a child for therapy or performs an assessment of the child and does not seek the permission of the guardian-ad-litem, that psychologist could be removed from the case by the court. This removal could be damaging to the child, if the psychologist has developed an ongoing therapeutic relationship with the child, or damaging to the case itself.

When a psychologist and a guardian-ad-litem are both involved in a case, it becomes necessary for both the psychologist and the guardian-ad-litem to know the state law requirements of the state in which the case is venued. It is incumbent upon the psychologist and the guardian-ad-litem to know what state law requires of each of these individuals for the following issues:

1. Does the state require that the guardian-ad-litem be an attorney?
2. If the guardian-ad-litem is an attorney, does the state allow the attorney to represent the child's wishes as well as the child's best interest, or one without the other?
3. When a state does not require a guardian-ad-litem to be an attorney, what will the interplay between the guardian-ad-litem and the psychological expert be?
4. What authority does the guardian-ad-litem have with regard to placement issues and time with parents, grandparents, and significant others?

Theoretically, the guardian-ad-litem (GAL) and the court appointed expert should operate as a team. Because both of them are considered to be neutral and working for the best interest of the child(ren), it is expected that they will work together. To this end, the guardian-ad-litem and the psychological evaluator should meet and discuss the case before either writes a report. The assumption is that the guardian-ad-litem will know things about the case that the psychologist does not and the psychologist evaluator will know things about the case that the guardian-ad-litem does not. A meeting would facilitate an exchange of information and an exchange of ideas. Engaging in such practice can be a valuable component of the evaluation process, which is lost if the GAL and psychologist do not work as a team.

§ 2.31 Case Digest

Page 140, insert after ***Oklahoma:***

Texas

Thapar v. Zezulka, Texas Supreme Court (994 S.W.2d 635) No. 97-1208 (June 24, 1999). The Texas Supreme Court refused to impose a duty on mental health professionals to warn third parties of a patient's threats.

Renu K. Thapar, a psychiatrist, treated Freddy Ray Lilly with psychotherapy and medication for Posttraumatic Stress Disorder, alcohol abuse, and paranoid and delusional beliefs concerning his stepfather, Henry Zezulka, and people of certain ethnic backgrounds. Dr. Thapar's notes from August 23, 1988, indicated that Lilly "feels like killing" Henry Zezulka, but that he "has decided not to do it but that is how he feels." Lilly then spent seven days in the hospital and was discharged. Less than a month later he shot and killed Henry Zezulka. Thapar had never warned Zezulka or any member of Zezulka's family, nor any law enforcement agency. Lyndall Zezulka, Henry's wife and Lilly's mother, sued Thapar for negligence.

The trial court granted summary judgment for Thapar based on the Supreme Court's decision in *Bird v. W.C.W.*, 868 S.W.2d 767 (Tex. 1994) that "no duty runs from a psychologist to a third party to not negligently misdiagnose a patient's condition." Zezulka appealed. The Texas court of appeals "held that the no-duty ground asserted in Thapar's motion for summary judgment was not a defense to the cause of action pleaded by Zezulka. . . ."

> [W]e are asked whether a mental-health professional owes a duty to warn third parties of a patient's threats. . . . The Legislature has chosen to closely guard a patient's communications with a mental-health professional. . . . Zezulka complains that Thapar was negligent in not warning members of the Zezulka family about Lilly's threats. But a disclosure by Thapar to one of the Zezulkas would have violated the confidentiality statute because no exception in the statute provides for disclosure to third parties threatened by the patient. . . . Under the appli-

cable statute, Thapar was prohibited from warning one of his patient's potential victims and therefore had no duty to warn the Zezulka family of Lilly's threats.

Zezulka also complains that Thapar was negligent in not disclosing Lilly's threats to any law enforcement agency. There is an exception in the confidentiality statute that provides for disclosure to law enforcement personnel in certain circumstances. The statute, however, *permits* these disclosures but does not *require* them. . . . Because of the Legislature's stated policy, we decline to impose a common law duty on mental-health professionals to warn third parties of their patient's threats.

CHAPTER 3

WHAT CONSTITUTES A PSYCHOLOGICAL EVALUATION?

§ 3.19 Child Custody Evaluation Practices

Page 193, add the following text at the end of the section:

The Comparison of Psychologists', Judges', and Attorneys' Surveys

Over the past two decades, child custody evaluation practices have been addressed through various models.[58.1] Between 1986 and 1994, many states developed child custody evaluation practice guidelines.[58.2] These efforts culminated in the development of the American Psychological Association (1994) Guidelines for Child Custody Evaluations in Divorce Proceedings and the Association of Family and Conciliation Court (AFCC, 1995) Guidelines.

The APA Guidelines are applicable specifically to psychologists. Recognizing this, the Association of Family and Conciliation Courts (AFCC) developed a model standard of practice for child custody evaluations. This organization includes psychologists, psychiatrists, social workers, court evaluators, judges, mediators, and attorneys. As a result, the standards are

[58.1] Chasen R. & Grunebaum, H., *A Model for Evaluation in Child Custody Disputes*, The American Journal of Family Therapy, 9(3), 43–49 (1981). Jackson, A.M., Warner, N.S., Hornbein, R., Nelson, N., & Fortescue, E., *Beyond the Best Interests of the Child Revisited: An Approach to Custody Evaluations*, Journal of Divorce, 3, 207–222 (1980). Landberg, G., *Proposed Model for the Intervention of the Mental Health Specialist in the Resolution of Difficult Child Custody Disputes*, Journal of Preventive Psychiatry, 1(3), 309–318 (1982).

[58.2] Georgia Psychological Association (1990). Recommendations for Psychologists' Involvement in Child Custody Cases. Atlanta, GA, Author. Nebraska Psychological Association (1986). Guidelines for Child Custody Evaluations. Lincoln, NC., Author. New Jersey State Board of Psychological Examiners (1993). Specialty Guidelines for Psychologists in Custody/Visitation Evaluations. Newark, NJ, Author.

not as narrowly focused as the APA Guidelines. It should be pointed out that the AFCC Guidelines are very similar to the APA Guidelines, but are much more broad based.

There has been considerable research performed over the years addressing child custody evaluation practices. One of the seminal works in this area was a study performed by Keilin & Bloom in which psychiatrists, psychologists, and social workers were surveyed.[58.3] Although there was a relatively small N, and the three mental health disciplines were grouped together, the Keilin & Bloom study quickly became the standard of practice in child custody evaluation practices and was widely quoted. Ackerman & Ackerman (1997) replicated and extended the Keilin & Bloom study and found:

- Child custody evaluators still prefer to serve in an impartial capacity, with almost 100 percent indicating they prefer to be retained by both parents, the guardian ad litem, or the court.
- The average child custody evaluation, with report writing, takes 26.4 hours, which is 7.6 hours greater than in the 1986 study. However, almost all of this difference comes from the increased amount of time spent reviewing materials and report writing.
- Psychologists spend an additional 3 to 4 hours consulting with attorneys and testifying in court.
- The average fee for a custody evaluation is $2,646, almost triple the fee in 1986.
- Each child generally receives an intelligence test; personality tests such as the Children's Apperception Test (CAT), Thematic Apperception Test (TAT), or Rorschach; an achievement test; a sentence completion test; and the Bricklin Perceptual Scales (BPS).
- Each adult generally receives the MMPI/MMPI-2, Millon Clinical Multiaxial Inventory-II (MCMI-II/MCMI-III), Rorschach, intelligence test, and the TAT.
- The Ackerman-Schoendorf Scales for Parent Evaluation of Custody (ASPECT) is the most frequently used custody test for adults; and the BPS is the most frequently used custody test for children.
- Ninety-five percent of psychologists require some or all of the testing fee to be paid in advance, with 50 percent requiring it be paid totally in advance.

[58.3] Keilin, W.G., & Bloom, L.J., *Child Custody Evaluation Practices: A Survey of Experiences Professionals*, Professional Psychology: Research and Practice, 17(4), 338–346 (1986).

- Eighty-three percent of psychologists require full payment of fees prior to testifying in court.
- When making sole-custody recommendations, active substance abuse, parental alienation, parenting skills, psychological stability, and emotional bonding with parents are considered most important when a forced choice is presented. When an open-ended choice is presented, geographical distance between parents and evidence of physical and sexual abuse are added to the above list.
- Joint custody is preferred based on parents' ability to separate interpersonal difficulties from their parenting decisions, quality of relationship with child, problems with substance abuse, psychological stability of parents, amount of anger and bitterness between parents, and the parents' willingness to enter into joint custody arrangements when presented to respondents on a forced-choice basis. On an open-ended basis, joint custody is preferred based on parents' ability to cooperate, attachment with both parents, psychological health of parents, ability to engage in more child rearing, and desire of the parents.
- Parenting cooperation is the factor that is presented most frequently on open-ended choices of sole versus joint custody.
- Joint custody is much more preferred now than it was in 1986.
- Mediation is recommended by almost 50 percent of the evaluators.
- The mean age at which children should be allowed to choose the parent with whom they will live is 15.1.
- Evaluators are much less likely to make a recommendation based on a single issue.
- Evaluators today rely more on psychological testing than they did in 1986.
- Alcoholism is a major negative factor, while being in recovery is not.[58.4]

Ackerman and Ackerman concluded "that psychologists have become more sophisticated in the custody evaluation process, and that they utilize more test results, review more materials, and are less likely to make recommendations based on a single variable" (p. 144).

The work of Keilin & Bloom, and later Ackerman & Ackerman, was further explored in two recent studies. In the Ackerman & Steffen study, the questions asked of psychologists in Ackerman & Ackerman were addressed to family law judges with 159 acceptable questionnaires being

[58.4] Ackerman, M.J. & Ackerman, M.C., *Custody Evaluation Practices: A Survey of Experienced Professionals (Revisited)*, Professional Psychology, 28(2), 137–144 (1997).

returned.[58.5] These same issues were addressed in the Ackerman & Kelley study with family law attorneys with an N of 153.[58.6] Since the Ackerman & Ackerman study was published, the LaFortune and Carpenter (1998) and the Bow (2000) studies have been performed.[58.7] Both studies addressed child custody evaluation practices from similar perspectives as the Keilen & Bloom and Ackerman & Ackerman studies. The results of those studies were relatively similar to the Ackerman & Ackerman study. However, the use of specialized tests has changed dramatically. Bow found that the PCRI is used four times more frequently, the ASPECT 50 percent more frequently, and the Bricklin Perceptual Scales 20 percent less frequently. Bow concludes:

- Clinicians do not overly rely on psychological testing in custody evaluations.
- Trends in test usage.
  - Increased use of objective personality measures with adults.
  - Decreased testing of children in general, with significant decrease in the use of intelligence tests in particular.
  - Increased use of parent rating scales to measure children's level of social-emotional functioning.
  - Increased use of parenting inventories.
  - "Custody tests" continue to be used on a limited basis.
  - Use of psychological testing appears consistent with APA Guidelines for Child Custody Evaluations.[58.8]

Few studies have been performed surveying the expectations of family law judges. There is a general reluctance among judges to answer questionnaires of this nature for fear that their responses will identify biases from the bench and compromise their ability to serve as a trier of fact. Studies were performed by Reidy, Silver, & Carlson; Hellman; Shear;

[58.5] Ackerman, M.J. & Steffen, L.J., Child Custody Evaluation Practices: A Survey of Experienced Judges (2000). Unpublished manuscript.

[58.6] Ackerman, M.J. & Kelley, S., Child Custody Evaluation Practices: A Survey of Experienced Attorneys (2000). Unpublished manuscript.

[58.7] LaFortune, K. & Carpenter, B., *Custody Evaluations: A Survey of Mental Health Professionals*, Behavioral Sciences and the Law, 16, 207–224 (1998).

[58.8] Bow, J.N., Quinnell, F.A., Child Custody Practices—Five Years Post APA Guidelines. Symposium presented at the 2000 Annual Convention of the American Psychological Association, Washington, DC, August, 2000.

Crosby-Curren; and Kuehnle & Weiner.[58.9] Their findings, in general, were very similar to the results of the Ackerman & Steffen (2000) study.

Similarly, few investigators have specifically addressed the opinions of family law attorneys with regards to child custody evaluation practices. However, Smart & Salts; Koopman, Hunt, Favoretto, Coltri, & Britten, Richard; Lee, Beauregard, & Hunsley, have all studied family law attorneys' opinions about child custody evaluation practices.[58.10] None of their findings were significantly different from the Ackerman & Kelley study.[58.11]

Ackerman & Ackerman, Ackerman & Steffen, and Ackerman & Kelley

The results of the studies were combined for a total N of 513 that addressed all of the issues identified in the Ackerman & Ackerman study as a replication of the Keilin & Bloom study. Eight-hundred surveys were sent to psychologists, family law judges, and family law attorneys each. A total N of 513 usable questionnaires were returned. The results of the Ackerman & Ackerman study were previously reported as well as the results of the Ackerman & Steffen study.[58.12] However, the results of the Ackerman & Kelley study have yet to be reported. The survey that was utilized with Ackerman & Ackerman was a modification from the Keilen & Bloom

[58.9] Reidy, T., Silver, R., & Carlson, A., *Child Custody Decisions: A Survey of Judges,* Family Law Quarterly, 23, 75–87 (1989). Hellman, J., *A Survey of Judges, School Psychologists, Private Psychologists and Attorneys Regarding the Child Custody Determination Process,* University of Northern Colorado (1987). Shear, L.E., *Children's Lawyers in California Family Law Courts: Balancing Competing Policies and Values Regarding Questions of Ethics,* Family and Conciliation Courts Review, 34(2), 256–302 (1996). Crosby-Currie, C.A., *Children's Involvement in Contested Custody Cases: Practices and Experiences of Legal and Mental Health Professionals,* Law and Human Behavior, 20(3), 289–311 (1996). Kuehnle & Weiner (1996).

[58.10] Smarts, L.S. & Salts, C.J. *Attorney Attitudes Toward Divorce Mediation,* Mediation Quarterly, 6, 65–72 (1984). Koopman, E.J.; Hunt, E.J.; Favretto, F.G.; Coltri, L.S.; & Britten, T., *Professional Perspectives on Court-Connected Custody Mediation,* Family and Conciliation Courts Review, 29, 304–317 (1991). Lee, C.M.; Beauregard, C.P.M., & Hunsley, J., *Lawyers' Opinions Regarding Child Custody Mediation and Assessment Services: Implications for Psychological Practice,* Professional Psychology, 29(2), 120–155 (1998).

[58.11] Ackerman, M.J. & Kelley, S., Child Custody Evaluation Practices: A Survey of Experienced Judges (2000). Unpublished manuscript.

[58.12] Ackerman, M.J. & Ackerman, M.C., *Custody Evaluation Practices: A Survey of Experienced Professionals (revisited),* Professional Psychology, 28(2), 137–145. Ackerman, M.J. & Steffen, L.J., Child Custody Evaluation Practices: A Survey of Experienced Judges (2000). Unpublished manuscript.

Table 3–13

Demographics

	A & A Psychologists	**A & S Judges**	**A & K Attorneys**
N	201	159	153
Age	49.1	53.5	51.6
% Males	69.0	73.9	70.9
% Females	31.0	26.1	29.1

questionnaire.[58.13] This questionnaire was further modified for the family law judges' and family law attorneys' surveys in that "expectations" were measured instead of "practices."

Table 3–13 summarizes the demographics of the participants in the three studies.

Table 3–14 addresses the issue of conditions of retainment. It should be noted that both attorneys and judges rate court appointed, mutually agreed upon, or GAL appointed psychologists significantly higher than second opinion or rebuttal witness psychologists. The court appointed, mutually agreed upon, and GAL appointed psychologists are all given approximately the same weight, while the second opinion and rebuttal witness psychologists are also given the same weight, but significantly lower.

Table 3–14

Conditions of Retainment

	A & S Judges	**A & K Attorneys**	**Grand Mean**
Court Appointed	4.19	3.93	4.42
Mutually agreed upon	3.94	4.22	4.08
GAL appointed	3.89	3.50	3.70
2nd opinion	2.94	2.89	2.92
Rebuttal witness	2.90	2.81	2.86

[58.13] Keilin, W.G. & Bloom, L.J., *Child Custody Evaluation Practices: A Survey of Experienced Professionals*, Professional Psychology: Research and Practice, 17(4), 338–346 (1986).

§ 3.19 COMPARISON OF EVALUATIONS

Table 3–15 summarizes the time psychologists spend in each of the activities required as part of a custody evaluation. (Ackerman & Ackerman, 1997, 138).

Table 3–16 compares the results between the family law judges and the family law attorney expectations about evaluation procedures that psychologists utilize. Judges and attorneys alike expect psychologists to observe children of all ages, review mental health records, review children's school and medical records, perform psychological testing of parents, children, and significant others, consult with the guardian ad litem, interview parents, children, and significant others, and write a report along with testifying in court. However, attorneys feel that psychologists should review criminal records and contact collateral sources, while judges do not expect psychologists to perform these tasks. Neither judges nor attorneys expect psychologists to review pleadings of family law cases, review legal records, review parents' medical records, perform home visits, or consult with the parties' attorneys.

The frequency of the psychological test usage with children and adults in child custody evaluations by psychologists is reported in Ackerman and Ackerman (1997 p. 139–40). It should be noted that neither attorneys nor judges have much knowledge about the use of psychological tests. The only test family law judges were able to identify with any frequency was the MMPI-2 and then only 34.6 percent of the time. Attorneys' understand-

Table 3–15

Time Spent in Evaluation Activities

Activity	Mean Number of Hours Spent in Activity
Observation	2.6
Reviewing material	2.6
Collateral contacts	1.6
Psychological testing	5.2
Report writing	5.3
Interviewing parents	4.7
Interviewing children	2.7
Interviewing significant others	1.6
Consulting with attorneys	1.2
Testifying in court	2.2

Table 3–16

Evaluation Procedures Percentage Expecting

	DO NOT EXPECT		NEUTRAL		EXPECT	
	A&S Judges	A&K Attys.	A&S Judges	A&K Attys.	A&S* Judges	A&K* Attys.
Observation of children under 6 with parent(s)	2.6%	0.0%	9.0%	6.0%	**88.4%**	**94.0%**
Observation of children 6–12 with parent(s)	1.9	0.8	11	6.5	**87.1**	**92.7**
Observation of children over 12 with parent(s)	7.7	5.0	23.2	26.0	**69.0**	**69.0**
Review mental health records	1.9	3.0	7.7	11.0	**90.3**	**86.0**
Review pleadings of family law cases	27.1	38.0	42.6	21.0	30.3	41.0
Review legal records	32.9	46.6	44.5	26.7	22.6	26.7
Review criminal records	21.9	21.3	35.5	18.0	**42.6**	**60.7**
Review children's school records	3.9	1.6	18.7	19.5	**77.4**	**78.9**
Review children's medical records	5.2	5.7	24.7	27.6	**70.1**	**66.7**
Review parents' medical records	17.4	16.4	52.2	45.9	30.3	37.7
Contact collateral sources	15.5	13.8	40.6	30.9	43.9	**55.3**
Perform psychological testing on parents	3.2	3.2	19.9	16.9	**76.9**	**79.8**
Perform psychological testing on children	2.6	1.6	23.5	12.9	**73.9**	**85.5**
Perform psychological testing on significant other	13.7	14.5	35.9	31.5	**50.3**	**54.0**
Home visit	31.4	35.5	39.7	32.2	28.8	27.3
Consult with guardian ad litem	13.0	8.6	24.7	28.4	**62.3**	**62.9**
Consult with party's attorneys	30.7	14.6	42.5	39.8	26.8	45.5
Interview parent	3.6	2.4	1.4	1.6	**95.0**	**96.0**
Interview children	0.0	0.8	1.8	1.6	**98.2**	**97.6**
Interview significant others	8.7	5.6	17.8	15.2	**73.5**	**79.2**
Write a report	0.6	0.0	7.2	4.0	**92.2**	**96.0**
Testify in court	3.9	2.5	29.6	13.4	**66.4**	**84.1**

*Numbers in bold represent a majority expected

ing of psychological tests was a little more broad based than that of judges. However, for the most part, they were unfamiliar with tests other than the MMPI-2. When judges and attorneys were asked about specific custody related tests, the Bricklin Perceptual Scales (BPS) was the most widely recognized by these two groups with the ASPECT relatively close. Although attorneys tended to recognize custody-related tests more frequently than judges, none of the custody specialty tests were recognized by a majority of the groups. The BPS and ASPECT are most recognized with judges and attorneys just as they are with psychologists. 38.1 percent and 37.7 percent of the BPS and the ASPECT, by attorneys, were the highest ratings. It should be noted that all of the judges' ratings were in the teens and twenties. See **Table 3–17.**

Psychologists' attitudes towards single/sole custody were assessed by having the subjects respond to 40 9-point Likert-type scales addressing a number of custody decision making areas. Furthermore, for each variable the respondents were asked to determine whether they would endorse "Parent A, Parent B, or Neither Parent," based on that item. **Table 3–18** compares the ratings of the three groups and rank orders the items from most important to least important.

Table 3–17

Familiarity with Custody Tests

		% Familiar With		
	Test	**A & S Judges**	**A & K Attorneys**	**Mean %**
1	Bricklin Perceptual Scales (BPS)	26.8	38.1	32.4
2	Ackerman-Schoendorf Scales of Parent Evaluation of Custody (ASPECT)	19.9	37.7	28.8
3	Parent-Child Relationship Inventory (PCRI)	28.6	22.9	25.7
4	Parent Awareness Skills Survey (PASS)	24.1	25.0	24.6
5	Custody Quotient	12.9	24.4	18.6
6	Perception of Relations Test (PORT)	17.0	16.1	16.5

Table 3–18

Mean Ratings of Sole- or Single-Parent Custody Decision-Making Criteria

		Ranks			Means			
Rank	**Item**	**A&A Psych.**	**A&S Judges**	**A&K Attys.**	**A&A Psych.**	**A&S Judges**	**A&K Attys.**	**Grand Mean**
1	Parent B is an active alcoholic.	1	1	1	8.35	8.14	8.41	8.30*ac
2	Parent B often attempts to alienate the child from the other parent by negatively interpreting the other parent's behavior.	2	2	3	8.12	7.87	7.95	7.99*a
3	Parent A exhibits better parenting skills than Parent B.	3	4	2	7.94	7.73	7.95	7.88
4	Parent A has not been cooperative with previous court orders.	6	3	4	7.62	7.74	7.81	7.71
5	Parent B appears to be more psychologically stable than Parent A.	5	6	7	7.70	7.47	7.44	7.55*ab
6	The child appears to have a closer emotional bonding with Parent B.	4	7	9	7.70	7.42	7.32	7.50*ab
7	Parent A actively participates in the children's education.	9	5	6	7.33	7.51	7.51	7.44
8	Parent B has a history of psychiatric hospitalizations.	14	8	5	7.14	7.38	7.64	7.36*b
9	Parent B is more tolerant of the other parent's visitation.	8	11	12	7.52	7.24	7.23	7.35
10	The 15-year-old-child would prefer to live with Parent A.	12	12	8	7.15	7.22	7.39	7.24

Table 3–18

Mean Ratings of Sole- or Single-Parent Custody Decision-Making Criteria *continued*

		Ranks			Means			
Rank	Item	A&A Psych.	A&S Judges	A&K Attys.	A&A Psych.	A&S Judges	A&K Attys.	Grand Mean
11	Parent A exhibits a great deal of anger and bitterness about the divorce.	10	13	13	7.24	7.18	7.19	7.21
12	Physical abuse allegation has been made against Parent B.	11	10	14	7.15	7.29	7.16	7.20
13	Sexual abuse allegation has been made against Parent A.	13	9	15	7.14	7.31	7.14	7.19
14	Before the divorce, Parent A had primary caretaking responsibility.	17	14	10	7.00	7.10	7.25	7.11
15	Parent A is threatening to move to another state with the children.	7	18	11	7.53	6.93	6.37	7.00*ac
16	Parent A is aware of the children's future needs.	16	15	16	7.03	7.06	6.81	6.97
17	Parent A has a criminal record.	15	19	18	7.06	6.78	6.67	6.86*b
18	The child appears to have a closer emotional bonding with Parent B.	19	16	19	6.83	7.03	6.58	6.81*bc
19	Parent B is aware of the children's developmental milestones.	21	17	22	6.74	7.02	6.53	6.76*ac
20	Parent A appears to be much more economically stable than Parent B.	18	22	21	6.86	6.38	6.54	6.62*ab
21	Parent B is significantly less intelligent than the children.	22	20	23	6.57	6.52	6.51	6.54

Table 3–18

Mean Ratings of Sole- or Single-Parent Custody Decision-Making Criteria *continued*

Rank	Item	Ranks			Means			Grand Mean
		A&A Psych.	A&S Judges	A&K Attys.	A&A Psych.	A&S Judges	A&K Attys.	
22	Parent A has significantly worse MMPI-2 results.	20	23	26	6.77	6.33	6.40	6.52*ab
23	Parent A is a recovering alcoholic.	23	21	27	6.38	6.40	6.37	6.38
24	Parent A's schedule would require placing the child in day care; Parent B's would not.	26	26	24	6.22	6.26	6.50	6.32
25	Parent B is taking psychiatric medication.	27	24	25	6.20	6.32	6.42	6.30
26	Parent A has remained living in the original family home, while Parent B has moved to a home in a different school district.	28	27	20	6.15	6.22	6.57	6.30*bc
27	Parent B has more extended family available.	25	25	29	6.23	6.26	6.23	6.24
28	Before the divorce, Parent B had the primary responsibility for disciplining the child.	24	28	30	6.26	6.21	6.17	6.22
29	Parent B is currently involved in a homosexual relationship.	32	29	17	5.41	5.99	6.71	5.97*d
30	Parent A appears to be much more economically stable than Parent B.	29	33	34	5.97	5.58	5.72	5.77*a
31	Parent A's new partner has children living with him/her.	31	34	28	5.52	5.57	6.27	5.76*bc

Table 3–18

Mean Ratings of Sole- or Single-Parent Custody Decision-Making Criteria *continued*

		Ranks			Means			
Rank	Item	A&A Psych.	A&S Judges	A&K Attys.	A&A Psych.	A&S Judges	A&K Attys.	Grand Mean
32	The 10-year-old child would prefer to live with Parent A.	29	30	33	5.70	5.80	5.79	5.76
33	Parent B is cohabiting with a person of the opposite sex (without marriage), while Parent A has remarried.	36	31	31	4.87	5.73	6.04	5.50*ab
34	Parent B is cohabiting with a person of the opposite sex (without marriage) while Parent A lives alone.	35	32	32	4.93	5.63	5.97	5.46*ab
35	Parent A is much more socially active than Parent B.	33	35	36	5.25	5.15	5.19	5.20
36	Parent A has remarried; Parent B lives alone.	38	36	35	4.66	4.70	5.22	4.84*bc
37	Parent B is the same sex as the child.	34	37	37	5.06	4.49	4.68	4.77*a
38	The 5-year old child would prefer to live with Parent B.	37	38	38	4.84	4.45	4.06	4.49*d
39	Parent A is the mother, Parent B is the father.	39	39	39	4.19	4.02	3.75	4.01
40	Parent A is 10 years older than Parent B.	40	40	40	3.28	3.51	3.73	3.49

* Significant difference
a–psychologists & judges significantly different
b–psychologists & attorneys significantly different
c–judges & attorneys significantly different
d–all three groups significantly different from each other

The underlined mean represents an item endorsed by that particular group as a determining factor in making a sole custody recommendation. Furthermore, the asterisks after the Grand Mean represent significant differences, with the letters "a" through "d" designating which pairs were significantly different from one another. An "a" signifies that psychologists and judges were significantly different from one another, but neither were significantly different from attorneys. A "b" indicates that psychologists and attorneys were significantly different from each other, but neither group was significantly different from the judges. A "c" indicates that judges and attorneys were significantly different from one another, but neither were significantly different from psychologists. A "d" represents that all three pairs were significantly different from one another. It should be noted, that for the most part, psychologists, judges, and attorneys tended to rate the same items as high, the same items in the middle, and the same items at the lower end of the continuum, with some exceptions. All three groups saw active substance abuse as being the greatest concern with alienation being the second greatest concern. All groups also agreed that the wishes of five and ten year olds were not to be taken seriously. Both attorneys and judges felt that lack of cooperation with previous court orders was more important than psychologists did. On the other hand, psychologists did not see a history of psychiatric hospitalizations as being as great a concern as judges and attorneys. Psychologists took a parent threatening to move to another state with the children as being a much greater concern than did judges or attorneys. Emotional bonding to one parent over the other was more important to psychologists than it was to judges or attorneys. One of the more noteworthy differences among these groups was with regards to the question of sexual preference. Psychologists and judges rated sexual preference as 32nd and 29th out of 40, respectively, whereas family law attorneys rated it at 17th out of 40.

Table 3–19 addresses the issue of joint custody placement comparing the three groups on 30 items. The asterisks and a, b, c, and d, represent the same types of significance as in **Table 3–18.** Both judges and attorneys found substance abuse to be the greatest concern in making a joint custody recommendation, while psychologists found the ability to separate interpersonal difficulties as being more important. Psychologists also found the quality of the relationship that each parent has with the children more important than judges and attorneys did. On the other hand, judges and attorneys found cooperation with previous court orders more important than psychologists did. Additionally, attorneys weighed the expressed wishes of a 15-year-old more than did psychologists or judges. Judges ranked current state law much higher than psychologists and attorneys did. As with sole custody, whether an individual was involved in a homosexual relationship or not was of much greater concern to attorneys than it was

Table 3–19

Rank Ordering of Joint Custody Decision-Making Criteria

		Rank			Means			
Overall Rank	Item	A & A Psych.	A & S Judges	A & K Attys.	A & A Psych.	A & S Judges	A & K Attys.	Grand Mean
1	Problems with substance abuse	3	1	1	8.15	8.06	8.19	8.13
2	Ability of parents to separate their interpersonal difficulties from their parenting	1	2	3	8.33	7.90	7.92	8.07*ab
3	The quality of relationship the child has with each parent	2	5	7	8.28	7.74	7.70	7.94*ab
4	The amount of anger and bitterness between the parents	5	6	5	7.98	7.73	7.77	7.84
5	Psychological stability of the parents	4	7	6	7.99	7.66	7.72	7.81*ab
6	Cooperation with previous court orders	8	3	2	7.42	7.89	7.94	7.72*ab
7	Expressed wishes of the child, age 15	7	8	4	7.65	7.41	7.77	7.61*c
8	The parents' willingness to enter joint custody arrangements	6	9	9	7.79	7.28	7.31	7.49*ab
9	Current state law (in your state)	10	4	12	7.24	7.75	6.80	7.27*d
10	Whether the child exhibits behavior problems at home or school	12	10	8	6.86	7.18	7.45	7.14*ab
11	Problems with the law	9	12	11	7.35	6.84	6.86	7.05*ab
12	Each parent's previous involvement in caretaking responsibilities	11	11	10	7.11	6.92	6.91	6.99
13	The geographic proximity of parental homes	13	13	14	6.81	6.62	6.54	6.67

Table 3–19

Rank Ordering of Joint Custody Decision-Making Criteria *continued*

Overall Rank	Item	Rank: A & A Psych.	Rank: A & S Judges	Rank: A & K Attys.	Means: A & A Psych.	Means: A & S Judges	Means: A & K Attys.	Grand Mean
14	Amount of flexibility in parents' work schedules	15	14	15	6.45	6.47	6.43	6.45
15	Differences between parental discipline styles	14	15	17	6.64	6.36	6.28	6.45*b
16	Influences of extended family members (e.g. in-laws and close relatives)	17	19	18	6.20	6.06	6.23	6.17
17	Economic stability of the parents	16	18	21	6.23	6.08	6.12	6.15
18	Intelligence of the parents	21	17	16	6.05	6.14	6.29	6.15
19	Whether or not one parent is involved in a homosexual relationship	22	21	13	5.98	5.97	6.55	6.15*d
20	Expressed wishes of the child, age 10	18	20	20	6.19	5.99	6.18	6.13
21	Age of the children	19	22	19	6.17	5.94	6.20	6.11
22	Availability of extended family members	20	16	23	6.09	6.19	6.03	6.10
23	Whether or not the child is placed in day care while the parent works	22	23	24	5.98	5.73	5.91	5.88
24	Economic and physical similarities or differences between parental homes	24	26	26	5.57	5.38	5.64	5.53
25	Differences between parents' religious beliefs	25	25	22	5.25	5.39	6.04	5.53
26	Marital status of each parent; remarried, single, or cohabiting	26	24	25	5.19	5.55	5.75	5.47*b
27	Number of children in the family	27	27	27	5.18	5.14	5.20	5.17

Table 3–19

Rank Ordering of Joint Custody Decision-Making Criteria *continued*

		Rank			Means			
Overall Rank	Item	A & A Psych.	A & S Judges	A & K Attys.	A & A Psych.	A & S Judges	A & K Attys.	Grand Mean
28	Gender of the child	29	30	29	4.91	4.41	4.56	4.65*a
29	Age of the parents	30	28	28	4.36	4.69	4.88	4.62*b
30	Expressed wishes of the child, age 5	28	29	30	4.94	4.46	4.31	4.60*ab

*Significant difference
a—psychologists & judges significantly different
b—psychologists & attorneys significantly different
c—judges & attorneys significantly different
d—all three groups significantly different from each other

to judges or psychologists. All three groups rated the age of the parents, the wishes of a five-year-old, the number of children in the family, and the gender of the child at the bottom of the list.

All three groups were asked reasons for supporting or ordering sole custody and reasons for supporting or ordering joint custody. See **Table 3–20.** All three groups rated the mental stability of the parents, inability to cooperate or communicate, and the presence of physical or sexual abuse as the top three areas of concern that would result in recommending sole custody.

Table 3–20

Reasons for Sole Custody

	A & A Psychologists	A & S Judges	A & K Attorneys	Grand Mean
Physical/sexual abuse	3	1	1	1
Inability to communicate/ cooperate	2	2	2	2
Parents psych./mentally ill	1	3	3	3
Substance abuse	4	4	4	4
Domestic violence	6	5	5	5
Geographical distance	5	7	6	6

There was some discrepency among these three groups with regards to recommending or ordering joint custody. See **Table 3–21.**

All three groups rated the ability to cooperate and communicate and the children's attachment to both parents as being the top two areas of concern. However, judges and attorneys ranked geographical proximity of the two parents much higher than psychologists did. The psychological health of both parties was rated much higher among psychologists than it was among family law judges and family law attorneys.

The three groups were asked what they considered to be the most appropriate conditions of placement, or the percentage of times that they recommended, ordered, or supported various placement plans. All three groups preferred the joint custody arrangement with primary placement to one parent over sole custody with visits. Shared 50/50-type placement schedules were preferred in only 15.47 percent of the participants across all three groups. Sole custody without visits, splitting the children, and placing the children in foster placement were recommended, ordered, or preferred in five percent or less of the cases for each category. See **Table 3–22.** Lastly, these groups were asked about whether mediation should or should not be used, the use of binding arbitration, at what age children should be allowed to choose which parent they live with, and at what age they should be allowed to choose whether they visit or not. **Table 3–23** summarizes the results.

Psychologists preferred mediation more than the other two groups. However, the lower number for ordering mediation by judges may be a reflection of the fact that by the time the judges see a case, it is likely to be beyond the ability to mediate. There appears to be considerable agreement

Table 3–21

Reasons for Joint Custody

	A & A Psychologists	A & S Judges	A & K Attorneys	Grand Mean
Coop/Commun	1	1	1	1
Attachment to both	2	2	2	2
Contact with both	4	2	2	3
Geographic proximity	6	3	3	4
Psychologically healthy	3	5	6	5
Desire of parents	5	4	5	5
Child's choice	7	6	4	7

Table 3–22

Conditions of Placement

	A & A Psychologists	A & S Judges	A & K Attorneys	Grand Mean Percentage
Sole custody without visits	2.71%	3.91%	2.69%	3.08
Sole custody with visits	32.35	36.33	33.02	33.78
Joint custody primary placement	46.38	45.00	52.40	47.75
Shared placement	17.52	12.27	16.10	15.47
Splitting children	6.41	4.45	3.78	5.02
Foster placement	2.90	2.17	0.71	2.02

among all three groups with regards to what age children should be allowed to choose with whom they live and the age at which they are permitted to choose whether to visit the other parent. The grand mean of 15.17 was very close to the means of each of the three groups separately. Furthermore, the grand mean for when children should be able to choose to visit or not is 15.95. It is somewhat peculiar that ratings indicate that children should be allowed to choose with whom they live at a younger age than they can choose whether they have placement time with a parent.

Table 3–24 addresses the preferred placement schedules of judges and attorneys. There is considerable difference in the favored schedules between these two groups. Judges are much more favorable to the traditional alternating weekend schedule, allowing for two overnights every two

Table 3–23

Mean	A & A Psychologists	A & S Judges	A & K Attorney	Grand Mean
Mediation	49.00	41.19	33.88	42.07
Arbitration	N/A	2.25	0.33	1.31
Live with	15.10	15.14	15.29	15.17
Visit	N/A	15.79	16.11	15.95

Table 3–24

Preferred Placement Schedule

	A & S Judges	A & K Attorneys
12/2 without midweek dinner	39.2%	14.0%
12/2 with midweek dinner	30.4	16.8
11/3	8.8	4.2
10/4	7.2	9.8
9/5	4.0	19.6
8/6	2.4	2.8
50-50	6.4	12.6
No favorite	20.0	21.0

weeks. They preferred this in a total of 70 percent of the cases, combining those who would include a midweek dinner with those who would exclude a midweek dinner. On the other hand, the most favored schedule for attorneys was the 9/5 schedule (Ackerman, 1997), which allows for a four-day expanded alternate weekend, and one midweek overnight every two weeks. This schedule was preferred by approximately 20 percent of attorneys.

There are a number of conclusions that can be drawn from these three studies.

1. Psychologists, judges, and attorneys prefer psychologists to be court appointed, mutually agreed upon, or GAL appointed, as opposed to hired as second opinion or rebuttal experts.
2. Both judges and attorneys expect psychologists to observe children of all ages, review mental health records, review children's school and medical records, perform psychological testing of parents, children, and significant others, consult with the guardian ad litem, interview parents, child, and significant others, and write a report along with testifying in court.
3. Only attorneys expect psychologists to review criminal records and contact collateral sources.
4. Judges and attorneys do not expect psychologists to review pleadings of family law cases, review legal records, review parents' medical records, perform home visits, or consult with the parties' attorneys.

5. Judges and attorneys are not knowledgeable about the wide variety of psychological tests utilized in custody cases, with a majority of them indicating that they did not know what tests they would rely upon or not responding to the question.
6. The only test that had any level of familiarity with attorneys and judges was the MMPI-2, but not by a majority.
7. The majority of judges were not familiar with the specialized custody instruments that had been developed. However, the two instruments that had the highest level of familiarity were the Bricklin Perceptual Scales (BPS) and the Ackerman-Schoendorf Scales for Parent Evaluation of Custody (ASPECT).
8. When a forced choice is presented concerning sole custody orders or recommendations, substance abuse, parental alienation, lack of cooperation with previous court orders, parenting skills, participation in the child's education, and parental stability are the most important for all three groups.
9. When an open-ended question is asked about sole custody, physical/sexual abuse, inability to communicate or cooperate, the parents psychological instability or mental illness, or substance abuse were the most frequently mentioned areas of concern.
10. When a forced choice was presented concerning joint custody orders or recommendations, problems with substance abuse, ability to separate interpersonal conflicts from parenting, quality of the relationship with the children, and the amount of anger and bitterness were the highest rated areas of concern.
11. In the open-ended question about the same issue, cooperation and communication, attachment to both parents, contact with both parents, and geographical proximity were the highest rated areas of concern.
12. All three groups preferred joint custody with primary placement to one parent over sole custody with placement time to the other parent or shared placement.
13. The overall mean age at which these groups feel that children should be allowed to determine who they live with is 15.17.
14. The mean age at which they should be allowed to choose to have placement or not among judges and attorneys is 15.95.
15. Alcoholism is a major negative variable, but being in recovery is not.
16. Sexual preference is not a major issue, but it is significantly more of an issue for attorneys than it is for judges or psychologists, who perceive it as a non-issue.

17. Psychologists appear to be more concerned about mental health related issues than attorneys and judges are.

18. Attorneys and judges appear to be more concerned about legally related issues than psychologists do.

Discussion

When addressing the sole custody criteria, there were 33 significant differences found. Twenty-six of those 33 significant differences were psychologists differing from attorneys or judges, whereas only seven of the 33 were judges differing from attorneys. On the joint custody questions, there were 23 significant differences; 22 of these 23 significant differences involved psychologists differing from judges or attorneys, while only one represented attorneys differing from judges.

Several issues should be addressed. With regards to psychiatric hospitalizations, psychologists would not use this criterion to endorse either parent, and rank it 14th, whereas judges and attorneys rank it 8th and 15th respectively, and would use this criterion to endorse one parent over the other. This suggests a better understanding of mental illness by psychologists and the stigma associated with mental illness with judges and attorneys.

Parenting skills was ranked high by all three groups (3rd overall). It is also one of the major factors in the custody evaluation guidelines. Since this is deemed such an important factor, we need to find better ways to assess parenting skills more directly, to better define what parenting skills are, and to operationalize exactly what parenting skills mean.

Alienation is ranked second overall as a major area of concern. More research needs to be performed in the area of alienation, its prevention, and its effects.

Psychologists found one parent threatening to move out of state as more of a concern than did judges or attorneys. This may be another attempt by one parent to alienate the children from the other parent. The sexual abuse issue was ranked the number one reason for sole custody, but was 13th in overall ranking with neither parent being endorsed.

Attorneys may have preconceived, and potentially misguided, beliefs about what psychiatric hospitalization means and what effects homosexuality may have on parenting skills. This may result in them being less tolerant in these areas of concern.

In general, all three groups agree with each other more than they disagree on factors that are important in sole and joint decision-making. However, judges and attorneys are more similar to each other, and psychologists differ more from these two groups. This makes sense in that judges and attorneys have the same basic educational background, with most judges having been practicing attorneys at one time or another. Although judges are likely to be seen as more neutral than attorneys, they are nonetheless more like attorneys than psychologists.

Several weaknesses must be identified in this study. The geographical distribution is not as close to the national demographics as would be desired. Furthermore, the vast majority of participants were Caucasian. The cumbersomeness of the original Keilen & Bloom questionnaire continues to be a problem in these subsequent surveys. However, when replicating a study, the original work must be utilized or it becomes a new study.

In conclusion, the comparison of these surveys demonstrates that psychologists, family law judges, and family law attorneys think more alike than differently in the vast majority of areas addressed by these surveys. Not surprisingly, the results skew in the direction of psychologists on mental health issues and in the direction of family law judges and family law attorneys on legal issues. As the complexity of child custody evaluation practices increases, it is hoped that this study will help facilitate the interdisciplinary cooperation among these professions.

§ 3.21 Judges' Custody Decision Criteria

Page 195, insert at beginning of section:

Mary Connell, Marsha Hedrick, Daniel Schuman, Stanley Brodsky, and Beth Clark participated in a symposium at the 2001 American Psychological Association Conference titled "Expert Witness Expertise—Three Vantage Points." During the presentation, Marsha Hedrick addressed the issue of what judges want from psychologists in custody cases. Her presentation was titled "What Judges Want to Hear from the Experts." She reported that judges want psychologists to state the basis for their opinions succinctly. Judges tend to be "lukewarm" about psychological tests. When psychological tests are administered, they do not want psychologists to report endlessly about the results. They look for psychologists to make realistic recommendations and are upset by recommendations that, for example, require parents to hire a secretary and a driver. Furthermore, diagnostic statements must be tied to the issues before the court. Although psychologists are trained to make a diagnosis or provide diagnostic impressions, judges generally are not interested in the diagnosis of the parents in that they do not perceive these diagnoses to be particularly helpful in family law cases. Dr. Hedrick also reported that judges are not interested in hearing about ethical violations of other psychologists involved in the case, unless the ethical violations directly effect placement recommendations. They want psychologists to state why the ethical violations matter to the court and the case at hand, not why the violation is a violation in and of itself. Judges also are not impressed when a psychologist's demeanor changes during cross-examination, when a psychologist exaggerates data, or when a psychologist responds in a hostile manner under cross-examination. Judges perceive the psychologist's job as being to teach them, not to persuade them. Psychologists must remember that judges have good conceptual ability, but may not have the vocabulary necessary to understand concepts. Judges want confident, intelligent, well-prepared testimony but do not like cleverness on the witness stand. Furthermore, they like visual aids to be utilized in helping explain issues.

Law professor Daniel Schuman addressed similar issues when he reported on juror assessments of the believability of expert witnesses. For jurors, qualifications are important. They perceive the more qualified expert as being the more believable expert. As a result, when juries are involved, considerable time should be taken to address an expert's qualifications. However, testifying to the ultimate issue did not persuade jurors in reaching their conclusions. Also, the more familiar the psychologist was with the facts of the case, the more credible the psychologist was. If a psychologist is asked a question that begins with, "Oh, Dr., you didn't know about. . .", the credibility of the psychologist is lessened. Last, jurors look for psychologists to be disinterested and impartial. As a result, if an opposing expert is able to demonstrate partiality or bias on the part of a psychologist, that psychologist's credibility is lessened.

As the discussant for this symposium, Dr. Beth Clark summarized and addressed many of the issues raised. Dr. Clark pointed out that preparation needs to be a mutual process, i.e., the attorneys need to prepare the psychologist and the psychologist needs to prepare the attorneys. She also pointed out that psychologists do not benefit from impugning the ethics or morals of the other expert. If there are ethical or licensure issues that need to be addressed, they should be directed to the ethics committees or licensure boards and should not be part of the case in court. She also pointed out that it is essential for the psychologist to know the case backwards and forwards. One way to do this is to obtain all of the discovery materials and review them prior to court. It can be costly to have the psychologist read all of the discovery materials, however, it can be more costly if the psychologist is ill prepared and has not had the opportunity to review the materials.

§ 3.23A —Second Opinion Evaluations (New)

*Page 197, add after **Other Considerations** (§ 3.23):*

It is not unusual for an individual who has received an unfavorable opinion from the court-appointed or guardian ad litem-appointed psychologist to seek a second opinion. However, this request should not be treated as a birthright, but something granted at the judge's discretion. It becomes the psychologist's responsibility to inform the parties seeking a second opinion evaluation that in a large majority of cases, the second opinion results should agree with the first opinion results, especially when the initial evaluation was performed by a competent psychologist. There is always room for the concept of "reasonable people can disagree," and there is also the possibility that there may be disagreement on minor points, but it is unlikely that there would be any significant disagreements on major points in a majority of cases when a standard competent evaluation is performed. However, there are times when a second opinion evaluation is warranted. These include:

1. When it has been more than one year since the first opinion evaluation has been performed, and there has been a substantial change of circumstances;
2. When a first opinion expert performs an evaluation outside the standard of practice;
3. When it can be demonstrated that inappropriate tests were administered, grossly inappropriate interpretations were given to the results, or if significant criminal, mental health, and/or substance abuse history affecting parenting skills was ignored.

Substantial Change

Unfortunately, in some circumstances, it can take more than a year for a custody case to reach court based on adjournments or other problems. It is also not unusual for the initial recommendations of the psychologist to be incorporated into temporary orders between the time of the evaluation and the start of the custody trial, and then for changes of circumstances to occur. For example, if a temporary order awarded placement of the children to the father, and during the ensuing year, the child dropped from being an A/B student to being a D/F student if there were numerous absences, and/or if homework was not being completed, this would represent a substantial change from when the mother was caring for the children. There are certainly other areas where substantial change can be identified including: medical care, parental responsibility, dangerousness, anger management, school problems, hygiene problems, and/or neglect-related problems.

Standard of Practice

There has been sufficient literature published in the last decade and a half about what represents an appropriate custody evaluation, in addition to the publication of the American Psychological Association Guidelines for Child Custody and Divorce Proceedings.[72.1] These research findings combined have helped form what is now identified as the standard of practice in performing custody evaluations today. If these standards have not been met, then a second opinion evaluation would be warranted.

Inappropriate Tests or Interpretations

With the advent of managed care plans, the ensuing reduction of therapy case referrals for psychologists, and the overall tightening of the health market, more and more psychologists without adequate training or experience have started to engage in performing custody evaluations when they previously did not do so. If an individual who may be a very competent neuropsychologist administers a battery of neuropsychological tests for a custody evaluation, that would represent the use of inappropriate tests. Furthermore, if the testing that is administered is inadequate, such as the Peabody Picture Vocabulary Test as a measure of cognitive functioning and the Bender-Gestalt as a personality measure, this would represent inadequate testing procedures. In addition, when extremely outdated tests are used to form the basis of an opinion, and research has demonstrated that those tests are not useful in custody cases anymore, this would represent an additional concern. Gross misinterpretations can be found on occasion where people are using their own stylized interpretations of the MMPI-2,

[72.1] Keilin, William G. & Larry J. Bloom, *Child Custody Evaluation Practices: A Survey of Experienced Professionals*, Professional Psychology: Research and Practice, 17 (1986): 338-46; American Psychological Association, "Guidelines for Child Custody and Divorce Proceedings." American Psychologist, 49 (1994): 677-80; Ackerman, Marc J. and Melissa C. Ackerman, *Child Custody Evaluation Practices: A 1996 Survey of Psychologists*, Family Law Quarterly, 30 (1996) 565-86; Ackerman, Marc J. and Linda J. Steffen. "Child Custody Evaluation Practices: A Survey of Family Law Judges" in preparation (2000).

the MCMI-2, or Rorschach without the literature supporting the interpretations. It may be necessary to utilize a psychologist as a consultant to determine if this is indeed the case.

When it has been demonstrated that a second opinion is warranted, it becomes essential for the second opinion psychologist to not appear as a "hired gun" who is hired solely for the purpose of opposing the first evaluation and is not as independent as would be desired. It is difficult to completely avoid the appearance of being a hired expert. However, there are ways to overcome this problem. When this author performs a second opinion evaluation, the attorney hiring this psychologist is informed that the evaluation will be handled in the same manner as a first opinion evaluation. This means that the results of the evaluation will be disseminated to all three attorneys, whether they are favorable or unfavorable to the hiring attorney's client, that the report will be addressed to the guardian ad litem, and that consultation will be held with the guardian ad litem prior to writing a report. If the attorney will not agree to these requirements for performing the second opinion evaluation, then this author will not do it, and will suggest that another psychologist be sought. Thus, if the second opinion evaluation renders results contrary to the first opinion evaluation, it will give more of an appearance of a neutral evaluation than a "hired gun" evaluation. When the report is written on the second opinion evaluation, it is explained that the second opinion evaluation was handled in this manner, and the reasons for doing so.

Another form of second opinion evaluation can occur when the aggrieved parent hires a second opinion evaluator and the non-aggrieved parent also hires a second opinion evaluator in an attempt to counter the perception that the first second-opinion evaluator will agree with the aggrieved parent. Thus, a battle of the experts among mom's expert, dad's expert, and the court appointed expert results. However, it is important to understand that there is a dynamic operating under these circumstances that will affect the results of the second opinion evaluations. Understand that when the mother and father go to her expert, she will be in what is perceived as "friendly territory" and the father will be in what is perceived as "hostile territory." When the two go to the father's expert, the father will be in what is perceived as "friendly territory" and the mother will be in what is perceived as "hostile territory." As a result, both sets of evaluations carry with them different dynamics. It would not be expected, under those circumstances, that the mother's results and the father's results in each of these settings would be identical. Therefore, the mother is likely to look better with her expert, and the father better with his expert. The psychological evaluators may naively interpret this to mean that there are substantial differences between the mother and the father, with the mother's expert recommending for the mother and the father's expert recommending for the father, with each asserting the other expert is wrong. Instead, what we have is a comparison between how the parents perform on psychological testing in comfortable environments and how they perform on psychological testing in uncomfortable environments. Therefore, the results of the mother's evaluation with her expert should be compared with the father's evaluation with his expert. This will allow the examiners to compare the parents in comfortable environments. Then the father's results with the mother's expert should be compared with the mother's results with the father's expert to understand how the parents react under stress. (See **Table 3–25**) Unfortunately, experts who are not aware of this cutting edge method of interpreting these results will battle this out in court with the mom's expert saying mom is better, and the father's expert saying dad is better, when that indeed may not be the case.

For psychologists to make the type of comparison that is discussed above, it is essential for them to exchange raw data. When the court order is obtained requiring that the second opinion evaluations be performed, it should also include the requirement that the raw data be exchanged between the first opinion expert and the second opinion expert, or among the first opinion expert and the two second opinion experts. Attorneys should not get caught up in the professional controversy of requiring psychologists to provide raw data to attorneys, when this exchange of information among psychologists can easily be accomplished by the raw data being sent directly to each psychologist.[72.2] In the case of a psychologist with a history of being noncompliant with either meeting deadlines or exchanging data

Table 3–25

Compare 1 & 2 and 3 & 4.

Mother's Expert	Father's Expert	
1. Mother's findings Performance positive	2. Father's findings Performance positive	Parents when comfortable
3. Father's findings Performance negative	4. Mother's findings Performance negative	Parents when under stress

[72.2] Ackerman, Marc J. and Andrew W. Kane. "Psychological Experts in Divorce Actions, Third Edition" Aspen Law and Business, New York, NY (1998), 114-42; Ackerman, Marc J. "The Essentials of Forensic Psychological Assessment." John Wiley & Sons, Inc., (1999), 14-22.

on a timely basis, the court order should indicate that if the raw data have not been exchanged by a certain date, or the reports have not been written by a certain date, then that psychologist will not be allowed to testify in the matter or the report will not be utilized.

When a second opinion evaluation is warranted, some of the psychological tests may be repeated while others should not. Tests of cognitive functioning, which include intelligence tests and achievement tests, should not be repeated less than six months to a year after the original evaluation is performed due to what is referred to as "practice effect." Practice effect occurs when an individual is exposed to a unique task in a first opinion evaluation and performs relatively poorly. However, having engaged in the task on one occasion, the individual will be educated to the task and will perform better the second time, not because he or she is more intelligent, but because of having practiced the task. Thus, they will end up with an inflated IQ score. There is no identifiable reason other than gross incompetence on the part of the first opinion psychologist to repeat tests of cognitive functioning in less than six months to a year. However, personality tests, such as the MMPI-2, MCMI-2, and Rorschach can easily be repeated based on the fact that if the individual chooses to be cooperative and open, the results will be valid, and if the person chooses to be guarded and defensive, there will be questions about validity, whether they are the results of the first opinion or a second opinion evaluation. Personality tests also respond to changes in circumstances, while intelligence tests and achievement tests generally do not.

The issue of practice effect not only involves a particular test, but the evaluation as a whole. The first opinion evaluation educates the participants about how to respond the second time around. For example, if a parent's MMPI-2 shows a significant amount of depression, and the examiner indicated that the depression was a factor in recommending placement to the other parent, when reading the MMPI-2 items during the second opinion evaluation, the party would likely not answer the depression questions in a scorable direction as had occurred the first time. Therefore, the parent who is seeking the second opinion evaluation is likely to look better the second time around, not because the first opinion evaluator was incorrect, but because the party has been educated by the results of the first opinion evaluation. Again, the second opinion evaluator often naively interprets these results to mean the first opinion evaluator was *wrong*, ignoring the educative aspect of the first opinion evaluation for one parent and the negative impact of the second opinion evaluation on the other parent.

When a second opinion evaluator disagrees with first opinion evaluators in a majority of cases, this is likely to say more about the second opinion evaluator than the quality of the first opinion evaluations, based on the fact that a large majority of second opinion evaluations should agree with competent first opinion evaluations. This type of second opinion evaluator will often gain the reputation of being a "hired gun."

The attorney is left with helping the client make the difficult decision of whether a second opinion evaluation should be performed or not. There is not only a significant financial cost to performing a second opinion evaluation, but there is also the psychological cost of subjecting the parties, especially the children, to the stress of additional evaluations. There is no birthright that necessarily gives the aggrieved parent the right to seek a second opinion evaluation if the first opinion evaluation does not suit their liking. It then becomes the judge's and the guardian ad litem's responsibility to determine whether there is sufficient reason to allow for a second opinion evaluation. It is this author's opinion that second opinion evaluations are used far too frequently and, in many cases, unnecessarily. As a result, the second opinion evaluation is likely to be of little value in standard cases with standard evaluations and is likely to be given little weight except for the above noted concerns. In a recent national survey, family court judges reported that they give significantly less weight to second opinion evaluations than neutral court or guardian ad litem appointed evaluations.[72.3]

[72.3] Ackerman, Marc J. and Linda J. Steffen. "Child Custody Evaluation Practices: A Survey of Family Law Judges," in preparation (2000).

CHAPTER 4

HOW DIVORCE AFFECTS FAMILIES

§ 4.7 Physical Placement and Visitation Schedules

Page 214, add the following text at the end of the section:

An issue that has been hotly debated in recent years is whether infants should be required to have overnights with the non-primary placement parent. There have been many learned treatises written by many scholars in this area. The vast majority point to the issue of frequent short contacts between non-primary placement parents and infant children. Unfortunately, this flies in the face of being able to implement a shared placement schedule with children this age. Criticisms have been leveled about the fact that there is no empirical research that demonstrates what type of schedule is beneficial in these cases. However, we cannot overlook that fact that it is difficult, if not impossible, to do research with infants, due to their inability to communicate. One would have to rely on reports of the parents, which would be subject to bias in the direction that the parent wished the placement to occur.

When children are between birth and 12 months of age, the frequent contacts should be four to five times a week for two to three hours in duration. To be most advantageous, these contacts should be at various times, scattered throughout the week. This would allow the non-placement parent to feed the child on occasion, bathe the child on occasion, and bed the child down on occasion. To make this work most efficiently, it may be necessary for the non-placement parent to come into the placement parent's home for this brief period of time to allow for these contacts. It is understood that this could be disruptive and difficult. However, when weighed against the negative effects of overnights and recognizing that this will occur for a limited period of time, the child's best interest should take precedence.

The purpose for not allowing overnights at this age is based on development theory which suggests that the most important factor children must engage in during these first two years is learning to trust the environment. The more stable the environment, the more predictable the environment, and the more consistent the environment, the better able children will be to trust the environment and develop a sense of security.

The long-term negative affects of these early disruptions can be seen in young adults in their late teens and early twenties who enter into therapy based on their inability to trust relationships, inconsistent work histories, and unresolved feelings about their parents' divorce. Simply stated, it appears that there is too much at risk in forcing the overnights at this young age when a short-term inconvenience can possibly prevent these lifelong problems.

Between 12 and 24 months, overnights should be minimized, but can occur occasionally. Children are still in the formative stages of being able to learn to trust the environment and feel comfortable with themselves and others around them. However, once children reach two years of age, up until six years of age, the number of overnights that the non-primary placement parent receives can be gradually increased. As the number of overnights increase, the frequency of the contacts can reduce, and the duration of the contacts can increase. The ultimate goal would be a joint custody/ shared placement plan identified later as the Ackerman Plan.

In a meta-analysis, Paul Amato and Bruce Keith reviewed 92 studies that evaluated how divorce affects children. They addressed the issues of parental absence, economic disadvantage, family conflict, and other related issues, with several interesting results. The authors concluded that "children who experience parental death tend to be better off than children who experience divorce."[24.1] When examining socioeconomic factors, the hypothesis that children are better off living with stepfathers rather than with single mothers was not supported for girls, but was for boys. However, "some support was found for the hypothesis that children have a higher level of well-being in father-custody families than mother-custody families."[24.2] The authors' meta-analysis supported the conclusion that family conflict remains a significant factor in how children function. The impact of post-divorce conflict between parents was strongly associated with children's maladjustment, receiving the widest support among the general concerns.

Neil Kalter and his associates discussed the predictors of post-judgment adjustment.[24.3] They found that parents' adjustment directly affects children's adjustment. They also report that negative changes in the mother's life negatively affect boys' adjustment to divorce, and severity of problems negatively affects girls' adjustment to divorce.

[24.1] P. Amato & B. Keith, Parental Divorce and the Well-Being of Children: A Meta-Analysis 39 (1991).

[24.2] *Id.* at 40.

[24.3] N. Kalter et al., *Predictors of Children's Post-Divorce Adjustment,* 59 Am. J. Orthopsychiatry No. 4, at 605–18 (Oct. 1989).

§ 4.7 PLACEMENT AND VISITATION

Research performed by David Demo and Alan Acock[24.4] determined that a child's emotional adjustment, gender role identification, and antisocial behavior appeared to be affected by the divorce process. However, other dimensions of a child's well-being remain unaffected. Like other authors, Demo and Acock concluded that the level of family contact may also be a factor in the adjustment of children.

Unfortunately, judges, family court commissioners, or mediators who do not have background in developmental theory may get caught up in the notion of equality of placement without recognizing the negative affect that some equal placement schedules will have on the child(ren). A number of years ago, while being involved in therapy, a 12-year-old girl talked to this author about what happens when she's at her mother's house and what happens when she's at her father's house. The parents had an alternating two week on/off week off schedule. The therapist stated, "you talk about what happens at your mother's house and what happens at your father's house, which house is your house?" The child responded "my mother has a house and my father has a house, but I don't have a house." What a sad commentary for a 12-year-old child to express. One of the advantages of the Ackerman Plan is that it allows for relatively equal placement, but also allows the child to have a sense of home base.

It would be ideal if all family court judges were required to take a course in child development. However, realistically this is not a possibility. Some examples of judges' orders designed to equalize the time, without taking into consideration the negative impact on the children follow. In one case this author was involved with, the judge ordered the children to be with the mother every Monday and Wednesday, the father every Tuesday and Thursday, and alternate weekends. There are few adults that could handle this frequency of moving and remain adjusted. Why then would we assume that children would be capable of doing this? Another example of poor scheduling is an increasingly popular schedule of a three day alternating schedule. Unfortunately, while equalizing the placement time, this puts the children on a seven week rotating schedule, which is far too much for anyone to be able to adequately manage.

In developing placement schedules, we must remember that the most important task for children is their education. Any schedule developed, as a result, must minimize the interference with their education, while at the same time maximizing the amount of time with each parent.

[24.4] D. Demo & A. Acock, *The Impact of Divorce on Children,* 50 J. Marriage & Family 619–48 (Aug. 1988).

§ 4.31 Parental Alienation Syndrome

Page 240, add the following text at the end of the section:

Parental Alienation Syndrome: Does It Really Exist and If So What Is It?

The concept of "Parental Alienation Syndrome" (PAS) has been in the public arena for more than a decade. There has been considerable controversy generated regarding the use or misuse of this term. A discrimination needs to be made between the concept of alienation and the possible existence of Parental Alienation Syndrome. If alienation occurs in a case, the reader must be aware that there are three possibilities of why the alienation occurs. The first is embodied in Gardner's lengthy explanations which follow. However, children can also be alienated from the disfavored parent because of that parent's behavior. Lastly, the alienation could be occurring as a combination of both. Thus, it becomes the professional's responsibility to determine which of these factors is operative in alienation cases.

Gardner also points out that mothers may program their children against their fathers in subtle and unconscious ways. By using the subtle manner, she can then proclaim innocence to any accusations of brainwashing. These subtle criticisms often take the form of indirect communications, such as, "There are things I could say about your father that would make your hair stand on end; but I am not the kind of person who criticizes a parent to his children."[95.1] Or "What do you mean you are going to your father's house? Oh, what am I saying, what's wrong, I shouldn't have said that. I shouldn't discourage you from seeing your father."[95.2] Parents who allow children to make the decision regarding visitation may indirectly tell them not to visit. Or a mother may say, "You have to go see your father. If you don't, he'll take us to court."[95.3] This is all done without mentioning any positive benefits that may result from visiting with the father.

Another indirect way of alienating the father occurs when the mother moves a considerable distance away for no other reason than to be far from the father. It must be noted that these mothers are much less loving of their

---

[95.1] Richard Gardner, Family Evaluation and Child Custody, Mediation, Arbitration, and Litigation 226 (1989) [hereinafter Gardner].

[95.2] *Id.* at 239.

[95.3] *Id.* at 240.

children than their actions would indicate, because a loving parent appreciates the importance of a relationship with the noncustodial parent.

Gardner identifies emotional factors within the child that may lead to Parental Alienation Syndrome. For instance, the child's psychological bond with the loved parent may simply be stronger than the bond with the hated parent. If the child fears that this bond will be disrupted and that the preferred parent will become angry, the child may love the "loved" parent more and hate the "hated" parent more. Because he already feels abandoned by one parent, the child is unwilling to risk being abandoned by the other parent. "This fear of the loss of mother's love is the most important factor in the development of the symptoms . . . of Parental Alienation Syndrome."[95.4] What fathers do not realize is that this obsessive hatred is really a disguise for deep love; the child does not hate the father, but is afraid of losing the mother's affection. Although Gardner does not use the term, this is often described as a loyalty issue.

Finally, Gardner identifies situational factors that can contribute to Parental Alienation Syndrome. He points out that the longer a child remains with a particular parent, the more the child will resist moving to the other parent. Another common situation is one "in which the child will develop complaints about the 'hated' parent in which the child has observed a sibling being treated harshly or even being rejected for expressing their affection for the 'hated' parent."[95.5]

In severe cases, "the mothers of these children are often fanatic. They use every mechanism at their disposal (legal and illegal) to prevent visitation. They are obsessed with antagonism towards their husbands. In many cases they are paranoid."[95.6] Unfortunately, these mothers do not respond to logic or appeals to reason. Children of these mothers end up being equally fanatic as a result of modeling their behavior. As a result, they can become panic-stricken when asked to visit their fathers. These panicked states become so severe as to render the possibility of visitation improbable. Unfortunately, cases of severe Parental Alienation Syndrome do not respond to traditional therapeutic approaches. Traditional therapy for the children is also not beneficial because the

> therapeutic exposure represents only a small fraction of the total amount of time of exposure to the mother's denigrations of the father. This is a sick psychological bond here between the mother and children that is not

[95.4] *Id.* at 246.
[95.5] *Id.* at 249.
[95.6] *Id.* at 361.

going to be changed by therapy as long as the children remain living with the mother.[95.7]

Gardner believes that the first step in the treatment of children in this situation is to remove them from the mother's home and place them with the father. He also identifies very structured and drastic recommendations to facilitate this process:

> [F]ollowing this transfer, there must be a period of decompression and debriefing in which the mother has no opportunity at all for input to the children. The hope here is to give the children the opportunity to re-establish the relationship with the alienated father, without significant contamination of the process by the brainwashing of the mother. Even telephone calls must be strictly prohibited for at least a few weeks, and perhaps longer. Then, according to the therapist's judgment, slowly increasing contacts with the mother may be initiated.[95.8]

Gardner notes that in some cases, the children may eventually be returned to the mother. However, if the mother continues to alienate the children, it may be necessary to consider never returning the children to the mother.

The fathers in these situations also need to be involved in individual therapy. The fathers must understand that the children do not sincerely hate them. A strong, healthy bond was established when the children were much younger, and the current allegations of hatred are merely a facet of a loyalty issue.

In moderate cases of Parental Alienation Syndrome, the mothers are not as fanatic:

> [T]hey are able to make some differentiation between allegations that are preposterous and those that are not. There is still, however, a campaign of denigration and a significant desire to withhold the children from the father as a vengeance maneuver. They will find a wide variety of excuses to interfere with or circumvent visitation.[95.9]

Children in this category are also less fanatic than those severely affected. Although they are likely to vilify the father in the presence of the mother, they are also likely to give up this attitude in the father's presence.

Gardner believes that these families should be seen in family therapy by one therapist rather than involving several therapists. The likelihood of

---

[95.7] *Id.* at 362–63.
[95.8] *Id.* at 363.
[95.9] *Id.* at 365.

manipulation may actually increase if several therapists take part. The therapist involved in this type of case must not succumb to the notion of "respecting the wishes" of the children and may actually have to be quite directive. The therapist must also be aware that "the older children may promulgate the mother's programming down to the younger ones."[95.10] The pathology extends itself when the mother relies on the older children to make sure that the younger children act accordingly with the father. If this becomes an ongoing problem, it can be recommended that the older children visit separately from the younger children.

If transition from the mother to father becomes difficult, a neutral place, such as the therapist's office, the guardian ad litem's office, or a social service agency office, can be used for the transfer of children. It is also important for the therapist to understand that the mother may be continuing the acrimony in the relationship as a way of remaining in a relationship with the former husband. Although it may appear to be a perverted reason for doing so, it allows the mother to continue a relationship with the father. It becomes the therapist's obligation, if this is occurring, to help the mother move beyond that type of thinking.

In cases of moderate Parental Alienation Syndrome, the fathers must learn not to take the children's vilifications too seriously. When the children engage in this type of denigration, the father must be encouraged to help avert their attention to healthier interchanges. The entire therapy process can be aided if a therapist can "find some healthy 'insider' on the mother's side of the family."[95.11] For example, "the mother's mother can become a very powerful therapeutic ally if the therapist is able to enlist her services."[95.12] Last, Gardner suggests that with moderate cases the therapist must be a strong individual who is not psychoanalytically oriented, but can be directive and structuring when necessary.

In mild cases of Parental Alienation Syndrome, mothers are generally more psychologically healthy than the mothers in the moderate or severe cases. They recognize that alienation from the father may not be in their children's best interest and they are less likely to become involved in ongoing litigation. These mothers also recognize that protracted litigation could cause everyone in the family to suffer. Nevertheless, there may still be some minor acts of programming, but without paranoia. These children tend to be more interested in strengthening their position with their mother than in openly denigrating their father. When a final court order results in

---

[95.10] *Id.* at 368.
[95.11] *Id.* at 372.
[95.12] *Id.*

primary placement with the mother, the fear of being transferred to the father is reduced and the Parental Alienation Syndrome generally disappears.

Gardner points out "that without the proper placement of the child (for which a court order may be necessary) treatment may be futile."[95.13]

Gardner states that the guardian ad litem's role in these cases can be very important. He sees the guardian ad litem as being a potentially powerful ally for the therapist in working with families where Parental Alienation Syndrome is present. However, he also points out that if the guardian ad litem is not familiar with the consequences of Parental Alienation Syndrome, the guardian ad litem may become manipulated into "supporting the children's positions" to their actual detriment. Because guardians ad litem are assigned to act in the best interest of their wards, they may have great difficulty in supporting "coercive maneuvers" such as "insisting that the children visit with the father who they profess they hate" because "it goes so much against the traditional orientation to clients in which they often automatically align themselves with their client's cause."[95.14]

In 1998, Richard Gardner wrote an article addressing the issue of recommendations that should be made for dealing with parents who induce Parental Alienation Syndrome in their children. He stated then, as previously, that in severe Parental Alienation Syndrome cases it is likely to be necessary to transfer the children from the alienating parent to the alienated parent. He adds a dimension in this article of providing a "transitional site" during this transfer period. He suggests that the transitional site could be the home of a friend or relative, a community shelter, or hospitalization, depending upon how restrictive the environment would need to be. He also suggests a six phase process for this transition. Phase 1 involves placement of the child in the transitional site. Following Phase 1, the child will begin to visit with their father for short periods of time at their home (Phase 2), eventually leading to the child leaving the transitional site to live with their father on an ongoing basis (Phase 3). During this time, there would be no contact with their mother. During Phase 4, carefully monitored contact with the mother could commence on a trial basis, leading to monitored visits with the mother in the father's home (Phase 5). Eventually, these monitored visits can be attempted in the mother's home (Phase 6).

In his concluding remarks, Gardner states . . . the *diagnosis* PAS is not made on the basis of the programmer's efforts, but the degree of the "success" in each child. The *treatment* is based not only on the degree to which

---

[95.13] *Id.* at 374.
[95.14] *Id.* at 375.

the child has been alienated but also on the mother's degree of attempted indoctrinations. In most cases the mother will remain the primary custodial parent. It is only when she cannot, or will not, inhibit herself from such indoctrinations that custodial transfer and the transitional site program should be implemented.[95.15]

A number of authors have written about Parental Alienation Syndrome on recent years. Several of those authors' comments will be addressed. In 1997, Deirdre Conway Rand wrote a two-part article talking about the spectrum of Parental Alienation Syndrome.

Dr. Rand offered a thorough review of the literature and provided case studies that support the diagnosis of Parental Alienation Syndrome. Much of the literature that she quotes does not directly address the issue of Parental Alienation Syndrome, but deals with parallel issues from which she generalizes. Many of the supportive articles that are discussed are anecdotal reports as opposed to complete research studies. She also points out that one of the byproducts of Parental Alienation Syndrome, in some cases, is parents making false sexual abuse allegations. She makes a tie-in between Parental Alienation Syndrome and Munchausen Syndrome by Proxy.

A very thorough discussion in Rand's articles about how children respond to high conflict divorce is valuable, but not necessarily supportive of the existence of a Parental Alienation Syndrome. It is difficult to determine why Rand generalizes Garbarino's descriptors for childhood maltreatment as being adapted to describe Parental Alienation Syndrome. When Rand discusses the involvement of third parties, the reader is made aware of the fact that additional parties can promote, foster, or expand the alienation process. New partners, mental health professionals, and therapists can all directly or indirectly foster the alienation process. A lengthy discussion of attorneys writing articles about Parental Alienation Syndrome follows. However, the fact that attorneys may have written such articles does not necessarily add to the credibility or the validity of the concept. The author relies too heavily on using professional writings that reference Parental Alienation Syndrome as an indication of its acceptance. She also quotes a study by Nicholas that utilized 21 completed surveys. The results of a survey that utilizes such a small sample are put in question.

In summary, Rand relies on anecdotal information, studies with small samples, and the inclusion of Gardner's Parental Alienation Syndrome concept in literature as being equivalent to acceptance and validity of the concept.

[95.15] Richard Gardner, *Recommendations for Dealing with Parents Who Induce a Parent Alienation Syndrome in Their Children*, A Journal of Divorce and Remarriage, 22–23 (1998).

Dr. Lowenstein, a consulting psychologist in the United Kingdom, addresses the use of mediation in dealing with Parental Alienation Syndrome as an alternative. He points out that "warring parents are a problem and that little can be achieved through this approach, and certainly those who suffer the most as a result are likely to be the children who are confused by warring parents, or who are poisoned by one parent against the other."[95.16] He points out that engaging in the mediation process takes the case out of the legal arena and puts it into the mental health arena. He also points out, however, that it is advantageous to have the court oversee the mediation process.

Kathleen Coulborn Faller has written extensively on sexual abuse related issues. Her 1998 article addresses the use of Parental Alienation Syndrome in various settings. She points out that the "Parental Alienation Syndrome offers an explanation for reports of sexual abuse when parents are divorcing or are divorced."[95.17] Faller is hard on Gardner's claims indicating that Gardner uses many percentages that are not supported by research, stating, for example, that "90 percent of the time the accusing parent is the child's mother."[95.18]

Faller spends a considerable portion of her article addressing Gardner's Sexual Abuse Legitimacy Scale (SALS). She states that "the SALS has been used by Gardner and others who accept his ideas, in conjunction with the Parental Alienation Syndrome."[95.19] There are 84 factors included in the SALS. Faller postulates that "further examination of the 84 factors in the SALS indicates that its primary function is diagnosis of the Parental Alienation Syndrome."[95.20] She further states, "because the SALS has not been validated and, in fact, had not been the subject of any research; because it was based on Gardner's assumptions about divorce allegations; and because its language lacked neutrality, it has been the subject of considerable criticism."[95.21]

Faller further states that "Gardner does not provide any research findings to substantiate his assertions about the proposed characteristics and dynamics of the Parental Alienation Syndrome. . . it is important to appreciate the consequence of the fact that Gardner publishes the vast majority of his work himself. His own press, Creative Therapeutics, only

---

[95.16] L.F. Lowenstein, *Parental Alienation Syndrome: A Two-Step Approach Toward a Solution*, Contemporary Family 514 (1998).

[95.17] Kathleen Coulborn Faller, *The Parental Alienation Syndrome: What Is It and What Data Support It?*, Child Maltreatment 100 (1998).

[95.18] *Id.*

[95.19] *Id.* at 105.

[95.20] *Id.*

[95.21] *Id.*

publishes his material and no works of other writers. . . . Thus, his ideas are not critically evaluated by others knowledgeable in the field before they appear in print."[95.22] Although there is a body of literature that exists on false sexual allegations, none of it references Gardner's work.

Much of the article is devoted to research findings that do not support Gardner's points of view. Faller states, "again, the research findings from large samples with defined methodology do not support Gardner's assertion that large numbers of mothers (or others) involved in divorce make false allegations, either by design or because they are mentally ill.[95.23] She later states, "therefore, it appears that experts in sexual abuse disagree with Gardner's (1991) assertion that sexual statements and sexualized behavior are characteristic of nonabused children and can be spontaneously generated by sexual fantasy."[95.24] Furthermore, she states, "there are no data that support a conclusion that because children have sexual knowledge, they will use this information to make a false allegation of sexual abuse."[95.25]

Faller concludes by dealing with the diagnostic label Parental Alienation Syndrome itself, pointing out that the Diagnostic and Statistical Manual of Mental Disorders-Fourth Edition (DSM-IV) does not include a diagnosis of Parental Alienation Syndrome. She states that "the Parental Alienation Syndrome is a nondiagnostic syndrome. It only explains the behavior of the child and the mother, if the child has not been sexually abused."[95.26] She goes on to state, "an additional problem with the Parental Alienation Syndrome is that virtually every symptom described by Gardner is evidence of its presence, and consequent false charges against the accused parent are open to opposing interpretations.[95.27]

As further substantiation of the concerns generated by Kathleen Faller, this author experienced Dr. Gardner's approach first hand in a divorce case that included a sexual abuse allegation. He provided over 100 criteria that could be used for evaluating whether sexual abuse had occurred or not. He provided no scientific research support, validation studies, or replication by other researchers to support his contentions of the more than 100 criteria. As a result, we were faced with the gospel according to Dr. Richard Gardner. The 100 criteria were clearly supportive of findings of false allegations. Some representative examples include Dr. Gardner's statement that sexual abuse perpetrators are often intellectually impaired. Since the father was not intellectually impaired, this would be an indication of a

---

[95.22] *Id.* at 106.
[95.23] *Id.* at 108.
[95.24] *Id.* at 110.
[95.25] *Id.*
[95.26] *Id.* at 111.
[95.27] *Id.*

false allegation. Merely because of the allegation was part of a child custody dispute, Gardner gave an additional false rating. Because the child did not tell the story exactly the same way each time, this was further indication for Gardner that it was a false allegation. He stated that victims of sexual abuse will show depersonalization, dissociation, attitude towards one's genitals, sexual organ anesthesia, and stigmatization. Since the four-year-old victim did not report any of these types of symptomatology, these would be five additional indications that it was a false allegation, according to Dr. Gardner. Eight of the items were also considered to be indications of false allegations because of Dr. Gardner's interpretation of the projective drawings. Furthermore, since the four-year-old victim did not run away from home, and victims often run away from home, this would be a further indication of a false allegation. He also used mutually exclusive criteria, stating that perpetrators are coercive and dominating, and passive and have impaired self-assertion. A person cannot be both of these. Therefore, at least one of them would be rated to come up with an indicator of a false allegation.

When Dr. Gardner finished his evaluation, he indicated that 52 criteria suggested a false allegation, two criteria suggested a true allegation, and four of the criteria were equivocal. When those same variables were scrutinized separately by two other mental health professionals, one rated 12 of them as indicating false allegation, and 19 of them as indicating true allegation, with 23 being equivocal, and six nonapplicable, while the other found 30 of the criteria to suggest a true allegation.

Richard Gardner is an accomplished mental health professional about divorce-related issues. He has published many books, developed therapeutic techniques, and been innovative in his approaches. However, some feel that he has gone astray in the past five to ten years with his work in the area of sexual abuse allegations, especially as it relates to the concept of Parental Alienation Syndrome (PAS). Furthermore, there has been an "unholy alliance" developed through conscious efforts or association between the concepts of "False Memory Syndrome" (a la Ralph Underwager) and "Parental Alienation Syndrome" (a la Richard Gardner). There are divorce cases where the professional opinions have been rendered that a false sexual abuse allegation is false because of Parental Alienation Syndrome and/or the False Memory Syndrome.

In addition, criticism has been leveled against Gardner for using the term diagnosis in relation to Parental Alienation Syndrome. Authors have written about the fact that there is no diagnostic manual that lists Parental Alienation Syndrome and/or its symptoms, thus stating that Parental Alienation Syndrome does not exist. This may be a rather hollow argument in that parents do alienate children from the other parent; the concept of alienation exists, whether we give it a diagnostic label of Parental Alienation Syndrome or not. Richard Gardner has raised the level of consciousness of psychologists, attorneys, and courts to recognize the fact that alienation occurs. The danger, however, is when it becomes the answer every time a parent is concerned that visitation or placement is not going as he/she would like it to. Research and therapeutic efforts need to focus on how to identify when alienation is or is not occurring, therapeutic interventions, and outcome studies instead of embroiling psychologists in the controversy of whether a diagnostic label exists or does not.

Three different case studies follow. Case Study #1 demonstrates the father's initial behavior as being behavior that would alienate children from him, but is followed by the mother's alienating behavior. Case Study #2 is a case where, although the father is accused of alienating the children from the mother, the mother's behavior has clearly alienated the children from her. Case Study #3 is an example of a situation where the mother's behavior exclusively has alienated the children from their father, and she has completely interfered with them being able to see their father.

Case Study #1

Tom and Helen Garrison were married to one another for 10 years. Their children, Nancy and Edward, lived with them throughout the marriage. Tom, a professional in the community, became addicted to prescription medications through a number of legal and illegal activities. His behavior became erratic, abusive, and withdrawn. As a result, Helen decided to divorce Tom. There was no question at the time that Nancy and Edward would live with their mother.

Over a four-year period of time, Helen engaged in an unending campaign against the father, identifying how bad a person he was, how abusive he had been, and that he was nothing more than a drug addict. Although Tom's license had been suspended, he had his license returned, had been clean and sober for more than five years, and was back to functioning as a professional in the community.

One contempt motion after another was brought against Helen by Tom for interfering with his placement rights. He had not seen his children for four years. Finally, after many contempt warnings, the court issued an order which essentially said "for every time your children do not visit with their father at the prescribed placement times, you will be found in contempt and spend three days in jail." This author was appointed as the therapist to help reunite Tom with his children, and help foster a relationship among them.

It should be noted that once the "jail" order was issued, the children never missed a placement period with their father.

During the four-year period of time that the children did not see their father, Helen would require the children to write letters to their father in their own handwriting, which she dictated, indicating they did not want to see their father. On other occasions, she would write the letters herself and ask the children to copy them in their own hand. On still other occasions, she perjured herself in court when giving testimony about what the children had said their father had done.

When the therapy commenced in Fall of 1996, the children's denigration of their father during the sessions was merciless and very hard to listen to. As time went on, visits with their father at the office were commenced; followed by several hour visits that commenced at the office, moved into the community, and terminated at the office; followed by all-day visits; followed by overnight visits; followed by visits with their father in an adjacent city. As time passed, the children came to realize that their father was not the ogre their mother had portrayed, that he was not still a drug addict, and that he was actually quite pleasant. Nancy and Ed became more integrated into their father's life, spent more time with their father, and eventually traveled with their father, his new wife, and their new step-sister.

When Nancy reached 16 years of age, she was unable to handle being with her mother and stepfather anymore, and requested to live with Tom. In the process of doing so, she disclosed to this author and the guardian ad litem all of the lies that had been perpetrated by her mother and carried out by her, all the manipulations that had occurred, and how she needed to leave that environment. She shook and sobbed uncontrollably as she described this entire set of circumstances. An immediate emergency transfer of placement was made and Nancy went to live with her father, stepmother, and half-sister.

Unfortunately, the damage had already been done. Moving in with her father did not appear to be the "magical" answer that Nancy had hoped it would be. She eventually ended up going through a series of mental health interventions including inpatient hospitalizations, day hospital, and residential treatment. To this date, she has not fully recovered from the adverse affect of the alienation that her mother fostered towards her father.

Although this is a case where the father initially engaged in behavior that could result in being alienated against, it was the mother's incessant need to punish the father for his previous "sins" and ongoing alienation that adversely affected the children. Unfortunately, one of the factors that parents do not consider when they are alienating their children against the other parent is the long-term negative psychological impact of requiring their children to engage in such behavior.

Case Study #2

Kelly is an accountant and Michael a dentist. Both have reached the upper levels of professional competence and respect within the community. They have been divorced for seven years. As of the writing of this chapter, Kelly has not spent any meaningful time with her children in the last four-and-a-half years, and claims that it is a function of alienation of the children by Michael against her. When the divorce was originally granted, Kelly was given primary placement of the children (2 boys and 2 girls), and Michael was seeing them on an alternating weekend basis. As time passed, Kelly's behavior became more erratic and of concern to the guardian ad litem. By mutual agreement of the attorneys, this author was appointed the therapist for the children to help them deal with the fallout of divorce and the acrimony that existed between their parents. As a result of this therapy, it quickly became apparent that Kelly's erratic behavior had a psychotic-like or dissociative quality about it. There were times that she would go into incoherent screaming rages; call her children by non-family member names; not provide food for the children; lock the children out of the house, leave town for the weekend, and leave a six- and eight-year-old to wander the neighborhood and other similar behaviors. After approximately six months of attempting to work with this problem, the guardian ad litem, with this author's help, filed a motion to transfer placement of the children from the mother to the father.

As part of the court order, Kelly was required to engage in therapy prior to being allowed to have visits with her children. She indicated that she did not need therapy and that it was her ex-husband who had the psychological or psychiatric problems. As a result, a considerable period of time passed before Kelly was willing to engage in therapy and before the process of reuniting Kelly with her children was commenced. A series of meetings were held with Kelly, her therapist, her attorney, the guardian ad litem, and this author.

The mother had not seen the children for four months. She was informed that the ground rules for the meeting would include no discussion about substance abuse, physical abuse, the legal matters, or name calling. She was also informed that she would be warned twice if she engaged in these types of behavior, and after the third occurrence the visit would be terminated.

The visit commenced with the mother complaining about the fact that the contact started four minutes late. All of the children crowded on a small sofa designed to seat two people in an effort to prevent their mother from sitting on the sofa with them. She asked for hugs from the children, they refused, and she began forceably pulling them off of the sofa in an attempt to get them to hug her. She brought a deck of cards with her to play a game with the children. She had a specific game in mind; the children did not want to play the game, wanted to play a game of their own, and she was unable to be flexible enough to defer to their wishes.

Five minutes into the visit, the mother found it necessary to tell the children that she did not trust this psychologist and that this psychologist had lied to her. It was apparent that this behavior on the mother's part upset three of the children, two of them asking to leave, and one sitting in a corner with her back to her mother. With the remaining child, the mother walked over to about four to six inches from her face, and started berating her about something that she said. The topic again turned to this psychologist and accusing the children of having misinformation. At this point, one of the children reported that she felt like she was going to throw up and two of the others were begging to have their mother stop saying what she was saying. After several warnings about her yelling at the children, criticizing her ex-husband, and other inappropriate behaviors, it was announced that the visit would end 19 minutes after it started. The children literally ran out of the room to leave the session when they were told they could. Following the termination of the visit, the mother was out of control, yelling, making accusatory statements, and telling people in the waiting room how "cruel" this psychologist was.

In the middle of this process, Kelly decided to sue the guardian ad litem and the therapist for malpractice for prohibiting contact with the children. The suit was found to be frivolous, and was dismissed on a summary judgment. Unfortunately, the filing of the suit delayed the time for reconnecting the children with their mother.

After a delay of a year and a half, the process was reinstituted and a series of meetings with the same set of individuals was commenced. These meetings resulted in a schedule of sessions between the mother and her children in this therapist's office with the mother's therapist present to help out with the process. The contacts were so stressful that the children all suffered adversely. One of the children became suicidal, one developed an eating disorder, and two had to repeat a grade in school. As a result, it was decided by all of the professionals that these contacts should once again be terminated.

Following these failed contacts, it was decided that each child, upon reaching 16 years of age, would be free to contact their mother if they chose. Since, at 16 years of age, each of the children would have their driver's license, it was felt that this freedom of contact should be acknowledged, instead of requiring a child to sneak to see his or her mother in an attempt to make a contact, if they desired to do so.

During the period of time between transfer of placement and the writing of this chapter (approximately 4-1/2 years), there have been hundreds, if not thousands, of violations of the court order by the mother. There were times that she would call the children's home as many as 25 times in an evening; she showed up at children's activities, drove past the house, tried to intercept one of the children at a school bus stop, and wrote inappropriate letters to the children, among many other damaging activities, all of which were prohibited by the existing court orders.

It should be understood that Michael was not without fault in the way that he handled these matters. There were times that he lost his temper with Kelly, and called her names in front of the children. He was not as encouraging as he could have been in having the children send pictures of themselves, report cards, and presents to their mother. In addition, although he recognized that Kelly was in contempt of court dozens of times, he refused to file contempt motions; he did not want to put his children through potentially seeing their mother arrested and jailed for these offenses, since they had already been through enough. Although not perfect, Michael's inappropriate behaviors, for the most part, were a reaction to Kelly's aberrant behavior and not a function of his desire to alienate the children from their mother. On more than one occasion, he sat in this therapist's office lamenting the fact that his children did not have a healthy mother or a healthy relationship with their mother, and were distressed over same.

This is clearly a case where any alienation that the children have towards their mother is a function of her own behavior and not a function of the father trying to keep them from their mother.

Case Study #3

Todd and Carol divorced after seven years of marriage with a one-, three-, and five-year-old. Four years later, this author was asked by the court to review the case since serious allegations of alienation had been made. Unlike many cases of this nature, neither party had funds to pursue an extended court battle. As a result, any services performed would be paid for by the County Court. Two years prior to my involvement, another psychologist performed an evaluation, opined that there was severe alienation, and recommended that the children be transferred from the mother to the father with no contact between the mother and the children for an extended period of time (a la Gardner).

During the four-year period of time during which the father had not seen the children, they accused their father of engaging in a whole myriad of inappropriate behaviors, including physical abuse, sexual abuse, psychological abuse, substance abuse, manipulation, and other behaviors. The children had assumed the last name of their stepfather, informed their father that he was not their father, and called their stepfather "Dad." The mother had not sent pictures, medical records, school records, or other important documents to the father since the time of the divorce. Furthermore, the five-year-old daughter claimed that she remembered being sexually abused by her father four years earlier. She also reported that her mother had told her about the sexual abuse. The nine-year-old boy threatened suicide if required to spend any time with his father. Upon observation of the children with their father in my office, there was a non-stop litany of denigrating statements towards the father, stated in a matter-of-fact, even-tempered, nonemotional manner. They all told the father that he was not their father, that they wished that he was dead, and that they never wanted to see him again.

The school social worker from the school the children attended had been drawn into the fray and became an ally of the mother's. A relative neophyte to the profession, the social worker gleefully reported to this psychologist that the children verified everything that the mother had said about the father. Carol also came to the school the first day of school and provided the social worker with the negative litany about the father. Lastly, the social worker felt it should be the children's choice as to which last name they used and she saw no problem with them selecting their stepfather's last name.

The guardian ad litem recognized a significant amount of alienation had occurred, but was fearful of forcing any contact between the father and the children for fear that the nine-year-old would follow through in his threat and attempt or commit suicide. This psychologist felt that although suicidal ideation should always be taken seriously, it was more a manipulation on the nine-year-old's part than an actual thought. The fact that he was able to sit in the room with the father without being upset, and express no suicidal ideation, during or after the contact, made this psychologist question the veracity of the suicidal claims.

A team of myself, another psychologist, and a psychology intern poured over the records, performed evaluations and interviews, and contacted collateral sources. Although there were a handful of behaviors that the father engaged in that could have alienated him from the children, they all had occurred more than five years prior to the evaluation. On the other hand, close to 50 alienating behaviors that the mother had engaged in during the past four years were identified through this process. As a result, it was concluded that the mother had engaged in an extraordinary ongoing campaign to alienate the children from their father. It was also apparent that the children could not live in their household without hating their father. Furthermore, it was opined that if the father magically dropped out of the children's lives they would not automatically become adjusted. They had already learned that the negative behaviors in which they were engaging would get them attention, and provide secondary gains for them. As a result, it was further stated that these negative behaviors would follow them into adulthood whether the father was present or not.

In conclusion, there were five options available to be recommended to the court in this case. They included:

1. Children remain with the mother and never see the father.
2. Children remain with the mother and be engaged in forced visitation with the father.
3. Children are transferred to the father without seeing the mother for an extended period of time.
4. Children are transferred to the father and have weekend supervised contacts with the mother.
5. Children are placed in foster care.

The report was made to the court that some drastic measure would be necessary to facilitate this process. As a result, the court was left with the choice of either transferring the children to the father without seeing their mother for an extended period of time or having the children remain with the mother with forced visits with the father coupled with severe sanctions against the mother, as in case number 1 above, for every time the children did not visit with their father. Since the children's therapist, the guardian ad litem and the school social worker are concerned about the suicidal ideation, the choice of remaining with the mother, coupled with severe sanctions, is the one the court will likely endorse.

The label of Parental Alienation Syndrome has been around for slightly more than a decade. It was initially greeted with enthusiasm by both the mental health and legal professions in the late 80s and early 90s as being a descriptor of loyalty-related issues. However, since that time, many authors and other mental health professionals throughout the country have been unable to find empirical studies that validate many of the notions presented by Richard Gardner. There are many authors, the present author included, who have reported, but none other than Gardner himself claims that research supports these claims. Furthermore, Richard Gardner does not enjoy the positive reputation in the mental health community that he did a decade or more ago. There are many mental health professionals who are disheartened by their perception of his misuse of the Parental Alienation Syndrome concepts as being indicators of false sexual abuse allegations.

As a result, it is suggested that Parental Alienation Syndrome be used by attorneys as nothing more than a descriptor for loyalty issue problems.

Lastly, this author is not aware of any judges who have embraced the harsh recommendations that Gardner suggests for resolving severe Parental Alienation Syndrome.

§ 4.40A Relocation ("Moving Away") (New)

Page 260, insert after last paragraph of § 4.40:

In 1996, the California Supreme Court decided, in *In re Marriage of Burgess*[143] that a primary-placement parent who wishes to relocate shall be permitted to do so without having to prove that the move is necessary. This was a substantial change in policy from previous court decisions in most jurisdictions around the country. The Supreme Court further ruled that it was not a substantial change of circumstances for the custodial parent to relocate. So long as the custodial parent has a "sound, good faith reason" to change his or her place of residence, that parent may do so unless, as a direct result, there will be significant detriment to the child. The ultimate decision of the trial court also needs to consider this, as it does all child custody matters, in the context of the best interests of the child.

This case has taken on particular importance in part because a number of courts in other states have made similar decisions that cited *Burgess*, and in part because of the major split in the mental health community regarding the probability that this policy would be harmful to the best interests of the child whose parent chooses to relocate.

The decision of the California Supreme Court was consistent with the recommendations of an amica curiae brief filed on behalf of Judith Wallerstein, Ph.D. in *Burgess*. Wallerstein's brief was based in large part on her extensive longitudinal research with children in the San Francisco Bay area, as well as two relocation cases that were studied in depth. Wallerstein notes that children are limited in their ability to travel to visit a distant parent, that children should not be made to travel a great deal during their developmental years, and that some parents relocate in bad faith, and should be enjoined from doing so. Her bottom line, however, is predicated on the principle that:

> It is altogether reasonable to assume that a parent and child who have been living together as a family unit and sharing the same household for several years are likely to have a close attachment to each other that

[143] 913 P.2d 473, 51 Cal. Rptr. 2d 444 (Cal. 1996).

> promotes a healthy sense of security and self-esteem in the child. It is reasonable to assume that more guidance and discipline from that parent will prepare the child for responsible participation in society.[144]

The best interests of the child, she indicates, are "best served within the nurture and protection provided by high-quality parent-child relationships–these relationships, rather than geographical convenience, should be paramount in custody cases."[145]

Over the past several years, a substantial backlash has developed against the *Burgess* decision, culminating in the filing in amici briefs by psychologist Richard Warashak *et al.*[146] and family law attorney Leslie Ellen Shear, *et al.*[147] in a case currently before the California Supreme Court, *In re Marriage of Navarro (LaMusga) v. LaMusga.*[148] The essential position of both the Warshak *et al.* and Shear *et al.* briefs is that (a) Wallerstein's briefs in both *Burgess* and *LaMusga*[149] do not represent the views of the majority of experts on child development and child custody; (b) the Supreme Court's decision in *Burgess* does not adequately permit trial courts to consider the individual needs of each child and what is in the best interests of that child; (c) the *Burgess* decision grossly underestimates the

---

[144] Judith Wallerstein & Tony J. Tanke, "To Move or Not to Move: Psychological and Legal Considerations in the Relocation of Children Following Divorce," 30 *Family Law Quarterly* 305–32 at 319 (1996). This article is an adaptation of Dr. Wallerstein's brief in *Burgess.*

[145] *Id.* at 320.

[146] Amici, along with Warshak, in *LaMusga,* are: Sanford L. Braver, Ph.D., Joan B. Kelly, Ph.D., James H. Bray, Ph.D., and William G. Austin, Ph.D.

[147] Amici, along with Shear, in *LaMusga,* are: Marjorie G. Fuller, J.D., Nancy Williams Olesen, Ph.D., Mamela Panasiti Stettner, J.D., CFLS, Michael E. Lamb, Ph.D., Dawn Gray, J.D., CFLS, Joan B. Kelly, Ph.D., Lawrence E. Leone, J.D., CFLS, William G. Austin, Ph.D., Constance R. Ahrons, Ph.D., M.S.W., Harold J. Cohn, J.D., CFLS, Sanford L. Braver, Ph.D., Frieda Gordon, J.D., CFLS, James M. Hallett, J.D., CFLS, CFCLS, Sidner J. Brown, Ph.D., Lynette Berg Robe, J.D., CFLS, Michael Gottlieb, Ph.D., Tammy-Lyn Gallerani, J.D., CFLS, Richard A. Warshak, Ph.D., Kenneth C. Cochrane, J.D., CFLS, Neil S. Grossman, Ph.D., David R. Lane, J.D., CFLS, Maureen Stubbs, J.D., CFLS, Fred Norris, Ph.D., Dianna Gould-Saltman, J.D., CFLS, Carol Silbergeld, LCSW, BCD, Susan Ratzkin, J.D., Jeffrey M. Lulow, Ph.D., Dale S. Frank, J.D., Leslye Hunter, M.A., LPC, LMFT, Ronald S. Granberg, CFLS, James R. Flens, Psy.D., Rebekah A. Frye, J.D., Renee A. Cohen, Ph.D., Tracy Duell-Cazes, J.D., CFLS, Marnee W. Milner, J.D., Jacqueline Singer, Ph.D., Erica L. Hedlund, J.D., James Livingston, Ph.D., Josephine A. Fitzpatrick, J.D., CFLS, Michael A. Fraga, Psy.D., Timothy C. Writht, J.D., CFLS, Avery Cooper, J.D., CFLS, Lawrence W. Thorpe, J.D., CFLS.

[148] Supreme Court Case No. S107355.

[149] *Amici,* along with Wallerstein, in *LaMusga,* are: Paulina F. Kernberg, M.D., Joyanna Lee Silberg, Ph.D., Julia M. Lewis, Ph.D., John B. Sikorski, M.D., and Stephanie Joan Dallam, R.N., M.S.N., F.N.P. *Amici,* along with *Burgess,* are: Trevor C. Thorpe, J.D., Steven R. Liss, J.D., Mark J. Warfel, J.D., and John R. Schiller, J.D., CFLS.

profound affect that relocation can have on a child and his or her development and welfare; and (d) relocation should be among the factors that are considered a change of circumstances requiring the trial court to make an assessment in the context of the best interests of the child.

The authors of the present text have a great deal of respect for Dr. Wallerstein, as witnessed by our lengthy discussion, above, of her pioneering research. However, we are also impressed by the arguments of Warshak *et al.* and Shear *et al.*, and by the fact that many prominent experts in child development and child custody are signers of one or both of those amicus briefs.

We do not have a problem with the principles in *Burgess* requiring a decision that is sound, in good faith, without significant detriment to the child, and in the best interest of the child. We do have a concern regarding the manner in which some courts have interpreted *Burgess*, permitting the primary placement parent to move away without the trial court carefully reviewing all four of these factors. We also believe that relocation should be considered as a possible change of circumstances requiring the trial court to make a formal assessment in the context of the best interests of the child. It is our position that each case should be evaluated on its own merits, and we have not supported positions that state that any placement decision that could have a major negative impact on a child should "always" or "never" be permitted.

Lawyers and psychologists must watch this issue as it evolves. We urge the readers of this text to review all of the briefs in *LaMusga*, as well as related research on the question of the affect of relocation on children. Those briefs, and some of the research articles, may be found at *http://psych.la.asu.edu/people/faculty/sbraver.html.*

Page 260, insert before § 4.43:

§ 4.42A Current Views on Controversial Issues (New)

During the 2002 American Psychological Association Convention, Marc J. Ackerman, Ph.D. gave a workshop to 45 experienced child custody evaluators from throughout the United States about controversial issues. As an outgrowth of that workshop Marc J. Ackerman, Ph.D. and Sheryl Dolezal, Psy.D. performed a study entitled *Experienced Custody Evaluators Views of Controversial Issues.*

The demographics of the subjects themselves are interesting. The mean age of the evaluators was 49.1 years, with 10.51 years of experience and an average of 181.95 custody evaluations having been performed. 57 percent of the group was male and 43 percent of the group was female. Because the average participant was almost 50 years of age and had slightly over 10 years' experience in the area, this suggests that psychologists tend to not get into the area of custody evaluations until they have 10 to 15 years of experience as a psychologist. If this hypothesis holds true, then young, neophyte psychologists are not often engaged in performing custody evaluations.

Risk Factors:

It has long been known that individuals who engage in custody evaluation work are likely to have complaints filed against them with State Licensing Boards, State Ethics Committees, the American Psychological Association Ethics Committee, and/or be sued for malpractice. 45 percent of the sample indicated that they had been reported to one of the above bodies or had been sued. 40 percent of the sample or 88 percent of those who had actions taken against them were reported to their State Licensing Boards. Of those individuals reported to State Licensure Boards, they had an average of three complaints per evaluator. Only 10 percent of the sample had complaints filed with their State Ethics Committees, while 5 percent had complaints filed with the American Psychological Association Ethics Committee. Lastly, 17.5 percent of the sample had been sued for malpractice. It appears as if there is a far greater likelihood that individuals will have reports filed with Licensure Boards than with Ethic Committees.

More alarming is the fact that 15.5 percent of the sample had been threatened with physical violence by litigants in custody cases. 13.3 percent of the sample indicated that they had had property destroyed by litigants in custody cases. Only one individual reported having been physically assaulted by a litigant in a custody case.

Placement Schedules:

One of the more controversial issues in recent years has centered around whether children under two years of age should be required to spend overnights with the non-primary-placement parent. In this particular presentation, the audience was asked three questions about placement before the discussion of this subject, and the same three questions were asked again after the discussion. When asked the question of whether children under one year of age should be required to go on regular overnight visits, 7.7 percent said yes, 76.9 percent said no, and 14.4 percent abstained. When asked whether children under two years of age should be required to go on regularly-scheduled overnight visits, 30 percent said yes, 32.5 percent said no, and 37.5 percent said they did not know. When describing an alternate-week schedule (week-on, week-off), 24.2 percent favored such as schedule, 66.7 percent did not favor it, and 9.1 percent were not sure. The common wisdom when overnights do not occur is to have frequent contacts of short duration. This is defined as four to five contacts per week with two to three hours at a time at various times of the day or evening. The discussion about placement schedules for this age group also addressed the issue of nursing mothers. Furthermore, *object constancy* was discussed. This concept basically refers to the environment remaining constant for the child with the same crib, same house noises, same room decorations, and same general environment. Attachment theory was also discussed. Although there are majority and minority positions about the effect of attachment, the most widely held position is that requiring overnights for very young children interferes with the attachment to the primary attachment figure. It was also pointed out that the inconvenience of such a schedule is only temporary. There is certainly a trade-off involving forcing overnights at too young an age and risking developmental problems, versus the inconvenience of a restricted schedule for the first year or two with reduced likelihood of developmental issues.

After the discussion about placement issues, the same three questions were asked. At that time, 7.5 percent felt that overnights should be required for a child one year of age and 92.5 percent felt that they should not. The percentage of those believing it should occur remained constant. However, those who did not previously know were swayed in the direction of not having the overnights. Furthermore, after the discussion 30.3 percent felt that there should be overnights for children under two years of age and 69.7 percent felt that there should not. Again, those who did not know were swayed in the direction of voting for no overnights. Lastly, after the discussion, only 3.2 percent felt an alternating week schedule would work, while 96.8 percent felt it would not. Research does not support the alternating week schedule. However, there is an ever-growing utilization of this schedule being used by family court judges.

During the discussion of placement schedules, the issue of the difficulty of dovetailing irregular work schedules with regular placement schedules was discussed. Individuals such as policemen, firemen, pilots, flight attendants, physicians with call schedules, and nurses often have irregular work schedules. These schedules may include 24 hours on followed by 48 hours off, call weekends with no availability to children, three days on/ three days off, or just about any other combination or permutation that could be imagined. When evaluating these situations, several questions must be asked. They include: (1) How willing are the parents to place the work schedule around the placement schedule? (2) How willing are the parents to work together and cooperate on the blending of these schedules? (3) Is this a control issue designed to continue the fighting? (4) What was the parental contact schedule prior to the separation? The evaluator might also want to call the schedule manager for the parent with a varied schedule as a collateral contact to determine the level of flexibility of the schedule.

In a recent case, both parents were obstetricians with call schedules. The parental attitude about the call schedule versus parenting time, however, was different between the two parents. The mother worked diligently to arrange her call schedule to coincide with the times that the father had placement of the children. On the other hand, the father's position was "this is my call schedule and my placement time with the children *must* be fashioned around my call schedule."

The consensus was that a schedule must be fashioned in the best interests of the children. Instead of developing a schedule that changes every week for six weeks based on the parent's work schedules, the consensus was to develop a regular placement schedule with the non-placement parent having the right of first refusal to provide childcare when the other parent was working. Thus, the children will know that on specific days they are to be with mom and on other days with dad. When a parent needs to work on a specific day, then the right of first refusal would be offered to the other parent.

The last controversial issue that was discussed involved placement issues centered around travel when the parents live in different cities. The post 9-11 era has brought far greater restrictions and an ever-increasing number of rules regarding flying. The number of cancelled flights has increased. The number of delayed flights has increased, resulting in more missed connections, and the overall number of flights between destinations has reduced. Parents can no longer accompany children flying alone to the gate, and security measures can often put children in frightening situations. What happens, for example, if a child is flying from Milwaukee to San Francisco through Denver and the last leg of the flight gets cancelled? The airlines will certainly be responsible and put up the children in a hotel overnight. However, where are the safety and security factors if the children are eight and ten years of age, having to stay alone overnight and being cared for by strangers under those circumstances? As a result, the common wisdom today is that children should not fly alone unless there is a parent to put them on the airplane at one end of the flight and one to take them off the airplane at the other end of the flight. If the children are on a direct, non-stop flight from one city to the other, this causes no problems for the parents. However, using the above example, if a child is flying from Milwaukee to San Francisco and has to change planes in Denver, then a parent would either have to fly with the children to Denver, or fly to Denver to pick up the children so they do not have to deal with the potential problems that can arise with post 9-11 flying.

Sexual Abuse Allegations:

One of the controversial issues about sexual abuse allegations is the manner in which they bring the entire custody determination process to a screeching halt. Unfortunately, the vast majority of false sexual abuse allegations are made in child custody cases. There are some experts who believe that once the sexual abuse allegation has been made, contact between the alleged perpetrator and alleged victim should be terminated until the completion of the investigation. This audience of experienced examiners was asked whether they felt that contact between the alleged perpetrator and alleged victim should be prohibited. No one in the group felt that contact should be prohibited. On the other hand, 96.8 percent of the group felt this contact should either be supervised or monitored, while only 3.2 percent felt that it did not need to be supervised or monitored. Half of the people in the audience had performed sexual abuse allegation interviews.

Not all sexual abuse allegations come with clear evidence of abuse. Many of the situations are vague, leaving the evaluator with the possibility of a false-negative or false-positive report. The group was asked whether in vague situations it is better to run the risk of erring by being too conservative and potentially restricting contact when it did not need to be restricted, rather than being too liberal and potentially not protecting the child when the child should be protected. 95.8 percent of the audience felt that it was better to be too restrictive and run the risk of protecting a child when the child did not need to be protected. The other 4.2 percent felt that it was better to be too liberal and perhaps not protect the child when the child needed to be protected.

Parental Alienation Syndrome:

Perhaps there are few areas of child custody evaluation that have been more controversial than that of parental alienation syndrome. This concept was originally developed by the late Richard Gardner, M.D. The controversy continues to rage about whether parental alienation syndrome exists and, if so, how to identify it with reasonable certainty.

The audience was asked how many thought that parental alienation syndrome existed as Gardner defined it. None of the audience felt it existed as Gardner defined it. The audience was then asked how many believe that the concept of parental alienation occurred. 100 percent of the audience felt that such alienation occurred. The most important notion that can be derived from this statistic is that whether or not we believe in parental alienation syndrome as Gardner defines it, he raised our level of consciousness about the concept of alienation and that all experienced examiners in this group recognize its existence.

§ 4.42A CURRENT VIEWS ON CONTROVERSIAL ISSUES (NEW)

Other than using the strict approach of removing the children from the alienator and not allowing the alienator to see the children for six months, as Dr.Gardner indicated, discussion ensued about ways to address the issue of alienation. A thorough analysis must be performed to determine why the alienation is occurring. In his writings, Gardner talks extensively about one parent alienating the children against the other parent. However, he ignores the fact that the alienated parent could be alienated because of his or her own behavior (abuse, name-calling, degrading). Alienation can also be caused by a combination of both factors, with one parent alienating the children against the other parent and the second parent engaging in behavior that would alienate him/herself from the children.

These experienced evaluators believe that therapy for all is beneficial. The alienated parent must be in therapy to help deal with the alienation and understand the effects of it. The alienated parent must also address what he or she may be doing to contribute to the alienation. The alienating parent must not only work on the issues of being an alienator, but, also, learn to help the child to understand that it is acceptable to like the other parent and still remain in the favor of the alienating parent.

A cost benefit analysis must be done to determine the psychological risk factors in forcing a child to spend time with the alienated parent. Even if it is not rational to avoid forcing placement, if the child engages in suicidal behavior to avoid the alienated parent, the risk of forcing the issues is too high.

In recent years, there have generally been two ways that courts have forced the issue without following Gardner's prescription. Some courts have looked upon the inability of one parent to get the child to visit with the other parent as being an indication of the child needing services from local social services departments. Courts have gone to the point of threatening the child by saying that if he or she does not engage in this placement the court will consider the child's behavior to be uncontrollable, will turn the case over to social services, and recommend foster placement for the child.

In one situation, a mother had kept the children from seeing the father for a two-year period of time. She had used about every ploy imaginable to prevent visitation from occurring. At one point the court looked at the mother and stated, "Ma'am for every time the father does not have placement when placement is scheduled you will spend three days in jail." After this threat had been made by the judge, no placement time was missed. It quickly became apparent why the mother was being as obstructionistic as she was, in that within a year of the beginning of the placement time with the father, the children ended up living with their father, by their request, following disclosure of the inappropriate behavior of the mother.

§ 4.43 Case Digest

Page 260, insert as the first case digest under ***National:***

In *Troxel v. Granville,* 99-138, 530 U.S. 57, 120 S. Ct. 2054, 147 L. Ed. 2d 49 (2000), the U.S. Supreme Court ruled on June 5, 2000, that a Washington state law that gives grandparents and others broad rights for visitation unconstitutionally infringes on the fundamental right of parents to raise their children. The Court wrote:

> The Fourteenth Amendment's Due Process Clause has a substantive component that "provides heightened protection against government interference with certail fundamental rights and liberty interests. . . , including parents' fundamental right to make decisions concerning the care, custody, and control of their children. . . . Washington's breathtakingly broad statute effectively permits a court to disregard and overturn *any* decision by a fit custodial parent concerning visitation whenever a third party affected by the decision files a visitation petition, based solely on the judge's determination of the child's best interest. A parent's estimation of the child's best interest is accorded no deference. . . .
>
> A combination of several factors compels the conclusion that [the state law], as applied here, exceeded the bounds of the Due Process Clause. . . . There is a presumption that fit parents act in their children's best interests, *Parham v. J.R.*, 442 U.S. 584, 602; there is normally no reason for the State to inject itself into the private realm of the family to further question fit parents' ability to make the best decisions regarding their children. . . . The problem here is not that the Superior Court intervened, but that when it did so, it gave no special weight to Granville's determination of her daughter's best interests. More importantly, that court appears to have applied the opposite presumption, favoring grandparent visitation. In effect, it placed on Granville the burden of *disproving* that visitation would be in her daughter's best interest and thus failed to provide any protection for her fundamental right. . . .

Page 261, insert as the first case under ***Arkansas:***

Hollandsworth v. Knyzewski, Case No. 02-720 (Ark. June 5, 2003). Hollandsworth, the mother of the couple's two children, wished to relocate 500 miles to Tennessee in order to live with the man she had married who lives in that state. Knyzewski filed a petition for change of custody to him, arguing that there had been a material and substantial change in circumstances. The trial court ordered a change of custody to the father on the basis that the mother had failed to show a real advantage to herself and to the children, and that it would be harmful to the children's relationship with their father and the strong ties the children had with family in Arkansas. The mother appealed, and the appellate court reversed. The father appealed to the Supreme Court.

The Supreme Court of Arkansas indicated that the factors to be considered when a custodial parent seeks to relocate with his or her child are: "(1) the reason for the relocation; (2) the educational, health, and leisure opportunities available in the location in which the custodial parent and children will relocate; (3) visitation and communication schedule for the noncustodial parent; (4) the effect of the move on the extended family relationships in the location in which the custodial parent and children will relocate . . . , and (5) preference of the child, including the age, maturity, and the reasons given by the child as to his or her preference." All of these are to be considered in the context of the best interest of the child.

The Supreme Court opinion indicates that courts in Minnesota, Tennessee, California, Colorado, Wyoming, Illinois, and New Jersey have indicated a presumption that a custodial parent may relocate so long as he or she has any good faith reason to do so. The New York Court of Appeals held that the trial court needs to weigh the evidence that a proposed relocation would serve the child's best interests. Texas and North Carolina courts have held that relocation, regardless of distance, does not constitute a substantial change of circumstances.

The Arkansas Supreme Court held that the relocation of a custodial parent is not a material change in circumstances, and that there is a presumption favoring the relocation of a custodial parent with primary custody. The custodial parent has no obligation to prove there is a real advantage to him- or herself or the children. The burden is on the noncustodial parent to rebut the presumption. In the instant case, the Supreme Court found that the father could have adequate visitation and could maintain an adequate relationship with his children after the relocation, that there was no evidence the children would be harmed by the move, and that the mother has a valid reason to relocate. The appellate court decision was reversed and remanded.

Page 261, insert above ***Arizona:***

Alaska

Kelly v. Joseph, Supreme Court No. S-10116 (Alaska, May 10, 2002). The Alaska Supreme Court ruled that when a custodial parent substantially interferes with the visitation rights of a non-custodial parent, that is sufficient to constitute a change of circumstances. One type of "substantial interference" is when the custodial parent engages in a detrimental, well-established pattern of behavior designed to erode the relationship between the non-custodial parent and the child(ren). In the instant case, the father had custody of the children, and did not take actions to ensure that the mother's rights under the visitation agreement were fulfilled, nor did he honor the spirit of the visitation agreement. The context for the modification of custody remains the best interests of the child(ren). A lack of compliance with court orders, by itself, is not sufficient to modify custody. That change requires a "best interests" analysis.

West v. West, 21 P.3d 838 (Alaska Supreme Court, Apr. 27, 2001). A trial court gave primary custody to a father, primarily because the father was about to remarry, while the mother remained single. When the parents separated the mother moved to Oregon, while the father remained in Alaska. The boy, of kindergarten age at the time of trial, moved between parental homes every few months. The custody evaluator found both parents to be appropriate and about equally positive, and recommended joint custody. She indicated her belief that the boy could flourish in either home, and that the boy remain in one home for the school year. Because of the distance between homes, she had to recommend one as preferred. She picked the mother, because the mother had a 16-year-old daughter who helped care for the boy, and other relatives nearby who would be available as needed. The trial court considered the recommendations, but found that the greatest stability for the boy would come from being with his father, who was "likely" to marry a woman with 12 years of experience as a nurse who would not be employed outside the home, providing a home with two adults present.

The state Supreme Court held that it was improper to award primary physical custody on the basis of the anticipated marriage. In the required context of the best interests of the child, the trial court found the parents to be essentially equal. The father's anticipated remarriage tipped the scale in his favor. The court indicated that other courts ruling on similar situations had generally indicated that custody should not be determined on the basis of a presumption of an advantage of a two-parent household. A custody determination may not be based on a presumption, without scientific evidence, that a working mother would not provide care equal to that of a father with a wife not employed outside the home. There was also no evidence that the convenience of in-home care would be better for the boy than being with his mother, stepsister, and maternal grandparents. The trial record contained no objective information that would indicate that either household would necessarily be better than the other. The case was remanded for a determination of custody on the basis of the current best interests of the child.

§ 4.43 CASE DIGEST

Page 262, insert after ***California:***

In re Guardianship of Z.C.W., 71 Cal. App. 4th 524. 84 Cal. Rptr. 2d 48 (Cal. App. 1999). The California First District Court of Appeals held that a lesbian partner does not have standing to sue for guardianship of her partner's children. One of the children was from a prior relationship of the partner, one was the product of a decision of the two that the partner be artificially inseminated. When they parted, the partner adhered to an agreement for visitation to four years, then terminated the agreement unilaterally. The court held that a non-parent does not have standing to obtain guardianship of or visitation with a partner's children.

Page 263, insert after ***Florida:***

Kantaras v. Kantaras, Case No: 98-5375CA (Fla. Cir. Ct. February, 2003). In a massive (809-page) decision, a circuit court judge ruled that Michael Kantaras, who had been born as a female, is a male under Florida law, is the legal father of two children born to his wife, and should be awarded custody and primary placement of his children.

Michael had completed sex reassignment surgery in 1986, and met Linda in 1988. They married in 1989, when the older child was six weeks old. Linda was aware of the sex reassignment. The older child was conceived by Linda Kantaras prior to her relationship with Michael. The younger child was conceived by artificial insemination using sperm from Michael's brother.

The trial court ruled that the marriage was valid, that the parents have joint custody, that Michael has primary residential custody and Linda has visitation, and that Michael shall remain in the family residence until the younger child reaches 18, at which time the house is to be sold and the proceeds divided between the parties.

The complete transcript is available at *http://www.transgenderlaw.org/cases/kantarasopinion.pdf.*

Page 264, insert after ***Indiana:***

Crafton v. Gibson, 752 N.E.2d 78 (Indiana Ct. of App. 2001). Crafton was awarded custody of her two children after a divorce in 1997. Gibson, the paternal grandmother, sought visitation, saying that Crafton would not permit any meaningful contact. The trial court granted visitation. In 1999, the father's parental rights were terminated and the children were adopted by their stepfather, Crafton's husband.

When the U.S. Supreme Court decided *Troxel v. Granville*, 530 U.S. 57, 120 S. Ct. 2054, 147 L. Ed. 2d 49, Crafton filed a motion for relief on the bases that Gibson's grandparent visitation was no longer equitable and that the trial court had failed to apply a presumption that Crafton's decision to limit Gibson's visitation was in the children's best interests. The trial court denied the motion. Crafton appealed.

The appellate court first indicated that it had previously found Indiana's Grandparent Visitation statute to be constitutional. They also held that it is not overly broad, unlike the Washington statute in *Troxel.* In the absence of an allegation that the mother is unfit, deference must be given to the mother's decision to deny visitation to Gibson, with the grandparent having the burden of rebutting the presumption that the decision to deny visitation was made in the children's best interests. The record does not suggest that the trial court gave the requisite special weight to Crafton's decision. The case was remanded to the trial court to address the requirements (1) that a presumption be made that the parent's decision to deny visitation was on the basis of the best interests of the child, (2) that consideration be given to Crafton's offer of limited visitation, (3) that special weight be given to Crafton's decision regarding grandparent visitation. The burden is on the grandparent to demonstrate that visitation should be permitted.

Page 264, insert as first case under ***Iowa:***

In re Stange, No. 1-390/00-1886 (Iowa Ct. App. June 13, 2001). Curt and Tammy Stange were divorced in 1997. The parties agreed that Curt would be the primary care parent for their son, Jacob (11/84), and Tammy would be the primary care parent for Janae (05/88). In 2000, Tammy filed a petition for modification of visitation because she had accepted a teaching position in the state of Washington.

After a trial, the district court awarded primary care of Janae to Curt. It indicated that the loss of her relationship with her father, brother, and relatives on both sides of the family outweighed any benefit she would obtain by moving with her mother. The court indicated that Curt provided her with greater stability, and noted that Tammy often placed her own interests before her daughter's. The court also indicated that Tammy showed "flagrant disregard" for Curt's joint custodial interests by failing to consult him before deciding to relocate. Tammy appealed.

The appeals court reviewed the case *de novo*. It noted that the criteria for custody in modification proceedings are the same as those in initial custody determinations, that is, the best interests of the child(ren). It indicated that Curt had a substantial role in Janae's life, and she would suffer if denied that involvement. She would also lose regular and frequent contact with her brother and the families of both parents. Further, the appeals court found that Curt offered significantly greater stability for Janae.

Tammy was often late to Janae's activities, had relocated on several occasions since the separation, and she did not investigate getting a teaching position in Illinois that would have given her a comparable salary to that in Washington state. She had also failed to support the relationship between Janae and her father. She arranged for Janae to be out of town on two Father's Days, had withheld visitation on one occasion because she was being punished—though Curt went to the planned event anyhow, and found that Janae was there. She also informed other parents of her planned move well before informing Curt. The court of appeals therefore affirmed the decision of the trial court.

Page 265, insert after ***Kansas:***

Ward v. Ward, __ Kan. App. 2d __ (Sept. 14, 2001), 30 P.3d 1001. Vanita and Stanley Ward were divorced on October 21, 1999. The mother was awarded sole custody and primary placement of their 7-year-old daughter, Jaclynn. The father had limited visitation (a maximum of three 3-hour afternoon periods per week). On January 11, 2000, Vanita Ward was killed in an accident. Jaclynn then lived with her maternal grandmother and maternal aunt and uncle. Her father saw her briefly four times between January 11 and 23. On January 23 he asked for a 3-hour visitation, but did not return Jaclynn to her grandmother and aunt and uncle. He filed a petition seeking to have his brother and sister-in-law appointed as co-guardians and co-conservators of Jaclynn. The trial court concluded that Jaclynn's father automatically received sole legal custody of Jaclynn upon the death of her mother. The maternal grandmother and aunt and uncle moved for reconsideration.

The appellate court initially noted the "admonition of Chief Justice Frank D. Celebrezze of the Ohio Supreme Court in *In re Wonderly*, 67 Ohio St.2d 178, 188, 423 N.E.2d 420 (1981), where, in a contest over a guardianship, he said:

> While statutes can be amended and case law can be distinguished or overruled, we take judicial notice of the fact that children grow up only once. When a mistake is made in a custody dispute, the harmful effects are irrevocable.

The appellate court indicated that it was clear that custody of Jaclynn belonged to her father upon the death of her mother, affirming the decision of the trial court.

Page 265, insert as the first case under ***Kentucky:***

Fenwick v. Fenwick and *Huck v. Huck*, Nos. 1999-SC-1055-DG and 2000-SC-0697-DG (Ky. Sept. 18, 2003). The Kentucky Supreme Court addressed these two cases together because both involved a primary custodian wishing to relocate with the children of the parties over the objection of the other parent. In *Fenwick*, the wife wished to relocate to a county 35 miles from her current home. In *Huck*, the wife wished to relocate to an adjoining state.

Acknowledging that relocation of a custodial parent is a thorny and divisive issue, the Supreme Court indicated that the issue had been resolved in the context of sole custody in 1992 in *Wilson v. Messinger*, 840 S.W.2d 203, noting that we live in a mobile society in which no one should be required to remain in a given location in order to retain custody. While earlier cases had placed the burden on the custodial parent who wanted to relocate, *Wilson* and the subsequent enactment of statute KRS 403.340 indicate that the custodial parent's relocation decision is presumptively permissible, and that a modification of the joint custody award is not necessary. The non-custodial parent would have to show that the child's present or proposed environment seriously endangers the physical, mental, moral, or emotional health of the child, and that a change of custody is therefore necessary. Accordingly, in both of these cases the custodial parent was permitted to relocate.

Page 267, insert above ***Missouri:***

Mississippi

Goodson v. Goodson, 816 So. 2d 420 (Miss. Ct. App. 2002). David and Judy Goodson were divorced in January, 2001. Judy was awarded primary custody of their daughter, born in 1986, by the chancery court. A visitation schedule was set up by the court. The chancellor found Judy to be in contempt of court when she did not force her daughter to follow the court's visitation schedule.

Sheri, age 14, told both of her parents that she refused to visit her father. At the trial, Judy testified that she urged Sheri to visit with her father, and that, short of physically putting Sheri in David's car, she could not do more to comply with the order of the court.

A finding of contempt is appropriate when there is a willful and deliberate ignoring of a court order, the appellate court indicated. The fact that Judy had attempted to get her daughter to comply with the court order, and that Judy was not responsible for Sheri's refusal, indicates that Judy did not willfully violate the court's order. The appellate court therefore reversed the contempt order.

*Page 267, insert as the first case under **Montana**:*

In re Marriage of Robinson, Case No. 00-744 (Mont. Sept. 10, 2002). Jill and Dixon Robinson divorced in 1999, after entering into a Final Parenting Plan that permitted Jill to live in the family home with their three children and set visitation and other conditions. The following year, Jill notified Dixon of her plan to move to Idaho and to remarry there. Dixon filed a motion to amend the parenting plan. A psychiatrist stipulated to by both parents indicated that both were fit parents and that the children needed regular contact with both parents. She also noted that Dixon's parents lived in Butte and had been involved with the care of the children. She recommended that Jill stay in close proximity to Dixon's home or work so that shared custody would be possible.

The trial court adopted the psychiatrist's recommendations, and concluded that the best interests of the children would be served by their remaining in Butte. Jill's residence would remain the children's primary residence if she remained in Butte, but if she moved to Idaho the children would remain with Dixon. Contrary to the court's order, Jill took the children to Idaho. Dixon went to Idaho and returned with the two youngest children, but the oldest refused to return with him. Jill was found in contempt for not returning the oldest child to Butte to live with her father. The parties later entered into a stipulation regarding the transportation of the children. Jill appealed the court's decision that the children must remain in Butte, alleging that she has a constitutional right to relocate with the children. Dixon argued that her right to travel does not supersede the best interests of the children.

The appellate court agreed that the "best interests of the child" was the standard upon which the decision rests. The district court had found that Dixon had a strong support system for the children in Butte, including the fact that his parents had a close relationship with the children. The support system also included neighbors, friends with children of similar ages, teachers, and day-care providers. In contrast, neither Jill nor her fiancé had any relatives in Idaho. The appellate court held that the best interests of the children outweighed Jill's constitutional right to travel. It further indicated that a parenting plan may be amended if there is a change in circumstances and an amendment is necessary to serve the best interests of the child. The district court order was affirmed.

*Page 267, insert as the first case digest under **New Jersey**:*

Wilde v. Wilde, 341 N.J. Super. 381 (N.J. Super. Ct. App. 2001). A father committed suicide. Some visitation occurred between the grandfather and grandchildren in the next few months, but was cut off by the mother four months after the suicide. The paternal grandfather and his second wife sued under the New Jersey Grandparent Visitation Statute. The mother filed a motion for dismissal on constitutional grounds. The trial court held the statute to be facially constitutional and constitutional as applied. The mother appealed.

The Appellate Division of the Superior Court of New Jersey declined to rule on the facial constitutionality of the statute. Citing *Troxel v. Granville,* 530 U.S. 57, 120 S.Ct. 2054, 147 L.Ed.2d 49 (2000), the court held that the Due Process Clause of the Fourteenth Amendment protects the right of a parent to make decisions regarding the care, custody and control of his or her children. The court further indicated that, when the fitness of the parent is not disputed, the grandparents have a responsibility to try to repair any breach between themselves and the parent before seeking a legal remedy. Litigation should also not be threatened prior to a denial of visitation with finality. The grandparents must also refrain from making severe criticisms of the parent, or impugning the parent's character. Since the grandparents had not proceeded according to these requirements, the Grandparent Visitation Statute was found unconstitutional as applied to the facts of this particular case.

Page 268, insert as the first case digest under ***New York****:*

New York v. Fortin, 706 N.Y.S.2d 611 (N.Y. County Ct. 2000). A man who was charged with sex crimes involving his 13-year-old niece sought to introduce testimony about "Parental Alienation Syndrome" (PAS). Psychiatrist Richard Gardner, who coined the term, testified that

> PAS typically arises when one parent programs a child in a campaign of denigration of the other parent, although PAS may also occur when other family members are involved. Under cross examination, Gardner admitted that he previously had written that psychodynamic psychiatry is the most speculative of all alleged sciences and that the concept of scientific proof is less important in that field than in other sciences, particularly with respect to persons charged with committing sexual abuse.

The court ruled that testimony regarding PAS was inadmissible, because the defendant failed to establish that the scientific community generally accepts PAS, "given the lack of a clear consensus by psychologists of the existence of this syndrome."[143]

---

[143] 24 Mental and Physical Disability Law Reporter 366 (2000).

§ 4.43 CASE DIGEST

Page 269, insert as the first case under ***North Dakota:***

Zeller v. Zeller, 640 N.W.2d 53 (N.D. Sup. Ct. 2002). Jenny and Doni Zeller are both members of the United States Air Force, stationed in North Dakota. They have joint custody, and Jenny was awarded physical custody of their children, born in 1994 and 1995. The parties had stipulated in their 1997 divorce that, if Jenny was transferred out of North Dakota, it would be a material change of circumstances and that physical custody would transfer to Doni. In 2000, Jenny was transferred to Fort Leonard Wood, Missouri, for a four-year teaching assignment. Jenny moved for an order allowing her to take the children to Missouri. The trial court denied the motion. Jenny appealed.

The North Dakota statute on relocation is designed to protect the non-custodial parent's visitation rights by requiring either a court order or consent of the non-custodial parent. The primary consideration is the best interests of the child. There are four factors to be considered:

1. The prospective advantages of the move in improving the custodial parent's and child's quality of life,
2. The integrity of the custodial parent's motive for relocation, considering whether it is to defeat or deter visitation by the non-custodial parent,
3. The integrity of the noncustodial parent's motives for opposing the move,
4. The potential negative impact on the relationship between the non-custodial parent and the child, including whether there is a realistic opportunity for visitation which can provide an adequate basis for preserving and fostering the non-custodial parent's relationship with the child if relocation is allowed, and the likelihood that each parent will comply with such alternate visitation.

While finding that Jenny's relocation request met the above criteria, the trial court ruled that the parties' stipulation, incorporated in the divorce decree, "is the law of the case," and that "[i]t is in the best interest of the children to be in the physical custody of their father if plaintiff relocates to Fort Leonard Wood, Missouri."

The supreme court cited *Zarrett v. Zarrett,* 1998 N.D. 49, 574 N.W.2d 855, which indicates that "[A] stipulation by the parents prohibiting or limiting the power of the court to modify future child support is against public policy and invalid." Therefore, the court ruled, the stipulation for "an automatic change in custody upon the occurrence of a future event is unenforceable and the district court retains control over the rights of children. . . ." The case was remanded to the trial court, which had already found that Jenny met the statutory criteria for location, for an order permitting her to take the children to Missouri.

Page 270, insert above ***Pennsylvania:***

Ohio

In re Bonfield, 773 N.E.2d 507 (2002). The Ohio Supreme Court addressed a request to recognize the lesbian partner of a mother of five children as equal to the parent in matters concerning the children.

Teri J. Bonfield and Shelly M. Zachritz have lived together since 1987 in a committed homosexual relationship. During that period, Teri adopted two children and gave birth to three children, conceived through anonymous artificial insemination. Shelly has actively participated in the planning and births of the children and in raising all five children. According to Teri, Shelly is the primary caregiver for the children, and is seen by the children as an equal parent with Teri. A licensed psychologist testified that Teri and Shelly are jointly raising the children and form a close, loving, committed family in which the children are strongly bonded to each of them. He opined that it would be devastating for the children to be separated from Shelly.

Unfortunately, under law Shelly has no legally recognized rights with regard to any of the children. She does not have equal access to medical or school records, and cannot authorize medical care or obtain medical insurance for the children. If Teri were to die, a relative of Teri's would have a greater right than Shelly to adopt the children.

In some states, but not Ohio, there is an option for a "second parent adoption." This is a mechanism for permitting a partner in a cohabiting, non-marital relationship to adopt the partner's biological or adoptive child without the parent having to relinquish any parental rights. In Ohio, Teri would have to lose her parental rights in order for Shelly to adopt the children.

The trial court concluded that it did not have jurisdiction to grant the petition to make Shelly a parent of the children. The appeals court indicated that the trial court does have jurisdiction, but ruled that the trial court does not have the authority to award parental rights or shared parenting to an individual who is neither a biological nor adoptive parent. The Supreme Court accepted the case on a discretionary appeal.

Appellants advocated a four-part test of whether an individual is a "psychological" or "second" parent, as is done in some other states:

> (1) whether the legal parent consents to and fosters the relationship between the "psychological" or "second" parent and the child, (2)

> whether the "psychological" or "second" parent has lived with the child, (3) whether the "psychological" or "second" parent performs parental functions for the child to a significant degree, and (4) whether a parent-child bond has been forged between the "second" parent and the child. *Bonfield* at 512.

However, the Supreme Court indicated that the word "parent" was used differently in existing statutes, and declined to accept that proposal. For similar reasons, the Supreme Court also rejected *in loco parentis* as a basis.

Noting its desire to honor the appellants' goal of providing a stable environment for the children, the supreme court indicated that the trial court has exclusive original jurisdiction to determine the custody of any child not a ward of another court. The court therefore held that the juvenile court has jurisdiction to determine the custody of the Bonfield children. Further, parents may waive the right to custody of their children, and are bound by an agreement to do so. Accordingly, the case was remanded to the juvenile court for proceedings to determine whether a shared custody agreement between Teri and Shelly is in the best interests of the children.

Page 270, insert as the first case under ***Pennsylvania:***

T.B. v. L.R.M., 786 A.2d 913 (Pa. 2001). T.B. and L.R.M., both females, had an exclusive, intimate relationship. They decided to have a child, and agreed that donor sperm would be used to impregnate L.R.M. The child, A.M., was born August 27, 1993. They raised the child together, but did not execute a formal parenting agreement. L.R.M. named T.B. as guardian of the child in her will. Both women did all of the things a parent would normally do in raising a child, including taking off work when the child was ill.

In May, 1996, they purchased a new home together. T.B. left that home shortly thereafter, and entered a relationship with another woman. In August, 1996, T.B. and L.R.M. formally separated. After T.B.'s visit with A.M. on September 4, 1996, L.R.M. refused all requests for visitation, all phone calls, and all gifts for A.M. On October 3, 1996, T.B. filed a "Complaint for Shared Legal and Partial Custody and Visitation." The hearing officer found that T.B. had standing to seek visitation and custody pursuant to the doctrine of *in loco parentis*, as well as finding that it would be in the child's best interests for T.B. to have partial custody for purposes of visitation. L.R.M. appealed. The *en banc* superior court agreed that T.B. stood *in loco parentis*, but indicated that the record did not provide an adequate basis to determine whether visitation was in A.M.'s best interests. The case was remanded for a full hearing. The Supreme Court agreed to solely address whether the lower courts correctly applied the common law doctrine of *in loco parentis*. It noted that, while third parties are often refused standing, actions for custody have been permitted when that third party stands *in loco parentis* to a child.

> The phrase "*in loco parentis*" refers to a person who puts oneself in the situation of a lawful parent by assuming the obligations incident to the parental relationship without going through the formality of a legal adoption. The status of *in loco parentis* embodies two ideas; first, the assumption of a parental status, and, second, the discharge of parental duties. . . . The rights and liabilities arising out of an *in loco parentis* relationship are . . . exactly the same as between parent and child. . . . The third party in this type of relationship, however, can not place himself *in loco parentis* in defiance of the parents' wishes and the parent/child relationship. *T.B.* at 916.

The Supreme Court rejected L.R.M.'s contention that T.B. lacked standing because the law does not apply to former partners of a biological parent. Rather, it found that

> [T]he nature of the relationship between Appellant and Appellee has no legal significance to the determination of whether Appellee stands *in loco parentis* to A.M. The ability to marry the biological parent and the ability to adopt the subject child have never been and are not now factors in determining whether the third party assumed a parental status and discharged parental duties. What is relevant, however, is the method by which the third party gained authority to do so. The record is clear that Appellant consented to Appellee's performance of parental duties. She encouraged Appellee to assume the status of a parent and acquiesced as Appellee carried out the day-to-day care of A.M. . . . Appellant further contends that Appellee can not stand *in loco parentis* to A.M. because Appellee merely acted as a caretaker and because A.M. was never in Appellee's sole care. . . . [However,] the record supports the hearing officer's finding that Appellee lived with Appellant and A.M. as a family unit and that Appellee assumed the role of co-parent. . . . Appellee has demonstrated that she assumed a parental status and discharged parental duties. *T.B.* at 918-19.

Finally, the Supreme Court addressed L.R.M's contention that the Court should adopt the position of the U.S. Supreme Court in *Troxel v. Granville*, 120 S. Ct. 2054 (2000). The Pennsylvania Supreme Court refused, indicating that the Pennsylvania statute was not overly broad, nor was there an abandonment of the presumption that a fit parent will act in the best interests of the child. Rather, the issue was whether the facts supported a determination that T.B. had standing to seek partial custody. The Supreme Court indicated that she did, affirming the lower court order.

Page 271, insert above ***Utah:***

Rhode Island

Rubano v. DiCenzo, 759 A.2d 959 Rhode Island Supreme Court No. 97-604-A (September 2000). The Rhode Island Supreme Court ruled that a woman may petition for visitation with the son she and her former lesbian partner raised together. The women agreed they wished to have a child, and one of them conceived via artificial insemination by an anonymous donor. They raised him together for four years, then separated. The biological mother agreed to visitation by her former partner, then changed her mind. The former partner petitioned the family court, seeking to establish her *de facto* parental status and to obtain court-ordered visitation. The women entered a consent order establishing "permanent visitation." The mother reneged again, and alleged that the visitation was harmful to the child. The Family Court certified the case to the Supreme Court due to its uncertainty regarding how to resolve the matter.

In this case of first impression, the Supreme Court held that the biological parent does not have an "absolute right to prevent all third parties from ever acquiring any parental rights *vis-á-vis* the child." In the instant matter, the fact that the biological mother allowed her partner to take on an equal role as a parent, and agreed to and signed an order granting the partner "permanent visitation" because it is in the "best interests of the child" indicate that the mother had, by word and deed, allowed her former partner to establish a parental relationship with the child. The case was remanded to the Family Court for adjudication consistent with the holding of the Supreme Court.

Tennessee

Casby v. Hazlerig, W2001-02073-COA-R3-CV (Tenn. App. July 24, 2002). A couple were divorced, and, based on the wife having engaged in "inappropriate marital conduct," emergency temporary custody of the two children was given to the father. After a hearing, joint custody was awarded to the father and to the maternal grandmother. After a trial, joint custody was awarded to the parents of the children, with the father as primary custodial parent. The mother, and later the father, filed motions to alter the custodial arrangement.

The trial court found that the mother had made allegations of abuse by the father that were without any factual basis, and that mother had attempted to manipulate the children. The court also noted that the mother's psychological evaluation had found her to be

> "self-focused" and to have a "narcissistic personality, with an overt agenda to portray [Father] in a negative light. She accepted little respon-

> sibility for her actions, and made frequent use of denial, minimization, rationalization, and projection of blame onto others. Based on the court's prior dealings with the mother, the court concurred in the evaluation's conclusions.

The evaluation also suggested that the mother would not be an appropriate custodial parent, and that she needed long-term psychotherapy. In contrast, the evaluation cast the father in a positive light, indicating that he would be an appropriate and protective parent who had created a safe, stable and nurturing environment for the children. The trial court awarded custody of the children to the father, giving mother limited visitation. Mother appealed.

Indicating that "the courts' paramount concern in a custody case is the welfare and best interest of the parties' minor children," the appeal court affirmed the ruling of the trial court.

Texas

In re C.P.J. and S.B.J., Case no. 05-02-01639-CV (Tex. App. 5th Dist. Aug. 4, 2003). Marshall Jackson agreed to allow his former parents-in-law visitation with his two children, their grandchildren, after his wife died. Nearly two years after a trial court approved the agreement, Jackson filed a motion to terminate the visitation order on the basis of the U.S. Supreme Court decision in *Troxel v. Granville*, 530 U.S. 57 (2000). The trial court reduced the amount of visitation, but refused to terminate it. Jackson appealed, stating that the grandparent visitation statute was unconstitutional.

The appellate court determined that *Troxel* was limited to the special facts of the Washington statute, and did not apply to the Texas statute. It further acknowledged that a parent has a special liberty interest in the care, custody and control of his or her child, and that the court is required by *Troxel* to accord some special weight to the wishes of the parent. However, it ruled that the trial court had accorded some special weight to the parent's own determination regarding visitation, and that the Texas statute was not unconstitutional on its face or as applied to the instant case.

Page 271, insert above ***Virginia:***

Vermont

Spaulding v. Butler, 782 A.2d 1167 (Vermont Sup. Ct. 2001). A trial court had ruled that, because a father had "a full parent/child relationship" with his son, while the mother was estranged from the boy, the father should be the "primary parent," with the mother having supervised visitation that would transition to unsupervised visitation. The mother appealed.

The Supreme Court reversed. While the facts supported the conclusion that the father had a full parent/child relationship with his son, that fact was undermined by the trial court's finding that the father had engaged in a long, persistent campaign to eliminate the mother-child relationship. Citing its decision in R*enaud v. Renaud*, 168 Vt. 306, 309, 721 A.2d 463, 465-66 (1998), the court indicated that "[a]cross the country, the great weight of authority holds that conduct by one parent that tends to alienate the child's affections from the other is so inimical to the child's welfare as to be grounds for a denial of custody to, or a change of custody from, the parent guilty of such conduct." The Supreme Court reversed and remanded the case to the trial court for further proceedings in the context of these rulings.

Page 272, insert as the first case digest under ***Wisconsin****:*

Richard D. v. Rebecca G., 228 Wis.2d 658, 599 N.W.2d 90 (Wis. Ct. App. 1999). The Wisconsin Court of Appeals held that the bond between a foster parent and a child must be considered as a critical element in determining with whom a child lives.

The case involved a four-year-old girl, who had seen her biological mother only twice during her first two years. The girl spent nearly all of her life with foster parents, who wanted to adopt her. The appellate court held that the trial court placed too much emphasis on the biological relationship with the mother rather than on the best interests of the child. The appellate court indicated that if a biological parent abdicates responsibility by abandoning the child or failing to fulfill "core parental responsibilities," it is up to the court to determine what is in the child's best interests. If there is determined to be "a strong bonding by a child with its caretakers," trial courts may "preserve the status quo and leave the child in a happy, nurturing home of a caring and loving non-parent." The appellate court further noted that "safety" and "best interests" are not synonymous, and that the latter governs the decision to be made by the trial court.

CHAPTER 8

INTELLIGENCE TESTING

§ 8.1 Classification Systems for Intelligence

Page 347, insert after last paragraph in § 8.1:

There have been significant advances in psychological testing during the past two years. All of the publishers of tests of cognitive functioning have provided new additions. Within the Wechsler family, the Wechsler Intelligence Scale for Children-Fourth Edition (WISC-IV), the Wechsler Pre-School and Primary Scale of Intelligence-Third Edition (WPPSI-III), and the Wechsler Abbreviated Scale of Intelligence (WASI) have been developed. Riverside Publishing has offered the fifth edition of the Stanford Binet. American Guidance Service will be publishing the Kaufman Assessment Battery for Children-Revised Edition (KABC-R), and the Kaufman Brief Intelligence Test-Revised Edition (KBIT-R). Furthermore, the new Clinical Scale Interpretation Model has been developed by Psychologist Auke Telligen for use with the Minnesota Multiphasic Personality Inventory-Second Edition (MMPI-2).

The WISC-IV, SB-5, and the WASI will be discussed in this supplement. The KABC-R, the KBIT-R, and the WPPSI-III, along with the new scales of the MMPI-2, will be discussed in the fourth edition of this text, which will be published in late 2004 or early 2005. These other instruments are being mentioned at this time to make the reader aware of the fact that they either have been published recently or will be published prior to the fourth edition of this text.

§ 8.10 Stanford-Binet Intelligence Scale: Fourth Edition

Page 354, insert after the last paragraph in § 8.10:

The Stanford Binet-fifth edition (SB5) is the latest version of the grandfather of intelligence tests. The original Binet instrument was published over one hundred years ago. Its current edition is applicable for individuals from 2 through 85 years of age. Unlike the Wechsler Scales, which require these tests, the WPPSI-III, WISC-IV, and WAIS-III cover this age range, all ages can be tested with one instrument with the SB5. As a result, the Stanford Binet still remains the best single instrument for exceptionalities.

For example, with a child over 6 years of age, functioning under 6 years of age, the WISC-IV could not be used. Furthermore, with a child under 16 years of age functioning beyond 16 years of age, the WISC-IV could also not be used. However, the SB5 could be used with both of these groups.

There are a number of changes between the fourth edition (SBFE) and the fifth edition. A fifth factor has been added to the four factors of the fourth edition. The five factors of the SB5 include Fluid Reasoning, Knowledge, Quantitative Reasoning, Visual-Spatial Processing, and Working Memory. The "manipulative toys" from pre-SB4 editions have been returned to the SB5. The authors have also expanded nonverbal assessments, with half of the sub-tests not requiring verbal responses, due to previous criticisms of the Stanford Binet Intelligence Scales alleging them to be too verbally oriented. Additional breadth has been added to more adequately measure the very low functioning and very high giftedness of subjects.

The SB5 cautions against using an intelligence test solely to diagnose mental retardation, learning disabilities, attention deficit hyperactivity disorder (ADHD), giftedness, and cognitive decline in the elderly. The professional standard now requires an assessment of functional ability as well.

The entry level into each of the sub-tests varies based on the age of the individual being tested. Furthermore, an abbreviated form of the SB5 can be used and is explained in the manual.

The five factors on the SB5 include: (1) Fluid Reasoning, which is the ability to solve verbal and nonverbal problems using inductive or deductive reasoning. Inductive reasoning is measured through Matrices or Verbal Analogies, while deductive reasoning is measured by the individual's ability to deduce underlying problems or situations. (2) Knowledge measures the general fund of knowledge that one acquires in such settings as work, school, and/or home. Because much of this information was acquired many years earlier, it is also a measure of acquired and stored memory, measuring fluid and crystallized intelligence. (3) Quantitative Reasoning utilizes the traditional arithmetic reasoning type sub-tests. (4) Visual-Spatial Processing measures the subject's ability to see patterns, relationships, and spatial orientations. These are acquired through administering the Form Board and Form Patterns sub-tests. (5) Lastly, Working Memory utilizes a number of different tasks to measure short-term memory. Each of these five factors is measured in the nonverbal and verbal domains. As a result, factor scores, domain scores, and a full scale I.Q. can be measured through the SB5.

§ 8.14 The Wechsler Scales

Page 359, insert text before § 8.15:

There has been a movement within the Wechsler family of tests away from giving selected sub-tests and prorating I.Q. results. As discussed in the section on the new WISC-IV, the publishers advise against prorating the WISC-IV. Instead, psychologists who do not wish to administer a full intelligence test are encouraged to give an abbreviated intelligence test such as the Wechsler Abbreviated Scale of Intelligence. The KBIT, also a useful instrument, is discussed in Section 8.24 of the text.

The WASI is made up of two scales and four sub-tests. The four sub-tests used on the WASI include Vocabulary, Block Design, Similarities, and Matrix Reasoning. This allows for a Verbal I.Q. as measured by the Vocabulary and Similarities subtests and a Performance I.Q. as measured by Block Design and Matrix Reasoning.

Vocabulary: This sub-test measures the individual's expressive vocabulary, verbal knowledge, and fund of information. It is considered to be a useful measure of crystallized intelligence and general intelligence.

Block Design: Block Design measures the abilities of visual/motor coordination, abstract conceptualization, and spatial visualization. It is also a good measure of perceptual organization and general intelligence.

Similarities: Similarities is a measure of verbal concept formation, abstract verbal reasoning ability and general intelligence functioning.

Matrix Reasoning: Matrix Reasoning is a measure of non-verbal fluid reasoning and general intellectual ability.

Although these sub-tests are available on the other Wechsler Scales, different items are used for the WASI. Thus, pulling the Vocabulary, Block Design, Similarities, and Matrix Reasoning sub-tests out of the WAIS-III, WISC-III, or WISC-IV and attempting to use them to obtain a WASI I.Q. score would be inappropriate and ineffective.

The WASI was designed for quickly and accurately estimating of individuals' intellectual functioning, and for screening people from ages 6 through 89 years of age. It does not substitute for the comprehensive measure of intelligence with the WISC-IV or the WAIS-III, and it is recommended that it not be used for "statutorily mandated diagnosis or determination of disability." The screening can be performed to help determine whether an in-depth evaluation is necessary or used at a later date to determine if there has been any change in cognitive functioning from a previously administered comprehensive evaluation. It is also designed to provide estimates of I.Q. scores for research purposes and vocational and rehabilitation purposes.

§ 8.16 —Wechsler Intelligence Scale for Children—Third Edition

Page 362, insert text before § 8.17:

The original Wechsler Scales were developed more than 50 years ago. Until now, all of the Wechsler family of intelligence tests have relied on a three-factor measure of intelligence that includes a Verbal Scale, a Performance Scale, and a Full Scale. With the introduction of the Wechsler Intelligence Scale for Children-Fourth Edition (WISC-IV) the developers of the instrument have presented an entirely new format for measuring intelligence. Gone are the Verbal and Performance Scales and their comparisons. Gone are the Picture Arrangement, Object Assembly, and Mazes. The Arithmetic and Information sub-tests have been relegated to supplemental status, and five new measures of intelligence have been added.

Instead of the Verbal Scale and Performance Scale comprising the Full Scale of the WISC-IV, the composite is now made up a Verbal Comprehension Index (VCI), a Perceptual Reasoning Index (PRI), a Working Memory Index (WMI), and a Processing Speed Index (PSI). The Verbal Comprehension Index is comprised of the Similarities, Vocabulary, and Comprehension sub-tests. The Perceptual Reasoning Index is composed of the Block Design, Picture Concepts, and Matrix Reasoning sub-tests. The Working Memory Index is made up of Digit Span and Letter-Number Sequencing, while the Processing Speed Index includes Coding and Symbol Search.

The new sub-tests include Word Reasoning, Matrix Reasoning, Letter-Number Sequencing, Picture Concepts, and Cancellation. Word Reasoning is a supplemental Verbal Comprehension sub-test measuring verbal reasoning by providing the subject with a series of clues. The task is designed to measure verbal comprehension, analogical and general reasoning ability, verbal abstraction, domain knowledge, the ability to integrate and synthesize different types of information, and the ability to generate alternative concepts. Picture Concepts is a core perceptual reasoning sub-test designed to measure abstract, categorical reasoning ability. Matrix Reasoning is also a core perceptual reasoning sub-test that is considered to be a good measure of fluid intelligence and a reliable measure of general intellectual ability.

Letter-Number Sequencing is a core working memory sub-test in which a sequence of numbers and letters is presented, with the requirement to recall them in ascending numerical order and alphabetical order. Cancellation is a supplemental processing speed sub-test that measures processing speed, visual selection attention, vigilance, and visual neglect.

The interpretation process for the WISC-IV is much more involved than the WISC-III, including a 10-step procedure. The first five steps include reporting and describing the Full Scale I.Q., the VCI, the PRI, the VMI, and the PSI. Step six evaluates the discrepancies between and among the various scales, followed by evaluating the relative strengths and weaknesses shown by the individual. Then sub-test level discrepancies need to be compared, along with evaluating the pattern of scores within the sub-tests. Lastly, a process analysis is performed.

Unlike the WISC-III, prorating I.Q. scores is discouraged by the developers of the WISC-IV. Instead, an instrument like the Wechsler Abbreviated Scale of Intelligence (WASI) could be used. The manual specifically discourages prorating based on the fact that there are only two or three sub-tests per index, making it difficult to achieve valid scores through prorating.

Generally, a new intelligence test should be incorporated into the psychologist's test battery within a year of development to comply with ethical standards. In the case of the WISC-IV, with the number of new sub-tests that have been added, the number of old sub-tests that have been eliminated, and the restructuring of scales from the traditional Verbal and Performance scales to the four new indices, the clinician must be cautious in rushing into the use of the WISC-IV until such time as research has been published on exactly what this instrument measures in comparison to what was measured by the WISC-III. As is always the case, Psychological Corporation has published some of its own research in its manual. However, it will be important to wait for independent research to be performed to address some of these issues. If this process follows its typical course, there should be sufficient information within the next year or so to know what the WISC-IV is measuring and what its utility will be.

§ 8.29 Case Digest

*Page 386, insert after **New York** heading:*

In re Loraida G., 1999 WL 1292948 (N.Y. Fam. Ct., Nov. 16, 1999). A family court in New York denied a petition by the Department of Social Services (DSS) alleging that Lori G., who has mild mental retardation, would not be capable of parenting her child. The child was taken from

Lori G. within days of birth. The court indicated that mild mental retardation is not *per se* or *ipso facto* child neglect. A finding of child neglect must be based upon evidence that there is impairment of a child's physical, mental, or emotional condition, or that the child is imminently in danger of impairment due to a parent's failure to exercise even minimally adequate care. The court granted Lori G. custody, with the proviso that she accept help from appropriate social services programs to ensure that the child will be properly cared for.

CHAPTER 9

OBJECTIVE PERSONALITY TESTING: MMPI, MMPI-2, MMPI-A, AND OTHER OBJECTIVE PERSONALITY TESTING

§ 9.19 Implications of the Studies and Findings from Other Research

Page 452, insert at the end of section:

In an invited address, James Butcher, an author of the Minnesota Multiphasic Personality Inventory—second edition (MMPI-2) gave a presentation titled "Assessment with MMPI-2: Research-based Decisions and Diversed Applications." Dr. Butcher presented ten suggestions that should be considered when using the MMPI-2 for assessment purposes:

1. He suggests not ignoring the vast wealth of research available from the MMPI, and indicated that he perceives that it is generalizable to the MMPI-2.
2. He pointed out that a number of people have criticized the MMPI-2 over the past ten years. However, he suggests that people should explore the underlying motivation of accepting the critique before falling into the trap of superficial criticism.
3. He is concerned that too much interpretation of the clinical scales of the MMPI-2 is done without paying sufficient attention to "invalidating conditions." He suggests making sure the interpreter uses the validity scales in the overall interpretation of the MMPI-2 and does not interpret an invalid test and protocol.
4. Dr. Butcher suggests that the user of the MMPI-2 avoid the attractive nuisance modifications of the test that are referred to as MMPI short forms. Although several MMPI short forms were developed for the original MMPI, there are no effective MMPI-2 short forms. If an attorney is involved in a case where the psy-

chologist purports to use a valid MMPI-2 short form, the attorney should insist on the administration of the full test, or should change psychologists.

5. He is concerned about the seemingly unending development of new MMPI-2 scales. He suggests that psychologists be careful in utilizing them, because many of them are not valid.
6. In the same vein, he encourages individuals to avoid "local norms" for MMPI-2 interpretation. For example, if someone has performed a study of MMPI-2 subjects in "small town middle America", those norms should not be used to substitute for the national norms.
7. Do not use insensitive test applications.
8. Questions have been raised about whether the MMPI-2 can be used across diverse populations. Dr. Butcher reports that research supports the use of the MMPI-2 with diverse populations, suggesting that it can be used with minority groups and other groups associated with diversity issues.
9. The examiner may be inclined to alter test items to help the subject understand the items. Dr. Butcher indicates that doing so reduces the meaning of the test items in general and may make the results for a particular client invalid.
10. The last, and perhaps most important, statement that Butcher made about the MMPI-2 was to not expect it to provide more than the test was developed to provide. Although it is the most widely used and most widely researched instrument in psychological assessment, it still has limitations and should not be expected to perform beyond the limitations that exist.

§ 9.21 MMPI/MMPI-2 Use in Child Custody Evaluations

Page 460, insert at end of section:

Roger Greene chaired a symposium titled "Complications in the Assessment of Test Results in Forensic Settings." The study was performed by Roger Greene and Marc Ackerman. The premise of the study was to compare the MMPI-2 results for individuals who were tested on more than one occasion in personal injury cases, divorce cases, and criminal cases. Focusing specifically on the results of divorce cases, it was demonstrated that, on average, the MMPI-2 profile was less pathological on the second administration than on the first administration. This supports the concept that was reported in the 2000 supplement of this text that individuals tend to perform better on a second administration of the MMPI-2, because they have seen the result of the first administration and know the profile that was achieved. Furthermore, they found that, upon second administration, only 25 to 30 percent of individuals had the same code type in the second administration as in the. This would suggest that the results would not remain the same in most cases from one setting to another. This too, may be the result of the education factor.

§ 9.36 Millon Clinical Multiaxial Inventory-III

Page 478, insert at end of section:

The Millon Clinical Multiaxial Inventory-II and III (MCMI-II,MCMI-III) continue to be among the most frequently-used tests in evaluation of adults in child custody actions.[323.1] Research continues to raise substantial questions regarding the appropriateness of this use.

The Thirteenth Mental Measurements Yearbook includes two reviews of the MCMI-III. The first is by psychologist Allen Hess, Distinguished Research Professor and Department Head, Department of Psychology, Auburn University at Montgomery, Montgomery, Alabama. He indicates that the MCMI-III is not psychometrically sound, because of (1) a lack of information on the true base rates of personality disorders in the general population and about the clinicians who did ratings, raising questions regarding the reliability and validity of the categories utilized in the test; (2) numerous problems with the item content, including too many items keyed "true" and having too many items appear on more than one scale, compromising statistical analysis of the data; and (3) inadequate differentiation among disorders, with a low sensitivity (ability to correctly identify people who have a disorder, with scales ranging from 12.5 percent to 53.1 percent and a mean sensitivity of 36.26 percent, i.e., error rates from 46.9 to 87.5 percent and a mean error rate of 63.74 percent) at the lowest level of

[323.1] Ackerman, Marc J. & Melissa Ackerman, *Child Custody Evaluation Practices: A 1996 Survey of Psychologists*, 30 Family Law Quarterly 565–586 (1996); Ackerman, Marc J. & Melissa Ackerman, *Custody Evaluation Practices: A Survey of Experienced Professionals (Revisited)*, 28 Professional Psychology: Research and Practice 137–45 (1997); LaFortune, K.A. & B.N. Carpenter, *Custody Evaluations: A Survey of Mental Health Professionals*, 16 Behavioral Sciences and the Law 207–224 (1998); Bow, James N. & Francella A. Quinnell, *Psychologists' Current Practices and Procedures in Child Custody Evaluations: Five Years After American Psychological Association Guidelines*, 32 Professional Psychology: Research and Practice 261–268 (2001); Hagen, Margaret A. & Castagna, Nicole, *The Real Numbers: Psychological Testing in Custody Evaluations*, 32 Professional Psychology: Research and Practice 269–71 (2001).

pathology (the "trait" or "features" level), and worse at a diagnostic level of severity.[323.2] Given the test's inability to accurately diagnose, its strong tendency to exaggerate psychopathology, its minimal likelihood of identifying anyone taking it as "normal," and its poor psychometric soundness, Hess concludes that "the user of the MCMI-III does so at his or her own risk."[323.3]

The second review is by psychologist Paul Retzlaff, Professor, Psychology Department, University of Northern Colorado, Greeley, Colorado. Retzlaff's review is nearly 180 degrees opposite that of Hess. He indicates that the test is "not only clinically useful but psychometrically the most sophisticated of any available product."[323.4] He does indicate that there is a problem associated with having only 175 items when the test derives 24 content scales, a reference to the number of items that appear on more than one scale. Retzlaff indicates that the internal consistency and reliability of the test are very high, as is the criterion validity. He also indicates that the positive predictive power of the test, based on the research done for the 1997 revision of the manual, ranges from the .50s to .70s (i.e., error rates from the .30s to the .50s). He concludes that "the MCMI-III is a clinically useful, well-constructed, and sophisticated test. It is particularly useful to diagnose the relatively difficult personality disorders."[323.5, 323.6]

Psychologist Anita Lampel evaluated the use of the MCMI-III in child custody evaluations. The test protocols of 50 couples were analyzed. It was found that 64 of the 100 parents had significant elevations on the defensiveness scale. Despite their defensiveness, 84 had elevations on one or more of the clinical scales. The author notes[323.7] that "litigating parents test with personality difficulties at a high rate compared to a nonclinical population."[323.8]

Psychologist Robert Craig wrote about testimony based on the MCMI-II and III. He notes that the "the MCMI was normed on patients being treated or evaluated in mental health settings. The normative clinical groups included about 10% of patients in forensic settings, but this does not mean

[323.2] *Id.* at 667.

[323.3] Hess, Allen, Millon Clinical Multiaxial Inventory-III. In James C. Impara and Barbara S. Plake, *The Thirteenth Mental Measurements Yearbook.* Lincoln, Nebraska: University of Nebraska-Lincoln (1998) at 665–667.

[323.4] *Id.* at 667.

[323.5] *Id.* at 668.

[323.6] Retzlaff, Paul, Millon Clinical Multiaxial Inventory-III. In James C. Impara and Barbara S. Plake, *The Thirteenth Mental Measurements Yearbook.* Lincoln, Nebraska: University of Nebraska-Lincoln (1998) at 667–668.

[323.7] *Id.* at 27.

[323.8] Lampel, Anita, *Use of the Millon Clinical Multiaxial Inventory-III in Evaluating Child Custody Litigants*, 17 American Journal of Forensic Psychology 19–31 (1999).

that the MCMI was normed or validated for use in forensic settings."[323.9] The only forensic areas for which there is a literature base, he indicates, are with regard to substance abuse and Post-traumatic Stress Disorder. He further indicates that "the test was not intended for use with nonclinical (e.g., normal) patients, and using the MCMI with this population tends to inaccurately describe and to overpathologize these groups."[323.10] He indicates that the limited research with a normal population finds that "non-clinical patients usually attain their highest elevations, often in 'clinical ranges' . . . on the Histrionic (4), Narcissistic (5) and Compulsive (7)" scales. That is, people with no known psychopathology may still score in the pathological range on the test.[323.11]

Psychologist James Schutte discussed the use of the MCMI-III in forensic evaluations. He indicates that "it is worth noting that unlike the MMPI-2 there are no non-clinical norms for the MCMI-III, and as such, the instrument's use is not recommended for individuals for whom assessment of pathology is not of interest (e.g., career choice counseling, self-exploration, executive coaching)."[323.12] He cautions that "assessing individuals who are likely to vary greatly from the normative sample runs the risk of overpathologizing. . . . [C]aution is advised in child custody . . . litigation."[323.13] He also notes that most of the MCMI-III test questions are "keyed positive," so that an individual must endorse many pathological traits in order to get a high score. He suggests mentioning this fact and that the individual being evaluated may be similar to the normative sample when a psychologist is questioned regarding the test's overdiagnosing of pathology.[323.14]

Psychologists Richard Rogers, Randall Salekin and Kenneth Sewell addressed whether the MCMI meets the *Daubert* standard. They note that other authors have recommended against using the MCMI-III in forensic assessments, and indicate that they concur, while adding "serious concerns about the diagnostic accuracy and construct validity of the MCMI-III."[323.15] They discuss the very substantial differences in content of the MCMI, the

[323.9] Craig, Robert J., *Testimony Based on the Millon Clinical Multiaxial Inventory: Review, Commentary, and Guidelines*, 73 Journal of Personality Assessment 290–304 (1999) at 291.

[323.10] *Id.* at 292.

[323.11] *Id.* at 295.

[323.12] Schutte, James W., *Using the MCMI-III in Forensic Evaluations*, 19 American Journal of Forensic Psychology 5–20 (2000) at 6.

[323.13] *Id.* at 15.

[323.14] *Id.* at 16.

[323.15] Rogers, Richard, Randall T. Salekin, and Kenneth W. Sewell, *Validation of the Millon Clinical Multiaxial Inventory for Axis II Disorders: Does It Meet the* Daubert *Standard?* 23 Law and Human Behavior 425–443 (1999).

MCMI-II, and the MCMI-III, and indicate that each test is a new instrument, not simply a revision of the previous version. They indicate that research has established a false-positive rate for the MCMI-III of 82 percent—that is, of 100 tests administered 82 will indicate psychopathology that is in fact not present. False-negatives, in contrast, are rare: only 7 percent of individuals for whom the test indicates a lack of psychopathology will in fact have serious psychological problems. The authors also indicate that the MCMI-III does not meet established standards for construct validity. Although the MCMI-II (the previous version of the test) has some limited utility for diagnosing three personality disorders (Avoidant, Schizotypal, and Borderline Personality Disorders), it has virtually no database of research in forensic areas, and should not be utilized in forensic matters.[323.16]

The article by Rogers et al. was commented upon by three articles in a later issue of the same journal. In the first, psychologists Frank Dyer and Joseph McCann indicate that Rogers et al. missed some important published research, particularly research contained in the 1997 revision of the MCMI-III manual, and suggest that MCMI-II and III have more validity than Rogers et al. identified. Dyer and McCann also identify criminal case law that refers to personality disorders as relevant to an individual's culpability for a crime. They suggest that the MCMI-III can provide "very useful data that can inform consideration of forensically related issues, including substance abuse, posttraumatic stress disorder, domestic violence, [and] violence risk assessment."[323.17, 323.18]

The second article is by psychologist Paul Retzlaff. He was concerned that Rogers et al. had not included information from the 1997 revision of the MCMI-III manual that supported the validity of the test. He also indicated that the number of scales with "positive predictive power" have risen from the three indicated by Rogers et al. to 11 of the 14 personality disorder scales.[323.19]

The third article is a rejoinder by Rogers et al. They indicated that Dyer and McCann appear to accept that the MCMI, MCMI-II, and MCMI-III are substantially different instruments, so that conclusions about one cannot be generalized to the others. Dyer and McCann also appear to have ac-

---

[323.16] *Id.* at 439.

[323.17] Dyer, Frank J. & Joseph T. McCann, *The Millon Clinical Inventories, Research Critical of Their Forensic Application, and Daubert Criteria*, 24 Law and Human Behavior 487–97 (2000).

[323.18] *Id.* at 490.

[323.19] Paul D. Retzlaff, *Comment on the Validity of the MCMI-III*, 24 Law and Human Behavior 499–500 (2000).

cepted the conclusions of Rogers et al. about the MCMI falling below the standards of the *Daubert* requirements, and did not argue with the allegations regarding the lack of content validity of the MCMI-III.

With regard to the 1997 revision of the MCMI-III manual, Rogers et al. indicate concern that (1) clinicians were free to decide whether to participate in the research, free to decide which of their cases to refer for inclusion, and free to decide whether to consult other clinicians to ensure the reliability of their conclusions—each a violation of normal research protocols. Rogers et al. indicate that none of the six studies cited by Dyer and McCann as "forensic studies" are in fact forensic studies. Rogers et al. acknowledge their oversight in failing to include a review of the revised MCMI-III manual. They indicate that a review of that revision indicates that (1) their previous statement regarding a lack of construct validity remains accurate, (2) there is a new concern about the normative group, with the original group of 998 patients being eliminated and a much smaller sample of 321 patients replacing it, and, therefore, (3) some of the diagnostic categories now have too few patients to permit great generalizability. Rogers et al. note that the revised manual claims an increase in "positive prediction" from .18 in the original manual to .70 in the new manual. The reason, they indicate, is that the test author eliminated the objective criterion of a base rate equal to or greater than 85, substituting a criterion of the "percentage of patients having a particular MCMI-III personality scale as the highest in their profile."[323.20] This criterion could allow an MCMI-III score that falls well below the cutoff for significance to be accepted as correct so long as it is the highest score. Recalculating the positive predictability from the data in the manual, Rogers et al. indicate that the correct figure is .31—that is, the test is wrong two out of three times. Further, Rogers et al. indicate that Millon et al. violated a fundamental rule of test validation by encouraging contributing clinicians to include MCMI-III protocols already in those clinicians' files, so that the clinicians may recall aspects of the test results while attempting to render an "independent" opinion regarding the validity of the test. Permitting a rater to have any knowledge of test scores is called "criterion contamination." Rogers et al. reassert their conclusion that the MCMI-III is not appropriate for forensic work and does not meet the *Daubert* criterion for admissibility in court.[323.21]

[323.20] Millon, T., R. Davis & C. Millon, *The Millon Clinical Multiaxial Inventory-III Manual* (2nd ed.). Minneapolis, MN: National Computer Systems (1997) at 98.

[323.21] Rogers, Richard, Randall T. Salekin, & Kenneth W. Sewell, The MCMI-III and the *Daubert* Standard: Separating Rhetoric from Reality. 24 Law and Human Behavior 501–506 (2000).

The overwhelming weight of the evidence is that the MCMI is not appropriate for a normal (non-patient) population. Further, given the continued evidence that the MCMI-II and MCMI-III overpathologize, the continued lack of a normal comparison group, the continued questions regarding the validity of the test, and the evidence that the test does not meet the Daubert criterion for admissibility in court, the present authors continue to strongly recommend against using the MCMI in any of its versions in a child custody evaluation.

CHAPTER 10

PROJECTIVE PERSONALITY TESTING

§ 10.10 Acceptance of the Rorschach by Mental Health Professionals

Page 509, insert at the end of § 10.10:

In a 2001 article, psychologists Francella Quinnell and James Bow indicated that the Rorschach remains the most frequently used projective test. Forty-four percent of the survey respondents used the Rorschach, and they used it in 64 percent of their evaluations.[105.1]

A New Rorschach Controversy

A 1999 study by psychologists Thomas W. Shaffer, Philip Erdberg and John Haroian had an impact far beyond the intent of the researchers. Noting that the professional literature has relatively few articles that indicate the response patterns of non-patients on the Rorschach, the Wechsler Adult Intelligence Scale-Revised (WAIS-R), and the Minnesota Multiphasic Personality Inventory, Second Edition (MMPI-2), they set out to provide data to address this need. Individuals were excluded who had a major medical illness in the past six months, who had ever been hospitalized in a psychiatric facility, who had been in psychological treatment in the past two years, who had ever been convicted of a felony, or who had psychological testing within the past year. The results of administration of these three tests to 123 non-patient adults were very similar to the standardization samples for the WAIS-R and the MMPI-2, but not extremely similar to those of the Comprehensive System (CS) for the Rorschach. Rather, the Comprehensive System identified these adults as having significant psychopathology, despite all the contrary indicators from other sources.[105.2]

105.1 Quinnell, Francella A. & Bow, James N., *Psychological Tests Used in Child Custody Evaluations*, 19 Behavioral Sciences and the Law 491-501 (2001).

105.2 Shaffer, Thomas W., Erdberg, Philip & Haroian, John, *Current Nonpatient Data For the Rorschach, WAIS-R, and MMPI-2*, 73 Journal of Psychological Assessment 305-316 (1999).

A study by psychologists Mel Hamel, Thomas W. Shaffer and Philip Erdberg[105.3] found similar problems in the assessment of children aged six to 12 years. One hundred children were identified who had never been referred for psychological or psychiatric treatment, had never been arrested, convicted, or put on probation for any offense, had no more than one suspension or expulsion from school, had never used alcohol or other drugs, and had a GPA of at least 2.0 for the current school year. To further ensure that this was a "normal" sample, the Conners Parent Rating Scale-93 (CPRS-93) was used to identify whether any of the children had significant behavioral problems. The results indicated that the parents of these children clearly indicated that the children did not have behavioral problems. Since these were mentally healthy children, from all indications, it was expected that the Comprehensive System would support that conclusion. It did not. The interpretive guidelines collectively described the children as "grossly misperceiving and misinterpreting their surroundings and having unconventional ideation and significant cognitive impairment. Their distortion of reality and faulty reasoning approach psychosis."[105.4]

Numerous articles addressing the Shaffer et al. and Hamel et al. results and other issues have been published in the past two years. Much of the criticism of the Comprehensive System has come from psychologists James M. Wood, M. Teresa Nezworski, Howard N. Garb, and Scott O. Lilienfeld. In articles published in 2000-2001,[105.5] they indicated that the norms for the Comprehensive System are not accurate, and that using those norms makes an individual appear to have more psychopathology than he or she actually has. All 14 variables they studied were found to differ significantly for non-patients in the Comprehensive System's normative groups and non-

---

[105.3] Hamel, Mel, Shaffer, Thomas W. & Erdberg, Philip, *A Study of Nonpatient Preadolescent Rorschach Protocols*, 75 Journal of Personality Assessment 280-294 (2000).

[105.4] *Id.* at 291.

[105.5] Wood, James M., Nezworski, M. Theresa, Garb, Howard N. & Lilienfeld, Scott O., *The Misperception of Psychopathology: Problems With the Norms of the Comprehensive System for the Rorschach*, 8 Clinical Psychology: Science and Practice 350-373 (2001); Wood, James M., Lilienfeld, Scott O., Nezworski, M. Teresa, & Garb, Howard N., *Coming to Grips With Negative Evidence for the Comprehensive System for the Rorschach: A Comment on Gacono, Loving, and Bodholdt; Ganellen; and Bornstein*, 77 Journal of Personality Assessment 48-70 (2001); Wood, James M., Nezworski, M. Teresa, Garb, Howard N. & Lilienfeld, Scott O., *Problems With the Norms of the Comprehensive System for the Rorschach: Methodological and Conceptual Considerations*, 8 Clinical Psychology: Science and Practice 397-402 (2001); Lilienfeld, Scott O., Wood, James M. & Garb, Howard N., *The Scientific Status of Projective Techniques*, 1 Psychological Science in the Public Interest 27-66 (2000).

patients tested by other researchers. They also found that the reliability of some Comprehensive System scores is far below acceptable levels. As a result, the authors "recommend that psychologists not use the present CS norms in clinical or forensic work, with either children or adults. Psychologists who use these norms run the risk of attaching false and negative labels to clients and thereby potentially harming them," an ethical violation. Any psychologists who continue to use the Comprehensive System norms, they indicate, have at the least an ethical obligation to describe the controversy and the possible limitations of those norms.[105.6] In another article, one of these authors, Howard Garb, has called for a moratorium on use of the Comprehensive System in clinical and forensic evaluations until further research has established new, valid norms for the System. The problem, Garb et al. indicate, is not that all Comprehensive System scores are invalid; rather, at this point in time no one knows with certainty which norms are valid and which are not. They criticize articles by other Rorschach researchers on various methodological grounds, indicating that none of the "pro-Comprehensive System" authors has produced methodologically sound data thus far. The authors also note that their own research supports the use of several Comprehensive System scales, though they also recommend further research on those scales.[105.7]

In addition to the above conclusions, Wood *et al.* indicate their belief that the Comprehensive System is no longer widely accepted by the scientific community, given the controversy regarding it, and, to a degree, the Rorschach itself is brought into question given that most psychologists now use the Comprehensive System norms. Questions regarding the accuracy of scoring the test using the Comprehensive System, in particular, make most of the CS scales highly inappropriate in forensic settings, they indicate. At minimum, they say, if the Comprehensive System's scoring is to be used in a forensic context, it should be scored independently by at least two experts on the test, to try to ensure the accuracy of the results. Finally, they indicate that there is substantial evidence that some variables in the Comprehensive System yield significantly different results for Caucasians, Blacks, Hispanics and other minorities, as well as non-Americans. Their recommendation is that the Comprehensive System (and perhaps Rorschach) not be used in court or, if used, that only the few well-validated

---

[105.6] *Id.* at 363.

[105.7] Garb, Howard N., Wood, James M., Nezworski, M. Teresa, Grove, William M. & Stejskal, William J., *Toward a Resolution of the Rorschach Controversy*, 13 Psychological Assessment 433-448 (2001).

Comprehensive System scales be utilized until new research produces the valid and reliable results that are essential to the forensic arena.[105.8]

Psychologists John Hunsley and J. Michael Bailey caution that *many authors confuse criticisms of the Comprehensive System with criticisms of the Rorschach Inkblot Test (or Method) itself.* While some researchers criticize aspects of the Rorschach, it is the Comprehensive System that is the object of most concerns.

They note that many psychologists do not attempt interpretations utilizing the Comprehensive System norms, preferring other systems or using idiographic (case specific) interpretations. They also suggest that the reputation of the Rorschach for identifying psychopathology may be based to a substantial degree on the apparent tendency of the Comprehensive System to overpathologize. They recommend great caution in use of the Comprehensive System at this time, while calling for a great deal of research to establish clearly for whom the Rorschach is an appropriate test, what outcome criteria are valid and reliable, and in what circumstances the Rorschach is an appropriate instrument (forensic, clinical, other).[105.9] John Hunsley, in an article authored with Gina Di Giulio, finds the arguments of Wood *et al.* "compelling," and urges that new research be done as soon as possible to determine which Comprehensive System scales are valid and reliable and which are not.[105.10]

Psychologists R.K. McKinzey and Victoria Campagna asked 30 psychologists with extensive experience using the Comprehensive System to score a single Rorschach protocol. The Rorschach was also scored with the Rorschach Interpretation Assistance Program: Version 4 (RIAP4). Three of the psychologists considered the protocol unscorable, while 27 scored it. Of that 27, 19 made from one to seven scoring errors each, as identified by RIAP4. Many of the scoring errors changed the interpretation of the test results, in some cases dramatically. As a result of these findings, McKinzey and Campagna recommend against use of the Comprehensive System for scoring and interpretation.[105.11] Similarly, V. Guarnaccia, C.A. Dill, S. Sabatino and S. Southwick had 21 graduate students and 12 psy-

---

[105.8] Wood, James M., Nezworski, M. Teresa, Stejskal, William & McKinzey, R.K., *Problems of the Comprehensive System for the Rorschach in Forensic Settings: Recent Developments*, 1 Journal of Forensic Psychology Practice 89-103 (2001).

[105.9] Hunsley, John & Bailey, J. Michael, *Whither the Rorschach? An Analysis of the Evidence*, 13 Psychological Assessment 472-485 (2001).

[105.10] Hunsley, John & Di Giulio, Gina, *Norms, Norming, and Clinical Assessment*, 8 Clinical Psychology: Science and Practice 378-382 (2001).

[105.11] McKinzie, R.K. & Campagna, Victoria, *The Rorschach, Exner's Comprehensive System, Interscorer Agreement, and Death*, WebPsychEmpiricist Apr. 27, 2002. Retrieved Aug. 14, 2002 from www.wpe.info/papers_table.

chologists score 20 Rorschach responses using the Comprehensive System. Nearly all scorers made errors.[105.12] In contrast, Gregory Meyer, Mark J. Hilsenroth, Dirk Baxter, John E. Exner, Jr., J. Christopher Fowler, Craig C. Piers and Justin Resnick examined scoring of the Rorschach by large samples of students, researchers, and clinicians, all using the Comprehensive System. They found a high level of accuracy across and reliability among the groups of scorers, particularly for summary (rather than individual) scores. Meyer et al. recommend that clinicians continually update the accuracy of their scoring, to ensure that errors do not occur.[105.13]

Several Comprehensive System proponents have responded to the above articles. Psychologist Irving B. Weiner, one of the foremost Rorschach experts, wrote that the Comprehensive System calls for a standardized administration and scoring, and that the test can be reliably scored. Further, the Comprehensive System does have reasonable norms, even if some of those about which questions have been raised are included, and the CS scoring of the Rorschach remains valid for most scoring purposes, he indicates. Further, he writes, the CS adds incremental validity in situations in which decisions must be made, including forensic evaluations. It must also be noted, he indicates, that many psychologists use the CS recommendations for administration and scoring of the Rorschach, but use different interpretive strategies from those recommended by John Exner, the primary author of the Comprehensive System. Even if all the criticisms of the CS norms were valid, use of these other interpretive strategies would not be affected. In addition, many psychologists use primarily or exclusively idiographic interpretations that are case-specific rather than comparing an individual's CS scores with Exner's or any other normative group. This method circumvents all of the criticisms of the Comprehensive System, since each Rorschach protocol is individually addressed, with or without formal scoring. Weiner also suggests that Exner's normative groups may be better-adjusted than is a representative sample of the U.S. population, which would also lead to the finding that more representative samples would appear more pathological. Weiner's suggestion is that both the MMPI-2 and the Rorschach should be used in most evaluations, because each may yield data that is missed by the other test, as well as helping to

---

105.12 Guarnaccia, Vincent, Dill, Charles A., Sabatino, Susan & Southwick, Sarah, *Scoring Accuracy Using the Comprehensive System for the Rorschach*, 77 Journal of Personality Assessment 464-474 (2001).

105.13 Meyer, Gregory J., Hilsenroth, Mark J., Baxter, Dirk, Exner, Jr., John E., Fowler, J. Christopher, Piers, Craig C. & Resnick, Justin, *An Examination of Interrater Reliability for Scoring the Rorschach Comprehensive System in Eight Data Sets*, 78 Journal of Personality Assessment 219-274 (2002).

confirm hypotheses based on either test.[105.14] Similar statements are made by other authors.[105.15]

Prominent researchers Gregory Meyer and Robert Archer indicate that no single measure of personality or psychopathology is so comprehensive that it may reasonably be used alone. Rather, one should look for incremental validity based on several overlapping measures. They indicate that research evidence has established that the Rorschach is a valid test, with validity coefficients similar to those of other frequently used instruments such as the MMPI-2 and the Wechsler intelligence scales. They acknowledge that the Comprehensive System may appear to overpathologize, because the reference group is made up of people who are both relatively healthy and functioning well, and recommend that a sample representative of the U.S. population be collected. They recommend an approach to test interpretation that places the greatest weight on those factors that have been empirically replicated, and the avoidance of conclusions based on factors with little or no empirical support. They also caution against drawing inferences regarding whether a child was sexually abused from Rorschach results.[105.16] Dr. Meyer, in another article, indicates that the coding for the Comprehensive System form categories ("good" vs. "bad" form) has changed substantially over time on the basis of ongoing research, and will change in the future on the same basis. Rather than dismissing the CS, he asserts, one should foster research to further improve it. He also compares the continuing improvements in the CS with the periodically changed norms of intelligence tests, on which an individual whose tested IQ two generations ago was 100 would score at or below 84 based on current norms. Meyer also reports that analysis of data based on thousands of Rorschachs from non-clinical settings around the world that were scored utilizing the CS norms found that there was little difference from Exner's non-patient data. Further, data on the first 100 people in the new non-patient sample were analyzed, with the result that they evidence very slightly more psychopathology than Exner's earlier non-patient sample, but

[105.14] Weiner, Irving B., *Advancing the Science of Psychological Assessment: The Rorschach Inkblot Method as Exemplar*, 13 Psychological Assessment 423-432 (2001).

[105.15] Rosenthal, Robert, Hiller, Jordan B., Bornstein, Robert F., Berry, David T.R. & Brunell-Neuleib, Sherrie, *Meta-Analytic Methods, the Rorschach, and the MMPI*, 13 Psychological Assessment 449-451 (2001); Viglione, Donald J. & Hilsenroth, Mark J., *The Rorschach: Facts, Fictions, and Future*, 13 Psychological Assessment 452-471; Ganellen, Ronald J., *Weighing Evidence for the Rorschach's Validity: A Response to Wood et al.* (1999). 77 Journal of Personality Assessment 1-15 (2001).

[105.16] Meyer, Gregory J. & Archer, Robert P., *The Hard Science of Rorschach Research: What Do We Know and Where Do We Go?* 13 Psychological Assessment 486-502 (2001).

less than Exner's patient sample. He characterizes the differences as trivial.[105.17]

Psychologist Thomas Widiger, who was the research coordinator for the DSM-IV Task Force, seeks a middle ground. While noting that the Comprehensive System was a major advance over other, less concrete systems, he acknowledges that the problems identified must be rectified. The Rorschach itself, he indicates, "does provide useful and valid information and, as a projective test, it is a very intriguing instrument that might be helpful in the assessment of dispositions, needs, or conflicts that the person is unable or reluctant to acknowledge."[105.18] He questions, however, making it the primary source of data indicating whether an individual should have custody of his or her child. He also indicates that the current debate about the Comprehensive System, and, to a lesser degree, the Rorschach, may be predicated in part on a larger dispute among psychologists regarding the use of projective tests at all, despite the Rorschach's being characterized by the American Psychological Association's Board of Professional Affairs in 1998 as the "single, most powerful psychometric instrument ever developed."[105.19] He suggests that the Rorschach remains both useful and effective as a source of hypotheses regarding intrapsychic problems that may then be explored and validated by data from other sources.

Psychologist Edward Aronow recasts the dispute by indicating that the error may be placing too much emphasis on the Rorschach as a psychometric instrument rather than as a rich source of clinical data and hypotheses. He urges that the primary use of the Rorschach be projective analysis, with the psychometric characteristics a secondary consideration.[105.20]

Psychologist John Exner, Jr., primary developer of the Comprehensive System, also responded to the criticisms by various authors. He acknowledges that there are differences between the data presented by Shaffer et al. and the non-patient data for the CS. He is critical of the methodology of Wood et al. and other CS opponents, and questions the validity of comparing samples that have widely disparate populations, ages, and other characteristics. With regard to the Shaffer et al. study, he notes that the non-patient sample appears to have been unusually defensive, thereby skewing the results. This would not explain all of the differences, however,

---

[105.17] Meyer, Gregory J., *Evidence to Correct Misperceptions About Rorschach Norms*, 8 Clinical Psychology: Science and Practice 389-396 (2001).

[105.18] Widiger, Thomas A., *The Best and Worst of Us?* 8 Clinical Psychology: Science and Practice 374-377 at 375 (2001).

[105.19] *Id.* at 376.

[105.20] Aronow, Edward, *CS Norms, Psychometrics, and Possibilities for the Rorschach Technique*, 8 Clinical Psychology: Science and Practice 383-385 (2001).

so he indicates that a new non-patient sample is being developed to address various issues. He is also critical of the notion that psychopathology is diagnosed based on the differences between the scores of the non-patient sample and those of an individual taking the test. Rather, he indicates, interpretation using the Comprehensive System involves reviewing seven clusters of data, developing hypotheses, and evaluating these hypotheses against data gathered from other sources regarding the individual.[105.21]

Exner has also published data on the first 175 individuals in the new non-patient sample he and his colleagues are developing. He indicates that the data from these individuals is quite similar to that from the original sample of 600 people, collected between 1973 and 1986. He notes that a major revision of the CS was undertaken in 1990 because it was determined that Rorschach records with fewer than 14 responses were likely to be invalid. From a database with some 1,100 records, 700 met criteria for number of responses and distribution of gender, geography, and socioeconomic level. Exner also acknowledges that a serious error was made: it was discovered in 1999 that 221 records were included twice among the 700, skewing the data. The "700" records represented only 479 individuals. Those duplicate records have since been replaced with others that maintained the gender, geographic and socioeconomic balance of the sample. The current normative group consists of 300 men and 300 women, with 120 individuals from each of five geographic areas of the United States, with partial stratification for socioeconomic level. In addition, data collection is proceeding for the new normative sample. Unfortunately, Exner indicates that data collection is proceeding at about the same rate as the original normative sample, which took 10 years to complete. That would put the end of the data-gathering in 2009, followed by publication of the results (though partial data could continue to be presented, as did this article).[105.22]

Exner is periodically revising certain tables in *A Rorschach Workbook for the Comprehensive System, Fifth Edition*, published in 2001. The latest revision, available for downloading from the Rorschach Workshops web site (www.ror-scan.com/workshop.htm), is dated April 27, 2002.[105.23]

The primary Comprehensive System critics (Garb, Wood, Lilienfeld and Nezworski) have published a 2002 article with several recommendations for current utilization of the Rorschach and other projective techniques:

[105.21] Exner, Jr., John E., *A Comment on "The Misperception of Psychopathology: Problems With the Norms of the Comprehensive System for the Rorschach*, 8 Clinical Psychology: Science and Practice 386-388 (2001).

[105.22] Exner, Jr., John E., *A New Nonpatient Sample for the Rorschach Comprehensive System: A Progress Report*, 78 Journal of Personality Assessment 391-404 (2002).

[105.23] Rorschach Workshops web site, Sept. 27, 2002.

> Clinical Guideline 1: Exercise caution when using the CS norms, as research indicates that their use is related to the overperception of psychopathology. In many instances, it may be best not to use the CS norms.[105.24]
>
> Clinical Guideline 2: Use scores that are valid for their intended purposes. Scores should be validated in well-designed studies, results should be consistent, and positive findings should be replicated by independent investigators.[105.25]
>
> Clinical Guideline 3: Do not use the Rorschach, TAT, or human figure drawings to detect child physical or sexual abuse.[105.26]
>
> Clinical Guideline 4: Use projective techniques differently depending on whether one is testifying in court as an expert witness, evaluating a client in clinical practice, or using a projective technique as an aid for exploration in psychotherapy.[105.27]

They also have some recommendations for assessments in general. With children, they recommend that data primarily be gathered via interviews with the children, with teachers, and/or with parents. The screening instruments they recommend are the Child Behavior Checklist or the Draw a Person: Screening Procedure for Emotional Disturbance (DAP: SPED). To diagnose children or adults, they recommend primary reliance on interviews and historical information, "but results from psychological tests, including self-report personality inventories and projective techniques, can sometimes be helpful," including careful use of the Rorschach with certain Comprehensive System variables or with criteria from non-CS methods. Behavioral predictions should primarily be predicated on interview and historical data, but projective techniques may help with prediction in certain areas. For assessment of psychiatric disorders and personality characteristics, they recommend reliance on history and interview information, brief self-report measures, and, if necessary, projective techniques. They again note the success of the Rorschach at identifying thought disorders

---

[105.24] Garb, Howard N., Wood, James M., Lilienfeld, Scott O. & Nezworski, M. Teresa, *Effective Use of Projective Techniques in Clinical Practice: Let the Data Help With Selection and Interpretation*, 33 Professional Psychology: Research and Practice 454-463, at 455 (2002).

[105.25] *Id.* at 457. The authors also indicate that the Rorschach has demonstrated validity at detecting thought disorders, e.g., a psychosis, as well as evaluating dependent personality traits. They also recommend it as a method for generating hypotheses in psychotherapy, for the purpose of identifying and addressing an individual's problems. They do not believe it valid at this time for other purposes.

[105.26] *Id.* at 459.

[105.27] *Id.* at 460.

and dependency tendencies. Finally, they recommend use of the Washington University Sentence Completion Test, which has extensive validation research behind it, but is not used by many clinicians as a source of data.[105.28]

Three of the experts cited above presented at a seminar at the 2002 Convention of the American Psychological Convention: Gregory Meyer, Howard Garb, and Thomas Widiger. Dr. Meyer began by noting that the degree of interrater reliability in medicine tends to fall between .21 and .57, with examples being the .42 agreement on abnormalities in mammograms, .45 agreement on the meaning of cardiac arrhythmias, and .42 agreement on the meaning of PAP smears. In comparison, interrater agreement on the scoring of the Rorschach exceeds .80 in several studies, far better than most reliability ratings in medicine. Further, test-retest reliabilities have been found to average .79 for intelligence testing of adults age 18-24; .85 the Rorschach, .82 for the Wechsler Adult Intelligence Scale, and .74 for the Minnesota Multiphasic Personality Inventory. Validity coefficients for the Rorschach also compare favorably with other psychological tests, he indicated.[105.29]

Dr. Garb began by indicating that clinicians should not draw any conclusions about the presence or absence of sexual abuse from the Rorschach. He also questioned the validity of several of the Comprehensive System scales, noted Exner's error in double-counting 221 Rorschach protocols among the 700 protocols in the normative study, and criticized Exner for refusing to give independent evaluators access to his raw data. He emphasized the tendency of the Comprehensive System interpretation guidelines to overpathologize, the CS often being the only data source that indicates psychopathology, even when numerous other sources clearly indicate that there is none.[105.30]

Dr. Widiger indicated that projective techniques *do* have validity, reliability, and usefulness *when used appropriately and conservatively.* Most problems associated with prominent psychological tests are problems related to the competence of test users rather than problems with the tests. He emphasized that the Rorschach is very good at generating hypotheses, which may then be validated or invalidated by other data. It is not unusual

---

105.28 *Id.* at 461.

105.29 Meyer, Gregory J., *Overview of Evidence on the Rorschach and TAT.* Paper presented at the 110th Annual Convention of the American Psychological Association, Chicago, Aug. 25, 2002.

105.30 Garb, Howard N., *Validity of Projective Techniques and Self-Report Tests.* Paper presented at the 110th Annual Convention of the American Psychological Association, Chicago, Aug. 25, 2002.

for the Rorschach to identify significant issues that are not identified by other tests or lengthy interviews, he indicated.[105.31]

Psychologists Jeffrey M. Lohr, Katherine A. Fowler, and Scott O. Lilienfeld wrote, in a 2002 article, about what they call "pseudoscience," which they characterized as involving use of various means of shielding hypotheses from falsification; rigidity in the face of negative findings; use of language that sounds scientific but is not; relying on anecdotes rather than on systematic scientific methodology; trying to place the burden of proof on critics, rather than providing evidence that a methodology is valid and reliable; and use of alleged experts rather than systematic data to "prove" their case. They note that "clinical techniques, per se (e.g., the Rorschach Inkblot Test) are not pseudoscientific. Instead, the concept of pseudoscience applies to the ways in which certain proponents of these techniques deal with evidence, particularly evidence that contradicts their hypotheses."[105.32] They indicate that,

> with the primary exception of indices relevant to detecting thought disorder, the indices derived from the Rorschach CS have been found to exhibit low or negligible construct validity. For example, although the Rorschach CS possesses some validity for detecting schizophrenia and related conditions, its validity for detecting depression, posttraumatic stress disorder, psychopathy, and other psychiatric conditions appears to be weak. Nor is there compelling evidence that the CS is helpful for the detection of child sexual abuse, even though it is used frequently for this purpose.[105.33]

The authors end with a recommendation that "The APA and other professional organizations must be willing to impose stiff sanctions, including expulsion if necessary, on practitioners who routinely use therapeutic and assessment practices that are devoid of scientific support."[105.34]

In response, psychologists Irving B. Weiner, Charles D. Spielberger, and Norman Abeles indicate that "the psychometric soundness of an assessment instrument is defined by standardized procedures, intercoder agree-

---

[105.31] Widiger, Thomas A., *Training Implications of Empirically Supported Assessments*. Paper presented at the 110th Annual Convention of the American Psychological Association, Chicago, Aug. 25, 2002.

[105.32] Jeffrey M. Lohr, Katherine A. Fowler, & Scott O. Lilienfeld, "The Dissemination and Promotion of Pseudoscience in Clinical Psychology: The Challenge to Legitimate Clinical Science," 55(3) *The Clinical Psychologist* 4–10 (2002) at 5.

[105.33] *Id.*

[105.34] *Id.* at 8.

ment, reliability, normative data, and validity."[105.35] They proceed to indicate that "meta-analytic reviews and studies with patient and nonpatient samples have identified mean Kappa coefficients [degree of agreement among multiple raters] across various Comprehensive System coding categories, ranging from .79 to .88, which is in the excellent range for Kappa." In addition, researchers have "found median and mean interrater coefficients of .92 and .90, respectively, for 164 structural summary variables in two independent ratings of 219 protocols containing 4,761 responses. . . . Without doubt, then, the RIM [Rorschach Inkblot Method] can be reliably coded using the Comprehensive System."[105.36] Next, they indicate that "almost all of the variables coded in the Comprehensive System and conceptualized as relating to trait characteristics show substantial short-term and long-term stability, with retest correlations in excess of .75."[105.37] They further note that the claim of critics that the CS overpathologizes is largely based on poor-quality research. The current restandardization project, they indicate, yields data that "closely resemble the earlier reference data and dispel any concerns about overpathologizing."[105.38] With regard to validity, the authors indicate that meta-analytic studies have produced unweighted mean validity coefficients similar to those for MMPI variables. Finally, while Lohr *et al.* criticized the CS for failing to provide specific diagnoses, the authors indicate that the Rorschach is not meant to be a diagnostic test; it addresses personality processes. It does well at addressing thought disorders, which could lead to a diagnosis of a psychosis. It does well at addressing mood dysfunctions, which could lead to a diagnosis of depression. Thus, they indicate, the Rorschach, and the Comprehensive System, do well at identifying processes that contribute to diagnoses, but neither is meant to lead, per se, to a specific diagnosis, without data from other sources.

Psychologist Stephen Hibbard criticized a paper by Lilienfeld, Wood, and Garb,[105.39] referenced at the beginning of this section, as making statements that are too broad considering the relatively narrow bases they have for those statements, and for ignoring the fact that at least some of the Comprehensive System (CS) norms that Lilienfeld et al. indicate "overpathologize" may, in fact, reflect accurately on the general level of psychopathology in the normative sample. Hibbard concurs with Lilienfeld *et*

[105.35] Irving B. Weiner, Charles D. Spielberger, & Norman Abeles, "Scientific Psychology and the Rorschach Inkblot Method," 55(4) *The Clinical Psychologist* 7–12 (2002) at 7.

[105.36] *Id.*

[105.37] *Id.* at 8.

[105.38] *Id.*

[105.39] Scott O. Lilienfeld, James M. Wood, & Howard N. Garb, "The Scientific Status of Projective Techniques," 1 *Psychological Science in the Public Interest* 27–66 (2000).

al. that the CS should be used with caution—or not used—with non-Caucasian populations, because there is minimal normative data for these groups. He is critical of Lilienfeld *et al.*'s claim that other researchers get lower test-retest coefficients for many scales than those reported by Exner. Three of the four studies cited by Lilienfeld *et al.* appear in refereed journals. None of those three studies actually provides test-retest data, Hibbard indicates. He does not comment on the fourth study.[105.40]

Psychologist Cato Gronnerod did a literature search for all journal articles, books, and dissertations that reported test-retest data from the Rorschach in English, Norwegian, Swedish, or Danish. He found 158 studies, with 23 studies providing 36 samples usable in meta-analyses. The average test-retest interval was just over three years. Eleven studies provided data on the Comprehensive System. Gronnerod found that "[t]he CS was consistently associated with higher temporal stability levels than other systems. Furthermore, the CS variable reliability coefficients were generally more consistent across samples than variables from other systems."[105.41]

The authors of the present text continue to believe that the Rorschach Inkblot Test has much to offer in child custody and other forensic evaluations. In our experience it has often yielded hypotheses about an individual that led to areas of inquiry that might have been missed without the input from this test. Test-taking attitude is also a valuable clinical component.

As indicated by most of the authors above, the Rorschach, like any single instrument, should not be used in isolation. There is strong evidence for its validity and reliability, and it can be a critical part of a complete evaluation. Its primary purpose should be to generate hypotheses regarding the individual taking the test, so that other sources of information (other tests, parent/child interviews, collateral interviews, historical information, and so forth) may be used to confirm or deny the hypotheses formed.

Given the difficulty with accurate scoring of the Comprehensive System, as documented above, we recommend that all Rorschach protocols scored with the Comprehensive System be scored twice: once by the evaluator, and once by either a local expert on the scoring of the test or, preferably, by the computer program designed for that purpose: the Rorschach Interpretation Assistance Program: Version 4-plus:S (RIAP4-plus:S). The available evidence indicates that the computer program is more accurate than the vast majority of clinicians at scoring the test.

[105.40] Stephen Hibbard, "A Critique of Lilienfeld *et al.'s* 'The Scientific Status of Projective Techniques,'" 80 *Journal of Personal Assessment* 260–71 (2003).

[105.41] Cato Gronnerod, "Temporal Stability in the Rorschach Method: A Meta-Analytic Review," 80 *Journal of Personality Assessment* 272–93 (2003) at 287.

While the Rorschach remains a valuable tool, the evidence that there are significant problems with interpretations based on the Comprehensive System is compelling, and psychologists should avoid making strong statements, including predictions, predicated on CS-based interpretive criteria until the research has established new guidelines. We recommend that psychologists use the CS interpretive guidelines with extreme caution or not at all, recognizing that there is now a substantial body of research indicating that those interpretations are likely to exaggerate the level of psychopathology actually present. If the conclusions based on the CS guidelines are the *only* source of evidence of psychopathology, even after careful investigation utilizing other tests, interviews, and reviews of historical information, the CS results should generally be given less weight or ignored.

CHAPTER 12

PHYSICAL ABUSE, DOMESTIC VIOLENCE, AND EMOTIONAL ABUSE

§ 12.7 Some Facts about Domestic Violence

Page 589, add at the end of § 12.7:

Herrenkohl, Egolf and Herrenkohl (1997) followed preschool children who had been maltreated in a 16-year longitudinal study. They found that "severity of physical discipline, negative quality of the mother's interaction with the child, and the experience of sexual abuse were related to adolescent assaultive behavior." (p. 422) Abusers tend to live in urban areas characterized by high rates of social problems and high unemployment (Healy and Smith, 1998). As a group, abusers have high rates of histories of juvenile aggression, criminal behavior, mental illness, and substance abuse. (Keilitz, Hannaford & Efkman, 1998; Klein, 1998; Simon, 1995).

Psychological Effect of Physical Abuse

Emotional Problems

- Higher levels of internalizing symptoms have been found among abused preschoolers (Fantuzzo, DelGaudio, Atkins, Meyers & Noone, 1998) and adolescents.
- 36 percent of maltreated children and youth met the criteria for a PTSD diagnosis. (Pelcovitz et al., 1994).
- 33 percent of those with PTSD were later found to have retained the diagnosis in a two-year follow-up. (Famulario, Fenton, Augustyn & Zukerman, 1996).
- A history of child maltreatment is associated with a diagnosis of Borderline Personality Disorder, ADHD, and Oppositional Defiant Disorder. (Famulario, Kinschereff & Fenton, 1991).

Interpersonal Relationships

- Maltreatment is associated with having an insecure disorganized/disoriented attachment. (Barnett, Ganiban & Cicchetti, 1999).

- Abused children displayed less overall intimacy, were more conflicted, and demonstrated more negative affect. (Parker & Herrera, 1996).
- Social withdrawal, academic underachievement, psychopathology (including depression), conduct disorder, attention deficit hyperactive disorder, oppositional defiant disorder, post-traumatic stress disorder, insecure and atypical attachment patterns, impaired relationships involving increased aggression. (Ciccherri & Toth, 1995).

Health

- Retrospective cross/sectional studies document heightened health problems, including poor current health status, are associated with being victims of physical abuse. (Lesserman, Li, Drossman, Toomey, Nachman & Glogau, 1997).
- There are increased hospital admissions and surgical procedures in adulthood of individuals who have been abused as children. (Salman & Calderbank, 1996).
- There is an increase in the reporting of chronic pain in victims of physical abuse. (Goldberg, Pachas & Keith, 1999).

§ 12.8 Myths about Domestic Violence

Page 590, add at the end of § 12.8:

When recognizing the adverse affects associated with abuse-related issues, it becomes the mental health professional's moral and ethical obligation to provide appropriate treatment interventions. Most of the treatment approaches currently in use have been developed as a result of necessity, or trial by fire. Carlson (1996) recommended 10 elements that should be included in treatment programs for children of battered women. They include: (1) individual assessments; (2) individual counseling; (3) referrals; (4) advocacy; (5) group work for children; (6) regular, structured recreational activities for children; (7) aftercare and follow-up services; (8) prevention services; (9) parenting education and support groups for mothers; (10) evaluation of all aspects of the program. In a survey, Carlson found that, on average, shelters for battered women provide 3.8 of these 10 components to their intervention programs. It is recognized by almost all researchers in the area that multi-faceted approaches are necessary. These approaches need to include both individual and group work with children, therapy with the mother, therapy with the father, and recognition of developmentally appropriate interventions. Therapy needs to involve modeling and social learning, resolution of stress and trauma-related symptoms, and psychoeducational training (Rossman, Hughes & Rosenberg, 2000).

Treatment is one important intervention in dealing with domestic violence-related circumstances. However, prevention activities may be more important in that preventing abuse from occurring results in a lower need for intervention programs. Unfortunately, both the intervention and prevention programs require sufficient financial resources. Since more socioeconomically depressed families are abusers, they are less likely to have the resources available to take advantage of these services. (Wolf & Jaffe, 1999) report that home visitor programs have been effective in not only promoting healthy child development but in reducing abusive behavior within the home for infants and preschool children. School age children can be reached more easily by including education about domestic violence issues within the social studies or social science curricula. An effective curriculum will include "defining violence and its impact; developing safety plans; learning to express feelings and opinions based on values of equality, respect, and sharing of power; learning non-violent conflict resolution; and gaining a sense of worth regardless of family difficulties" (Rossman, Hughes & Rosenberg, 2000, p. 130). When working with teens, Wolf & Jaffe report that emphasis needs to be on healthy relationships and alternatives to violence and abuse. These approaches are particularly helpful to teens who have grown up in families where family violence has occurred. Prevention at this age level focuses on dating and partner relationship building.

Case Study

Rhonda came to a psychologist at 56 years of age to help decide whether she should stay in a 25-year marriage or leave her husband. During the initial session, she reported that during the 25-year history of the marriage she had suffered from domestic violence at the hands of her husband.

During the first several sessions, Rhonda disclosed that she was the passive member of a twin set in which her twin sister would "beat her up" on a regular basis without parental intervention. Furthermore, she witnessed her father be verbally abusive to her mother on a regular basis and infrequently physically abusive.

When Rhonda married Larry it wasn't long after the wedding date that Larry started to engage in domestic violence towards Rhonda. She was often in "dammed if you do, dammed if you don't" situations. For example, her upper management executive husband came home from work one day and beat her black and blue. He instructed her not to leave the house until the bruises healed. The next day Larry came home, opened the refrigerator, and did not find his favorite beer in the refrigerator. He beat his wife for not going out and buying his beer for him even though he had instructed her not to go out until the bruises healed.

During the later years of the marriage, Rhonda became abusive of alcohol as a means of attempting to deal with the domestic violence. There was some question as to whether the alcohol abuse reached the level of alcoholism or not, but nonetheless it interfered with her activities. Rhonda became so secluded that she would not travel more than a mile from her home and purchased most goods over the phone for delivery. She even purchased furniture for the house based on what she saw in ads in the local newspaper.

After two years of therapy, Rhonda decided to leave the marriage. She filed for divorce and her husband continued a virtual non-stop barrage of verbal insults. She had to call the police on several occasions, because he physically forced his way into the home even though the doors and windows were locked and he had been ordered not to do so. During rages, Larry threatened to kill Rhonda's attorney, Rhonda's psychologist and his own boss.

On one occasion Rhonda's two adult sons came to the psychologist's office demanding to know what was occurring between the psychologist and Rhonda in therapy. The psychologist informed Rhonda's sons that information could not be disclosed without a signed release and invited them to leave. At one point the oldest son pushed the psychologist in the chest demanding answers to his questions. The police had to be called but no arrests were made since the son was from another state and the police were not about to attempt to extradite him for a minor misdemeanor violation.

After the divorce, Larry remarried a woman 20 years his junior who left the marriage in less than two years because he became physically violent towards her and she did not want to expose her children to said violence. At that point, three years after his divorce from Rhonda, Larry showed up at Rhonda's front door with a laundry basket full of dirty laundry. He rang the doorbell, she opened the door and he demanded, "do my laundry." She responded by saying "ok." He then stated, "while you're doing my laundry, make me some lunch," and she responded with "ok." Even though Rhonda spent two years deciding to divorce, and another three years since the divorce, she was not able to overcome the role of victim when he requested that she do his laundry. Within another two years, Rhonda died of complications of alcohol and Larry died of cancer.

§ 12.11 The Psychologically Maltreated Child

Page 593, add at the end of § 12.11:

Effects of Psychological Maltreatment

There are a number of psychological effects that are associated with being psychologically maltreated. They include emotional instability, impulse control problems, Borderline or Narcissistic Personality Disorder, unresponsiveness, substance abuse, anxiety, depression, low self-esteem, suicidal ideation, and/or eating disorders. (Braver, Bumberry, Green & Rawson, 1992; Crittenden, Claussen & Sugarman, 1994; Engels & Moisan, 1994; Mullen, Martin, Anderson, Romans & Herbison, 1996; Rorty, Yager & Rossotto, 1994; Gross & Keller, 1992; Briere & Runtz, 1990).

- The greater the amount of verbal aggression by parents, the more likely that the child would be physically aggressive, delinquent or experience interpersonal problems. (Vissing, Straus, Gellis & Harrop, 1991).
- Verbal aggression by parents was more strongly related to negative child outcomes than physical aggression unaccompanied by verbal aggression. (Vissing, et al., 1991).
- Psychological abuse was a stronger predictor than physical abuse for both depression and low self-esteem. (Vissing et al., 1991).
- Social competency problems and anti-social functioning may result from psychological maltreatment, in addition to self-isolating behavior, low empathy, sexual maladjustment and delinquency/criminality. (Herrenkohl et al., 1983, 1997; Hughes & Graham-Bermann, 1998; Briere & Runtz, 1990; Egeland & Erickson, 1987).
- There is a relationship between psychological maltreatment and physical health problems as related to an increase in somatic complaints. (Hughes, 1992; Krugman & Krugman, 1994).

Domestic Violence

- According to the American Medical Association, 25 percent of the women in the United States, or 12 million women, will be abused by a current or former partner during their lives.
- The incidence of domestic violence is estimated at four million cases annually, or one assault every 15 seconds.
- Women in the United States are more likely to be victimized by a current or former male partner than by all other assailants combined.

Over 50 percent of all women murdered are killed by male partners, and 12 percent of murdered men are killed by female partners.

- Over half of the defendants accused of murdering their spouses had been drinking alcohol at the time of the offense. Non-family murder defendants were even more likely to have been drinking. Also, almost half of the victims of spousal murder had been drinking alcohol at the time of the offense—about the same proportion as for the victims of non-family murder.
- Conditions associated with domestic violence include miscarriages, drug and alcohol abuse, attempted suicide and other forms of mental illness, low birth weight babies, pain, injuries, and permanent physical impairment.
- Forty-seven percent of men who beat their wives do so three or more times a year. Battering may start or become worse during pregnancy; more than 23 percent of pregnant women are abused during pregnancy.
- Twenty-one percent of all women who use hospital emergency and surgical services are battered.
- One in four married couples experience one or more incidents of domestic violence, and repeated severe episodes occur in one marriage out of every four. (Sattler, 1998, p. 698).

Effects of Domestic Violence on the Victim and Children

- Between 30 and 60 percent of children living in domestic violence homes are abused. (Eddelson, 1997).
- 30 to 60 percent of families where children are victims of abuse, mothers are also battered. (Eddelson, 1997).
- School age children demonstrate high rates of internalizing and externalizing behavior problems, low self-esteem and more difficulty in school than children raised in non-violent families. (Hughes & Graham-Berman, 1998).
- Children raised in violent homes demonstrate problems in interpersonal relationships, including fear and worry about those in the home and difficulty establishing and maintaining friendships with individuals outside the home. (Graham-Berman, 1996).
- Boys from violent families often exhibit abusive tactics in their teenage and young adult relationships. (Jouriles & Norwood, 1995).
  - Battering is the leading cause of injury in American women. (Jones, 1994).
  - Spousal abuse contributed to one fourth of all suicide attempts by women. (Jones, 1994).

- 50 percent of homeless women and children in the United States are fleeing from male violence. (Jones, 1994).

Walker (2000) reports that research suggests that there are several types of batterers including "the power and control" batterer who uses violence to get his partner to do what he wants; the mentally ill batterer who has a distorted "sense of power"; and the "anti-social personality disorder" batterer who has psychopathic tendencies. She reports:

- 15 percent of the batterers were reported as unemployed during the battering relationship.
- The violence escalated in frequency and severity over time.
- Battered women held attitudes towards women's roles that were more liberal than most of the population.
- Battering was present in two-thirds of the battered women's childhood homes, four-fifths of the batterer's homes, and one-quarter of the non-batterer's homes.
- One-half of the battered women reported being sexually molested or abused as children.
- There was high rate of arrest and conviction for batterers for offenses other than family violence.
- Women were more likely to be married to their batterers.
- Women were at high risk to be battered during pregnancy.
- Sex was used as a power weapon to dominate the women in the same manner they used physical violence.
- The batterer's unreasonable jealousy was almost always reported by the women.
- Battered women believe that their batterer would kill them.
- Children in battering-relationship homes were at high risk for physical child abuse and almost all were psychologically abused by living in the violent atmosphere.
- Battered women report experiencing more anger when living with a batterer than with a non-batterer.
- Eight times as many women report using physical discipline on their children when with their batterers than when living alone or in a non-battering relationship.
- Battered women are more socially and financially isolated when living with a batterer.
- Violence escalates over time. Use of weapons during battering incidents increases over time.

- The probability that women will seek help increases over time.
- There is more alcohol abuse reported than other drug abuse in battering relationships.
- The trend was that batterers who abuse alcohol were from lower socioeconomic status homes.
- Battered women reported themselves as high on depression indices. (pp. 215-218)

Children Who Witness Violence

- Preschool children exposed to parental violence had many more behavior problems, exhibited significantly more negative affect, responded less appropriately to situations, were more aggressive with peers, and had more ambivalent relationships with their caregivers than those from nonviolent families. (Graham-Bermann & Levendosky, 1998, p. 281).
- Children, especially boys who witness mothers being abused, have an elevated rate of emotional, developmental, and behavioral problems. (Fantuzzo & Mohr, 1999).
- The percentage of youth who report that they acted violently increases as the number of different types of violence in their family increases. (Thornberry, 1994).

Rosman, Hughes & Rosenberg (2000) did a meta-analysis of 28 age and gender studies. The samples were largely drawn from the community or shelters and dealt with children from three years of age through adolescence. They concluded, "in sum, both boys and girls show behavioral disruption associated with exposure. This appears to be more evident for boys during school age and, perhaps, for girls following school age." (p. 44). They found that gender issues and the affect of abuse were related to "the development of emotional security; being the recipient of personal abuse; children's reactions to battered and depressed mothers and attitudes toward woman more generally; selection of coping strategy; and children's perceptions of internal conflict." (p. 44).

Impact of Family Violence on Children

When children who are exposed to parental violence are compared with those who are not exposed, the following characteristics are found:

1. greater internalizing (i.e., depression, anxiety, or social withdrawal) behavior problems;

2. greater externalizing (e.g., hyperactivity, aggression) behavior problems;
3. more aggressive social problem solving strategies;
4. lower social competence;
5. lower self-esteem;
6. lower school performance and school achievement;
7. poorer informational intake capacities, lower levels of curiosity, and distortion of neutral information;
8. poorer performance on intelligence tests;
9. greater PTSD symtomatology;
10. more frequent attributions of self-blame and guilt for the domestic violence;
11. less secure attachments with caregivers;
12. lower sense of personal control.

(Rossman, Hughes & Rosenberg, 2000, pp. 67-68)

Cultural Diversity

Domestic violence is an area that has been researched not only with regards to the general population, but also with reference to specific ethnic groups. Similarities and differences occur within ethnic groupings.

African American Families

African American families represent the group for which the greatest amount of research has been performed. African American families frequently use physical punishment. (M.K. Ho, 1992). Although acceptable within the African American culture, these physical discipline methods can elevate to the level of domestic violence or physical abuse. Hampton & Gelles (1994) found that 17 percent of wives in African American families reported at least one violent incident within the past 10 years, and 7 percent had experienced severe violence. They were 1.23 times more likely to experience minor violence and 2.36 times more likely to experience severe violence than Caucasian wives. Even when controlling for demographic variables, African American females were most likely to report being victims and perpetrators of spousal abuse. (Neff, Holamon & Schluter, 1995). Sorenson, Upchurch & Shen (1996) found that being younger, less educated, a low-income earner and African American were risk factors for being more violent towards a spouse.

Latino Families

Culturally, the Latino families tend to place a strong emphasis on extended family. In addition, there is an emphasis on the respect for authority, with the father being superior and the head of the family. Kantor, Jasinski & Aldarondo (1994) found that as a group Latino families have similar rates of domestic violence as Anglo families. There is, however, considerable variation within different Hispanic ethnic groups. For example about 20.4 percent of Puerto Rican wives reported husband-to-wife violence, as do 10.5 percent of Mexican wives, 17.9 percent Mexican American wives, 2.5 percent of Cuban wives and 9.9 percent of Anglo wives in their survey. (Rossman, Hughes & Rosenberg, 2000, p. 94).

Asian Families

Asian families highly value the family and perceive any negative actions of a family member as reflecting negatively on the family as a whole. Self-control, humility, and inconspicuousness (Rossman, Hughes & Rosenberg, 2000) are values of Asian families. The expectation would be that, based on the emphasis on having a harmonious family, that physical and verbal abuse would be discouraged. However, C.K. Ho (1996) suggests that these activities occur in the privacy of the Asian families' homes with an emphasis on hiding such problems. Reported rates of family violence in Asian American families is low. However, it cannot be determined if the reported rates are low because of actual low frequencies or the emphasis on hiding such problems. It is reported that the Chinese culture perpetuates exploitation of women. (Lee & Au, 1998; Tang, 1997; C.K. Ho, 1996). Twenty to 30 percent of Chinese husbands hit their wives, with at least 60 percent of Japanese women reporting some type of physical abuse. (Yoshihama & Sorenson, 1994). Yoshihama concluded that domestic violence perpetrated by Japanese men against their partners was not only condoned, but was not viewed as a social problem.

Native American Families

While other cultures' identities are tied to their extended families, Native Americans identities are also tied to their tribe. Chester, Robin, Koss, Lopez & Goldman (1994) estimated between 50 and 55 percent of women were physically abused by their partners. They also reported that estimates were as high as 80 percent in urban areas. Native Americans in an urban Indian Health Center reported approximately 56 percent of their parents engaged in violence towards each other. (Norton & Mansen, 1995).

§ 12.14 Advisory Opinion and Case Digest

*Page 597, insert above **Rhode Island:***

Missouri

Dickerson v. Dickerson, 55 S.W.3d 867 (Mo. App. W.D., September 25, 2001). Brent Dickerson filed for divorce from his wife, Tamera. The wife alleged that the husband had physically abused her and physically and sexually abused the children. The court appointed a guardian ad litem (GAL) for the children. Each parent sought sole custody. Testimony by the wife and a number of other witnesses established the husband's history of physical and sexual abuse. The guardian ad litem, the husband, and the wife presented testimony from three psychologists who did custody evaluations, each of whom recommended joint custody, with the wife having primary residential custody and the husband initially having supervised visitation. At the close of twelve days of testimony, the court invited the guardian ad litem to make a final recommendation. Rather than limiting her remarks to that recommendation, the GAL gave unsworn testimony that included a statement that two of the three psychologists had changed their minds and now agreed with the GAL's recommendation that the husband should have primary physical custody of the children. The judge refused to permit the GAL to be cross-examined, indicating that she was an officer of the court. The trial court granted sole legal and physical custody to the husband. The wife appealed.

The appellate court held that (1) the trial court failed to make specific findings of fact regarding allegations of domestic violence, as required by Missouri statute, and (2) the trial court failed to make necessary written findings of fact and conclusions of law to justify awarding custody to the abusive parent and how that would serve the child's best interest. The court further ruled that the trial court committed error when it allowed the GAL to give unsworn testimony and recommendations based on hearsay medical opinions that were not admissible. The trial court could not accept those statements without applying the required procedural and evidentiary rules regarding competency and reliability, and admitting them was prejudicial error. The case was remanded for a new trial on the custody issue and related matters.

CHAPTER 13

SEXUAL ABUSE

§ 13.9 Psychological Effects of Sexual Abuse

Page 622, insert at the end of § 13.9:

Current research demonstrates that pedophiles rarely have diagnoses of psychotic disorders, but often have mood disorder diagnoses. (Raymond, Coleman, Ohlerking, Christenson & Minar, 1998). Child molesters who prefer boys or younger children are generally of lower intellectual functioning. (Blanchard et al., 1999). Alcohol abuse during the offense or in general is reported to appear frequently among child molesters. (Allnutt, Bradford, Greenburg & Currey, 1996). Marshall (1997) states that offenders rarely accept full responsibility for their offenses. They demonstrate deficits in empathy in general, and empathy towards their victims, (Marshall, Hudson, Jones & Fernandez, 1995), lack self-esteem (Marshall, Anderson & Champagne, 1996), lack intimacy and experience loneliness (Bumby & Hansen, 1997; Garlic, Marshall & Thornton, 1996), and have inadequate attachment styles (Ward, Hudson & Marshall 1996).

The Sexual Abuse Experience

- Multiple abuse episodes are very common, occurring in up to half of the cases in non-clinical samples. (Saunders et al., 1999)
- The mean age for the abuse victim is nine years old.
- Unlike other forms of child abuse, sexual abuse does not appear to be related to socioeconomic status.

Additional Research on the Effects of Sexual Abuse

- Histories of physical, and especially sexual, abuse are associated with severe psychological disturbances, Borderline Personality disorder in particular. (Polusny & Follette, 1995; Weston, Ludolph, Misile, Ruffins, & Block, 1990).
- Abused children have more depressive and anxiety symptoms and lower self-esteem than non-abused children. (Boney-McCoy & Finklehor, 1995).

SEXUAL ABUSE

- Sexually abused children report higher levels of PTSD symptomotology. (Boney-McCoy & Finklehor, 1995; Briere, 1996). More than half the children reached the diagnostic criteria for PTSD. (Dubner & Motta, 1999; Kilpatrick & Saunders, 1999).
- Sexually abused adolescents report more problems with their teachers. (Boney-McCoy & Finklehor, 1995).
- Sexually abused children are less socially competent. (Mannarino & Cohen, 1996).
- Between 10-24 percent of child victims either do not improve or deteriorate. (Berliner & Saunders, 1996).
- There is also a significant literature on the psychological disabilities of adult survivors of childhood sexual abuse.
- There is a relationship between childhood sexual abuse and adult depression. (Leviatian, Parikh, Lesage, Hegadoren & Adams, 1998).
- There is a relationship between childhood sexual abuse and adult anxiety disorders. (Lombardo & Pohl, 1997).
- Adult survivors of childhood sexual abuse often have somatically related symptoms such as headaches, gastrointestinal problems, back and pelvic pain and muscle tension. (Maynes & Feinauer, 1994; Salmon & Calderbank, 1996). Problems with anger control, chronic irritability, unexpected feelings of rage, and fear of their own anger are found in this group. (Briere & Runtz, 1987; Lisak, 1993; Scott & Day, 1996).
- Feelings of anger are expressed either internally through self-blame and self-injury (Briere & Gil, 1998) or externally resulting in perpetration of violence towards others (Duncan & Williams, 1998).
- As much as 36 percent of adult survivors of childhood sexual abuse experience PTSD symptomotology. (Saunders et al., 1999).
- Highly traumatic events may lead to dissociative disorders. (Elliott & Breire, 1992; Chu & Dill, 1990).
- This group provides less satisfaction in their relationships, greater discomfort and sensitivity and more maladaptive interpersonal patterns (Bartoi & Kinder, 1998; Ti Liolo & Long, 1999; Elliott, 1994).
- External emotional responses manifest through a variety of activities including self-mutilatory, such as cutting, burning, or hitting oneself or pulling out hair (Breire & Gil, 1998; van der Kolk, Perry & Herman, 1991; Walsh & Rosen, 1988); binging and purging to deal with feelings of emptiness (Piran, Learner, Garfinkel, Kennedy & Brouillette, 1998; Steiger & Zanko, 1990); and alcohol or other drug abuse (Breire et al., 1997).

§ 13.42 Case Digest

Page 673, insert as the first case under ***Federal:***

Mindombe v. United States, 795 A.2d 39 (D.C. Ct. App. 2002). The Court of Appeals for the District of Columbia ruled that the testimony of a clinical psychologist about the behavior of children who have been sexually abused was properly admitted with limitations that prevented the psychologist from stating conclusions regarding whether the victim was honest or the defendant was guilty.

The prosecution presented testimony by a clinical psychologist to provide the jury with a profile of the range of behaviors exhibited by victims of child sexual abuse. The victim was six or seven at the time of the abuse and eight at the time she testified. The psychologist testified that child victims do not always report abuse promptly, that children react with a range of responses that can include no visible reaction, and that children that age may not remember events in sequential order.

This expert testimony was appropriately admitted because significant evidence at trial is likely to be inconsistent with the expectations of a lay juror regarding how a victim of child sexual abuse should react to such abuse. Without such expert testimony, the jury may conclude from the secrecy, inconsistency, or recantation of the child that the testimony has been fabricated. Without the expert's testimony, the jury may not be able to judge the credibility of the victim.

Finally, the court indicated that experts are not permitted to make ultimate conclusions regarding the truthfulness of witnesses, whether a person was in fact abused, or whether the defendant is guilty. Those conclusions belong to the factfinder. 26 Mental and Physical Disability Law Reporter 614-615 (2002).

Page 678, insert above ***Texas:***

Oklahoma

Paulson v. Sternlof, 15 P.3d 981, 2000 WL 1810920 (Okla. Ct. App. Dec. 12, 2000). The Oklahoma appeals court ruled that a parent could not sue a psychologist for conducting an allegedly negligent evaluation of his child, because no doctor-patient relationship existed between the psychologist and the father.

A father won custody of his son in Virginia in 1991, based on the trial court finding that the mother had made continual and unsupported allegations of abuse of the child by the father. In 1993, the mother moved to Oklahoma with her son, but without consent of the father or a court. The mother's attorney got a recommendation of a psychologist, Dr. Sternlof, to evaluate the boy and then to testify at a custody hearing that the boy may have been sexually abused. The trial court granted summary judgment to the defendant.

The court of appeals affirmed. In this matter of first impression, the court adopted *Bird v. W.C.W.*, 868 S.W.2d 767 (Tex. Sup. Ct. 1994) (see p. 678 of *Psychological Experts in Divorce Actions*), which held that a psychologist has no professional duty to a third party for failing to properly diagnose the condition of a child, based on the lack of a physician-patient relationship.

South Dakota

State v. Edelman, 593 N.W.2d 419 (S.D. 1999). A father convicted of child sexual abuse of his stepdaughter argued that the trial court erred in admitting a psychologist's testimony regarding behavioral characteristics of sexually abused children and about the Child Sexual Abuse Accommodation Syndrome (CSAAS), on the basis that such testimony did not meet the *Daubert* standard. The Supreme Court unanimously ruled that other courts have accepted such testimony under the *Daubert* standard. In addition, the psychologist made the points that care must be taken not to overinterpret, and that behavior typical of the CSAAS did not prove that sexual abuse had occurred. The psychologist also did not directly compare the child's behavior with the CSAAS. Fairness was ensured, the court indicated, by virtue of the adversarial nature of the proceedings and the opportunity to demonstrate problems with expert testimony on cross-examination.

CHAPTER 14

SPECIAL CONCERNS: MENTAL DISORDERS

§ 14.6 Effect of Major Parental Mental Disorders on Children

Page 695, insert after last paragraph:

In one of the few longitudinal studies of children of schizophrenic mothers ever done, 50 children of schizophrenic mothers were studied over a period of 25 years. Half of the children were raised by their mothers and half were raised by foster parents with no psychiatric history. The researchers found a slightly higher incidence of psychopathology in the children *not* raised by their own mothers, while children raised by their schizophrenic mothers evidence a slightly higher level of psychosocial functioning. Twelve of the children raised by their own mothers had no evident psychopathology, while only seven of the children who were adopted have no evident psychopathology. The greater prevalence of children with psychopathology in the non-mother-raised group may have been due to a greater genetic predisposition. Although this was a small study, it clearly demonstrated that being raised by a mother who is chronically mentally ill does not necessarily lead to psychopathology in the child.[37.1]

§ 14.16 Munchausen Syndrome by Proxy

Page 716, add at the end of § 14.16:

Munchausen Syndrome by Proxy has two components involving the child victim and the adult perpetrator. When referring to the child victim, the condition is sometimes referred to as "pediatric condition (illness, impairment, or symptom) falsification." This is a form of child abuse in which the adult falsifies physical and/or psychological signs and/or symptoms in a victim, causing the victim to be regarded as ill or impaired by others.

[37.1] Higgins, J., R. Gore, D. Gutkind, *Effects of Child-rearing by Schizophrenic Mothers: A 25-Year Follow-up*, 96 Acta Psychiatrica Scandinavica 402–404 (1997).

(APSAC Task Force, 2002, p. 106). Individuals who intentionally falsify history, science, or symptoms in a child to meet their own self-serving psychological needs are diagnosed with Factitious Disorder by Proxy. "Some individuals appear to need or thrive on attention or recognition that results from being perceived as being the devoted parent of a sick child. Other's appear to be motivated by the need to covertly control, manipulate or deceive authority figures or those perceived to be powerful." (pp. 106-107).

When one evaluates whether Munchausen Syndrome by Proxy, is present, several factors are considered. They include: evidence of induction of symptoms, evidence of feigning of symptoms, recurrent illness that appears unusual, lack of continuity of care or appropriate communication, and inconsistencies. Inconsistencies include reported symptoms that do not match objective findings; reported medical history that does not match previous medical records; diagnoses that do not match objective findings; behavior of parents does not match expressed distress or report of symptoms; other history reported is determined to be false; medical record names and numbers do not match. (Sanders & Bursch, 2002, pp. 115-116).

Although profiling a Munchausen Syndrome by Proxy abuser is not failsafe, there are a number of factors that help identify when this malady occurs. They include parents whose lives revolve around a child's illness and who do not appear to be relieved with normal test findings, and who promote invasive tests or procedures. They tend to be overly familiar with physicians or staff members, seem to enjoy the excitement of being in the spotlight, and have an interest or expertise in medicine. In addition, they are likely to predict deterioration or relapses, and the signs and symptoms of the child's illness are related to the presence of the suspected abuser. Furthermore, the father is rarely or briefly seen (*Id.* at 117).

Schrier & Libow conclude that "infants are damaged for life, if they survive. Enormous energies are required by child protective workers, the police, lawyers, and the courts. Doctors are often scarred and increasingly scarce medical resources are wasted." (*Id.* at 68).

§ 14.26 Case Digest

*Page 729, insert after **Alabama** case digest:*

Alaska

R.J.M. v. State of Alaska, Dep't of Health and Soc. Servs., 973 P.2d 79, 1999 WL 35765 (Alaska Sup. Ct., Jan 29, 1999). While Alaska Statute Section 47.10.010(a)(2)(F) regarding children in need of aid (CINA) refers only to physical abuse, the Alaska Supreme Court expanded CINA jurisdiction by indicating that the statute includes situations in which no one is "caring or willing to provide care" for a child. Because the mother refused to get treatment for her mental illness, and the mental illness was found to interfere with her ability to care for her child, the state supreme court found that the mother was unwilling to care for her son.

CHAPTER 17

CLASSIFICATION SYSTEMS

Page 812, insert after ***Social, Occupational, and Relational Functioning*** *subsection:*

§ 17.8A —DSM-IV-TR (New)

In 2000 the American Psychiatric Association published the *Diagnostic and Statistical Manual of Mental Disorders, Fourth Edition, Text Revision* (DSM-IV-TR). All of the revisions are in the text sections, the narrative portion of the manual that describes the disorders and offers comments on such things as the associated features and disorders, cultural and age factors, prevalence, course, and differential diagnosis. No changes have been made in the diagnostic criteria for any disorder. The intent of the revision is to correct factual errors and to add information not available at the time of the 1994 publication of DSM-IV. Since the diagnostic criteria are the part of DSM-IV essential to the forensic process, it is not necessary for an evaluator to have the "text revision" edition in order to be fully up to date.

Page 822, insert after last paragraph:

§ 17.12A —ICIDH-2 (New)

The World Health Organization has completed a final draft of a functionally-based classification system, the *International Classification of Functioning, Disability and Health* (World Health Organization, Geneva, Switzerland, 2001). It is a revision of the *International Classification of Impairments, Disabilities and Handicaps* (ICIDH), so its acronym is ICIDH-2, even though that is not consistent with the revised title. The document is available on the Internet at www.who.int/icidh.

While the International Classification of Diseases, Tenth Revision (ICD-10) focuses on health conditions, the ICIDH-2 focuses on functioning and disability that are associated with health conditions. Because the new document focuses on an individual's level of functioning, it is of potentially great benefit in identifying factors that go beyond medical diagnosis that cause an individual to have a less-than-optimal level of functioning. The ICIDH-2 has been field-tested in 40 countries, and 22 sites in the United States. It is designed to be used along with ICD-10, since the medical diagnosis tells little about the level of functioning of a given individual. It may also be used alone to describe the functional level of an individual.

The ICIDH-2 consists of two sections. The first, Functioning and Disability, consists of two components: classification of body systems and body structures, and descriptions of the range of functional abilities from both individual and societal perspectives. The second section, Contextual Factors, consists of the components of Environmental Factors and Personal Factors. The former addresses everything from the individual's most immediate environment to the most general social environment. The latter addresses the fact that individual, unique factors must be taken into consideration, but does not go into detail because of the huge number of possibilities this implies. Thus, the ICIDH-2 classifies situations, not people, and does so within the context of the environmental and personal factors that impact upon everyone.

Although the ICIDH-2 has been published, it is still in the process of formal adoption by the governing bodies of the World Health Organization. That process may take a number of months; however, the ICIDH-2 is already in use in the United States and elsewhere.

APPENDIX B

PROFESSIONAL ORGANIZATIONS

Corrections:

Academy of Family Mediators, corrected address: 5 Militia Drive, Lexington, MA 02421.

American Academy of Forensic Sciences has a new ZIP Code and telephone number: Colorado Springs, CO 80904-2798. Phone: 719-636-1100.

American Association for Marriage and Family Therapy (AAMFT) has a new address and telephone number: 112 S. Alfred Street, Alexandria, VA 22314-3061. Phone: 703-838-9808.

American Association of Sex Educators, Counselors and Therapists (AASECT) has a new address: P.O. Box 5488, Richmond, VA 23220-0488.

American Association of Suicidology is at the same address but is now in Suite 408.

American Board of Assessment Psychology, new address and phone: 1401 Brickell Avenue, Suite 320, Miami, FL 33131-3504. Phone: 305-372-0010.

American Board of Forensic Psychiatry, new address and phone: 3301 Dundak Avenue, Baltimore, MD 21222. Phone: 410-282-3376.

American Board of Medical Psychotherapists and Psychodiagnosticians, new address: Park Plaza Medical Building, 345 24th Avenue North, Suite 201, Nashville, TN 37203-1520.

American Board of Professional Psychology has a new area code: 573-875-1267.

American College of Forensic Psychology has a new telephone number: 949-673-7773.

American Medical Association has a new address and telephone number: 515 N. State Street, Chicago, IL 60610. Phone: 312-464-5000.

American Orthopsychiatric Association has a new address and telephone number: 2001 N. Beauregard, 12th Floor, Alexandria, VA 22311. Phone: 703-797-2584.

American Professional Society on the Abuse of Children has a new address and telephone number: P.O. Box 26901, CHO 3B3406, Oklahoma City, OK 73190. Phone: 405-271-8202.

American Psychiatric Association has a new address and telephone number: 1000 Wilson Boulevard, Suite 1825, Arlington, VA 22209-3901. Phone: 703-907-7300.

American Psychological Association has two new telephone numbers: 800-374-2721; 202-336-5510.

Association of State and Provincial Psychology Boards has a new address: P.O. Box 241245, Montgomery, AL 36124-1245.

Canadian Psychiatric Association has a new address: 260-441 MacLaren Street, Ottawa, ON, Canada K2P-2H3.

Canadian Psychological Association has added a second telephone number: 888-472-0657.

National Organization of Forensic Social Work, new address: 5784 E. Silo Ridge Drive, Ann Arbor, MI 48108. Phone: 734-944-2820.

Additions:

American Academy of Forensic Psychology: see American Board of Forensic Psychology.

American Academy of Forensic Psychiatry, c/o ABPP, 2100 E. Broadway, Suite 313, Columbia, MO 65201-6082. Phone: 314-875-1267.

American Association for Marriage and Family Therapy (AAMFT), 110 17th Street NW, Tenth Floor, Washington, D.C. 20036-4601. Phone 202-452-0109.

Association of Social Work Boards, 400 South Ridge Parkway, Suite B, Culpepper, VA 22701. Phone: 800-225-6880, 540-829-6880.

National Association of Counsel for Children (NACC): 1825 Marion Street, Suite 340, Denver, CO 80218, phone 1-888-828-NACC, e-mail *advocate@NACCchildlaw.org*

National Council of Juvenile and Family Court Judges: P.O. Box 8970 Reno, NV 89507, phone: (775) 784-6012, fax: (775) 784-6628, e-mail *admin@ncjfcj.unr.edu.*, web site *http://ncjfcj.unr.edu/*

Youth Law Center: 417 Montgomery Street, Suite 900, San Francisco, CA, 94104-1121, phone 415-543-3379, fax 415-956-9022, e-mail *info@youthlawcenter.com*

Youth Law Center: 1010 Vermont Avenue NW, Suite 310, Washington, D.C. 20005-4902, phone: 202-637-0377; fax 202-379-1600, e-mail *info@youthlawcenter.com*

APPENDIX B

Web sites:

Academy of Family Mediators: *www.mediators.org* (see also Association for Conflict Resolution: *www.acresolution.org*)

American Academy of Forensic Psychiatry: *www.quincy.ca/forpsych.htm*

American Academy of Forensic Psychology: *www.abfp.com*

American Academy of Forensic Sciences: *www.aafs.org*

American Academy of Psychiatry and the Law: *www.emory.edu/AAPL*

American Association of Sex Educators, Counselors, and Therapists: *www.aasect.org*

American Association of Suicidology: *www.suicidology.org*

American Association for Marriage and Family Therapy: *www.aamft.org*

American Board of Assessment Psychology: *www.assessmentpsychologyboard.org*

American Board of Professional Neuropsychology: *www.abpn.net*

American Board of Professional Psychology: *www.abpp.org*

American Board/College of Forensic Examiners: *www.acfe.com*

American Board of Forensic Psychiatry: *www.quincy.ca/forpsych.htm*

American Board of Forensic Psychology: *www.abfp.com*

American Board of Psychiatry and Neurology: *www.abpn.com*

American College of Forensic Psychiatry: *www.forensicpsychonline.com*

American College of Forensic Psychology: *www.forensicpsychology.org*

American Medical Association: *www.ama-assn.org*

American Orthopsychiatric Association: *www.amerortho.org*

American Professional Society on the Abuse of Children: *www.apsac.org*

American Psychiatric Association: *www.psych.org*

American Psychoanalytic Association: *www.apsa.org*

American Psychological Association: *www.apa.org*

  APA Divisions: *apa.org/about/division.html*

American Psychology-Law Society: *www.unl.edu/ap-ls*

Association of Social Work Boards: *www.aswb.org*

Association of State and Provincial Psychology Boards: *www.asppb.org*

Canadian Psychiatric Association: *www.cpa-apc.org*

Canadian Psychological Association: *www.cpa.ca*

Clinical Social Work Federation: *www.cswf.org*

National Association of Counsel for Children: *http://nacchildlaw.org/*

National Association of Social Workers: *www.naswdc.org*

National Council of Juvenile and Family Court Judges: *http://www.ncjfcj.org/*

National Organization of Forensic Social Work: *www.nofsw.org*

National Register of Health Service Providers in Psychology: *www.nationalregister.com*

Youth Law Center: *http://www.youthlawcenter.com/*

APPENDIX C

ETHICAL PRINCIPLES OF PSYCHOLOGISTS AND CODE OF CONDUCT

Page 832, replace current ***Ethical Principles of Psychologists and Code of Conduct*** *with the following:*

APPENDIXES

Ethical Principles of Psychologists and Code of Conduct

CONTENTS

Vol. 57, No. 12, 1060–1073 DOI: 10.1037//0003-066X.57.12.1060

APPENDIX C

INTRODUCTION AND APPLICABILITY

The American Psychological Association's (APA's) Ethical Principles of Psychologists and Code of Conduct (hereinafter referred to as the Ethics Code) consists of an Introduction, a Preamble, five General Principles (A–E), and specific Ethical Standards. The Introduction discusses the intent, organization, procedural considerations, and scope of application of the Ethics Code. The Preamble and General Principles are aspirational goals to guide psychologists toward the highest ideals of psychology. Although the Preamble and General Principles are not themselves enforceable rules, they should be considered by psychologists in arriving at an ethical course of action. The Ethical Standards set forth enforceable rules for conduct as psychologists. Most of the Ethical Standards are written broadly, in order to apply to psychologists in varied roles, although the application of an Ethical Standard may vary depending on the context. The Ethical Standards are not exhaustive. The fact that a given conduct is not specifically addressed by an Ethical Standard does not mean that it is necessarily either ethical or unethical.

This Ethics Code applies only to psychologists' activities that are part of their scientific, educational, or professional roles as psychologists. Areas covered include but are not limited to the clinical, counseling, and school practice of psychology; research; teaching; supervision of trainees; public service; policy development; social intervention; development of assessment instruments; conducting assessments; educational counseling; organizational consulting; forensic activities; program design and evaluation; and administration. This Ethics Code applies to these activities across a variety of contexts, such as in person, postal, telephone, Internet, and other electronic transmissions. These activities shall be distinguished from the purely private conduct of psychologists, which is not within the purview of the Ethics Code.

Membership in the APA commits members and student affiliates to comply with the standards of the APA Ethics Code and to the rules and procedures used to enforce them. Lack of awareness or misunderstanding of an Ethical Standard is not itself a defense to a charge of unethical conduct.

The procedures for filing, investigating, and resolving complaints of unethical conduct are described in the current Rules and Procedures of the APA Ethics Committee. APA may impose sanctions on its members for violations of the standards of the Ethics Code, including termination of APA membership, and may notify other bodies and individuals of its actions. Actions that violate the standards of the Ethics Code may also lead to the imposition of sanctions on psychologists or students whether or not they are APA members by bodies other than APA, including state psychological associations, other professional groups, psychology boards, other state or federal agencies, and payors for health services. In addition, APA may take action against a member after his or her conviction of a felony, expulsion or suspension from an affiliated state psychological association, or suspension or loss of licensure. When the sanction to be imposed by APA is less than expulsion, the 2001 Rules and Procedures do not guarantee an opportunity for an in-person hearing, but generally provide that complaints will be resolved only on the basis of a submitted record.

The Ethics Code is intended to provide guidance for psychologists and standards of professional conduct that can be applied by the APA and by other bodies that choose to adopt them. The Ethics Code is not intended to be a basis of civil liability. Whether a psychologist has violated the Ethics Code standards does not by itself determine whether the psychologist is legally liable in a court action, whether a contract is enforceable, or whether other legal consequences occur.

The modifiers used in some of the standards of this Ethics Code (e.g., *reasonably, appropriate, potentially*) are included in the standards when they would (1) allow professional judgment on the part of psychologists, (2) eliminate injustice or inequality that would occur without the modifier, (3) ensure applicability across the broad range of activities conducted by psychologists, or (4) guard against a set of rigid rules that might be quickly outdated. As used in this Ethics Code, the term *reasonable* means the prevailing professional judgment of psychologists engaged in similar activities in similar circumstances, given the knowledge the psychologist had or should have had at the time.

This version of the APA Ethics Code was adopted by the American Psychological Association's Council of Representatives during its meeting, August 21, 2002, and is effective beginning June 1, 2003. Inquiries concerning the substance or interpretation of the APA Ethics Code should be addressed to the Director, Office of Ethics, American Psychological Association, 750 First Street, NE, Washington, DC 20002-4242. The Ethics Code and information regarding the Code can be found on the APA Web site, http://www.apa.org/ethics. The standards in this Ethics Code will be used to adjudicate complaints brought concerning alleged conduct occurring on or after the effective date. Complaints regarding conduct occurring prior to the effective date will be adjudicated on the basis of the version of the Ethics Code that was in effect at the time the conduct occurred.

The APA has previously published its Ethics Code as follows:

American Psychological Association. (1953). *Ethical standards of psychologists*. Washington, DC: Author.

American Psychological Association. (1959). Ethical standards of psychologists. *American Psychologist, 14*, 279–282.

American Psychological Association. (1963). Ethical standards of psychologists. *American Psychologist, 18*, 56–60.

American Psychological Association. (1968). Ethical standards of psychologists. *American Psychologist, 23*, 357–361.

American Psychological Association. (1977, March). Ethical standards of psychologists. *APA Monitor*, 22–23.

American Psychological Association. (1979). *Ethical standards of psychologists*. Washington, DC: Author.

American Psychological Association. (1981). Ethical principles of psychologists. *American Psychologist, 36*, 633–638.

American Psychological Association. (1990). Ethical principles of psychologists (Amended June 2, 1989). *American Psychologist, 45*, 390–395.

American Psychological Association. (1992). Ethical principles of psychologists and code of conduct. *American Psychologist, 47*, 1597–1611.

Request copies of the APA's Ethical Principles of Psychologists and Code of Conduct from the APA Order Department, 750 First Street, NE, Washington, DC 20002-4242, or phone (202) 336-5510.

APPENDIXES

In the process of making decisions regarding their professional behavior, psychologists must consider this Ethics Code in addition to applicable laws and psychology board regulations. In applying the Ethics Code to their professional work, psychologists may consider other materials and guidelines that have been adopted or endorsed by scientific and professional psychological organizations and the dictates of their own conscience, as well as consult with others within the field. If this Ethics Code establishes a higher standard of conduct than is required by law, psychologists must meet the higher ethical standard. If psychologists' ethical responsibilities conflict with law, regulations, or other governing legal authority, psychologists make known their commitment to this Ethics Code and take steps to resolve the conflict in a responsible manner. If the conflict is unresolvable via such means, psychologists may adhere to the requirements of the law, regulations, or other governing authority in keeping with basic principles of human rights.

PREAMBLE

Psychologists are committed to increasing scientific and professional knowledge of behavior and people's understanding of themselves and others and to the use of such knowledge to improve the condition of individuals, organizations, and society. Psychologists respect and protect civil and human rights and the central importance of freedom of inquiry and expression in research, teaching, and publication. They strive to help the public in developing informed judgments and choices concerning human behavior. In doing so, they perform many roles, such as researcher, educator, diagnostician, therapist, supervisor, consultant, administrator, social interventionist, and expert witness. This Ethics Code provides a common set of principles and standards upon which psychologists build their professional and scientific work.

This Ethics Code is intended to provide specific standards to cover most situations encountered by psychologists. It has as its goals the welfare and protection of the individuals and groups with whom psychologists work and the education of members, students, and the public regarding ethical standards of the discipline.

The development of a dynamic set of ethical standards for psychologists' work-related conduct requires a personal commitment and lifelong effort to act ethically; to encourage ethical behavior by students, supervisees, employees, and colleagues; and to consult with others concerning ethical problems.

GENERAL PRINCIPLES

This section consists of General Principles. General Principles, as opposed to Ethical Standards, are aspirational in nature. Their intent is to guide and inspire psychologists toward the very highest ethical ideals of the profession. General Principles, in contrast to Ethical Standards, do not represent obligations and should not form the basis for imposing sanctions. Relying upon General Principles for either of these reasons distorts both their meaning and purpose.

Principle A: Beneficence and Nonmaleficence

Psychologists strive to benefit those with whom they work and take care to do no harm. In their professional actions, psychologists seek to safeguard the welfare and rights of those with whom they interact professionally and other affected persons, and the welfare of animal subjects of research. When conflicts occur among psychologists' obligations or concerns, they attempt to resolve these conflicts in a responsible fashion that avoids or minimizes harm. Because psychologists' scientific and professional judgments and actions may affect the lives of others, they are alert to and guard against personal, financial, social, organizational, or political factors that might lead to misuse of their influence. Psychologists strive to be aware of the possible effect of their own physical and mental health on their ability to help those with whom they work.

Principle B: Fidelity and Responsibility

Psychologists establish relationships of trust with those with whom they work. They are aware of their professional and scientific responsibilities to society and to the specific communities in which they work. Psychologists uphold professional standards of conduct, clarify their professional roles and obligations, accept appropriate responsibility for their behavior, and seek to manage conflicts of interest that could lead to exploitation or harm. Psychologists consult with, refer to, or cooperate with other professionals and institutions to the extent needed to serve the best interests of those with whom they work. They are concerned about the ethical compliance of their colleagues' scientific and professional conduct. Psychologists strive to contribute a portion of their professional time for little or no compensation or personal advantage.

Principle C: Integrity

Psychologists seek to promote accuracy, honesty, and truthfulness in the science, teaching, and practice of psychology. In these activities psychologists do not steal, cheat, or engage in fraud, subterfuge, or intentional misrepresentation of fact. Psychologists strive to keep their promises and to avoid unwise or unclear commitments. In situations in which deception may be ethically justifiable to maximize benefits and minimize harm, psychologists have a serious obligation to consider the need for, the possible consequences of, and their responsibility to correct any resulting mistrust or other harmful effects that arise from the use of such techniques.

Principle D: Justice

Psychologists recognize that fairness and justice entitle all persons to access to and benefit from the contributions of psychology and to equal quality in the processes, procedures, and services being conducted by psychologists. Psychologists exercise reasonable judgment and take precautions to ensure that their potential biases, the boundaries of their competence, and the limitations of their expertise do not lead to or condone unjust practices.

Principle E: Respect for People's Rights and Dignity

Psychologists respect the dignity and worth of all people, and the rights of individuals to privacy, confidentiality, and self-determination. Psychologists are aware that special safeguards may be necessary to protect the rights and welfare of persons or communities whose vulnerabilities impair autonomous decision making. Psychologists are aware of and respect cultural, individual, and role differences, including those based on age, gender, gender identity, race, ethnicity, culture, national origin, religion, sexual orientation, disability, language, and socioeconomic status, and consider these factors when working with members of such groups. Psychologists try to eliminate the effect on their work of biases based on those factors, and they do not knowingly participate in or condone activities of others based upon such prejudices.

ETHICAL STANDARDS

1. Resolving Ethical Issues

1.01 Misuse of Psychologists' Work

If psychologists learn of misuse or misrepresentation of their work, they take reasonable steps to correct or minimize the misuse or misrepresentation.

1.02 Conflicts Between Ethics and Law, Regulations, or Other Governing Legal Authority

If psychologists' ethical responsibilities conflict with law, regulations, or other governing legal authority, psychologists make known their commitment to the Ethics Code and take steps to resolve the conflict. If the conflict is unresolvable via such means, psychologists may adhere to the requirements of the law, regulations, or other governing legal authority.

1.03 Conflicts Between Ethics and Organizational Demands

If the demands of an organization with which psychologists are affiliated or for whom they are working conflict with this Ethics Code, psychologists clarify the nature of the conflict, make known their commitment to the Ethics Code, and to the extent feasible, resolve the conflict in a way that permits adherence to the Ethics Code.

1.04 Informal Resolution of Ethical Violations

When psychologists believe that there may have been an ethical violation by another psychologist, they attempt to resolve the issue by bringing it to the attention of that individual, if an informal resolution appears appropriate and the intervention does not violate any confidentiality rights that may be involved. (See also Standards 1.02, Conflicts Between Ethics and Law, Regulations, or Other Governing Legal Authority, and 1.03, Conflicts Between Ethics and Organizational Demands.)

1.05 Reporting Ethical Violations

If an apparent ethical violation has substantially harmed or is likely to substantially harm a person or organization and is not appropriate for informal resolution under Standard 1.04, Informal Resolution of Ethical Violations, or is not resolved properly in that fashion, psychologists take further action appropriate to the situation. Such action might include referral to state or national committees on professional ethics, to state licensing boards, or to the appropriate institutional authorities. This standard does not apply when an intervention would violate confidentiality rights or when psychologists have been retained to review the work of another psychologist whose professional conduct is in question. (See also Standard 1.02, Conflicts Between Ethics and Law, Regulations, or Other Governing Legal Authority.)

1.06 Cooperating With Ethics Committees

Psychologists cooperate in ethics investigations, proceedings, and resulting requirements of the APA or any affiliated state psychological association to which they belong. In doing so, they address any confidentiality issues. Failure to cooperate is itself an ethics violation. However, making a request for deferment of adjudication of an ethics complaint pending the outcome of litigation does not alone constitute noncooperation.

1.07 Improper Complaints

Psychologists do not file or encourage the filing of ethics complaints that are made with reckless disregard for or willful ignorance of facts that would disprove the allegation.

1.08 Unfair Discrimination Against Complainants and Respondents

Psychologists do not deny persons employment, advancement, admissions to academic or other programs, tenure, or promotion, based solely upon their having made or their being the subject of an ethics complaint. This does not preclude taking action based upon the outcome of such proceedings or considering other appropriate information.

2. Competence

2.01 Boundaries of Competence

(a) Psychologists provide services, teach, and conduct research with populations and in areas only within the boundaries of their competence, based on their education, training, supervised experience, consultation, study, or professional experience.

(b) Where scientific or professional knowledge in the discipline of psychology establishes that an understanding of factors associated with age, gender, gender identity, race, ethnicity, culture, national origin, religion, sexual orientation, disability, language, or socioeconomic status is essential for effective implementation of their services or research, psychologists have or obtain the training, experience, consultation, or supervision necessary to ensure the competence of their services, or they make appropriate referrals, except as provided in Standard 2.02, Providing Services in Emergencies.

(c) Psychologists planning to provide services, teach, or conduct research involving populations, areas, techniques, or technologies new to them undertake relevant education, training, supervised experience, consultation, or study.

(d) When psychologists are asked to provide services to individuals for whom appropriate mental health services are not available and for which psychologists have not obtained the competence necessary, psychologists with closely related prior training or experience may provide such services in order to ensure that services are not denied if they make a reasonable effort to obtain the competence required by using relevant research, training, consultation, or study.

(e) In those emerging areas in which generally recognized standards for preparatory training do not yet exist, psychologists nevertheless take reasonable steps to ensure the competence of their work and to protect clients/patients, students, supervisees, research participants, organizational clients, and others from harm.

(f) When assuming forensic roles, psychologists are or become reasonably familiar with the judicial or administrative rules governing their roles.

2.02 Providing Services in Emergencies

In emergencies, when psychologists provide services to individuals for whom other mental health services are not available and for which psychologists have not obtained the necessary training, psychologists may provide such services in order to ensure that services are not denied. The services are discontinued as soon as the emergency has ended or appropriate services are available.

2.03 Maintaining Competence

Psychologists undertake ongoing efforts to develop and maintain their competence.

2.04 Bases for Scientific and Professional Judgments

Psychologists' work is based upon established scientific and professional knowledge of the discipline. (See also Standards 2.01e, Boundaries of Competence, and 10.01b, Informed Consent to Therapy.)

2.05 Delegation of Work to Others

Psychologists who delegate work to employees, supervisees, or research or teaching assistants or who use the services of others, such as interpreters, take reasonable steps to (1) avoid delegating such work to persons who have a multiple relationship with those being served that would likely lead to exploitation or loss of objectivity; (2) authorize only those responsibilities that such persons can be expected to perform competently on the basis of their education, training, or experience, either independently or with the level of supervision being provided; and (3) see that such persons perform these services competently. (See also Standards 2.02, Providing Services in Emergencies; 3.05, Multiple Relationships; 4.01, Maintaining Confidentiality; 9.01, Bases for Assessments; 9.02, Use of Assessments; 9.03, Informed Consent in Assessments; and 9.07, Assessment by Unqualified Persons.)

2.06 Personal Problems and Conflicts

(a) Psychologists refrain from initiating an activity when they know or should know that there is a substantial likelihood that their personal problems will prevent them from performing their work-related activities in a competent manner.

(b) When psychologists become aware of personal problems that may interfere with their performing work-related duties adequately, they take appropriate measures, such as obtaining professional consultation or assistance, and determine whether they should limit, suspend, or terminate their work-related duties. (See also Standard 10.10, Terminating Therapy.)

3. Human Relations

3.01 Unfair Discrimination

In their work-related activities, psychologists do not engage in unfair discrimination based on age, gender, gender identity, race, ethnicity, culture, national origin, religion, sexual orientation, disability, socioeconomic status, or any basis proscribed by law.

3.02 Sexual Harassment

Psychologists do not engage in sexual harassment. Sexual harassment is sexual solicitation, physical advances, or verbal or nonverbal conduct that is sexual in nature, that occurs in connection with the psychologist's activities or roles as a psychologist, and that either (1) is unwelcome, is offensive, or creates a hostile workplace or educational environment, and the psychologist knows or is told this or (2) is sufficiently severe or intense to be abusive to a reasonable person in the context. Sexual harassment can consist of a single intense or severe act or of multiple persistent or pervasive acts. (See also Standard 1.08, Unfair Discrimination Against Complainants and Respondents.)

3.03 Other Harassment

Psychologists do not knowingly engage in behavior that is harassing or demeaning to persons with whom they interact in their work based on factors such as those persons' age, gender, gender identity, race, ethnicity, culture, national origin, religion, sexual orientation, disability, language, or socioeconomic status.

3.04 Avoiding Harm

Psychologists take reasonable steps to avoid harming their clients/patients, students, supervisees, research participants, organizational clients, and others with whom they work, and to minimize harm where it is foreseeable and unavoidable.

3.05 Multiple Relationships

(a) A multiple relationship occurs when a psychologist is in a professional role with a person and (1) at the same time is in another role with the same person, (2) at the same time is in a relationship with a person closely associated with or related to the person with whom the psychologist has the professional relationship, or (3) promises to enter into another relationship in the future with the person or a person closely associated with or related to the person.

A psychologist refrains from entering into a multiple relationship if the multiple relationship could reasonably be expected to impair the psychologist's objectivity, competence, or effectiveness in performing his or her functions as a psychologist, or otherwise risks exploitation or harm to the person with whom the professional relationship exists.

Multiple relationships that would not reasonably be expected to cause impairment or risk exploitation or harm are not unethical.

(b) If a psychologist finds that, due to unforeseen factors, a potentially harmful multiple relationship has arisen, the psychologist takes reasonable steps to resolve it with due regard for the best interests of the affected person and maximal compliance with the Ethics Code.

(c) When psychologists are required by law, institutional policy, or extraordinary circumstances to serve in more than one role in judicial or administrative proceedings, at the outset they clarify role expectations and the extent of confidentiality and thereafter as changes occur. (See also Standards 3.04, Avoiding Harm, and 3.07, Third-Party Requests for Services.)

3.06 Conflict of Interest

Psychologists refrain from taking on a professional role when personal, scientific, professional, legal, financial, or other interests or relationships could reasonably be expected to (1) impair their objectivity, competence, or effectiveness in performing their functions as psychologists or (2) expose the person or organization with whom the professional relationship exists to harm or exploitation.

3.07 Third-Party Requests for Services

When psychologists agree to provide services to a person or entity at the request of a third party, psychologists attempt to clarify at the outset of the service the nature of the relationship with all individuals or organizations involved. This clarification includes the role of the psychologist (e.g., therapist, consultant, diagnostician, or expert witness), an identification of who is the client, the probable uses of the services provided or the information obtained, and the fact that there may be limits to confidentiality. (See also Standards 3.05, Multiple Relationships, and 4.02, Discussing the Limits of Confidentiality.)

3.08 Exploitative Relationships

Psychologists do not exploit persons over whom they have supervisory, evaluative, or other authority such as clients/patients, students, supervisees, research participants, and employees. (See also Standards 3.05, Multiple Relationships; 6.04, Fees and Financial Arrangements; 6.05, Barter With Clients/Patients; 7.07, Sexual Relationships With Students and Supervisees; 10.05, Sexual Intimacies With Current Therapy Clients/Patients; 10.06, Sexual Intimacies With Relatives or Significant Others of Current Therapy Clients/Patients; 10.07, Therapy With Former Sexual Partners; and 10.08, Sexual Intimacies With Former Therapy Clients/Patients.)

3.09 Cooperation With Other Professionals

When indicated and professionally appropriate, psychologists cooperate with other professionals in order to serve their clients/patients effectively and appropriately. (See also Standard 4.05, Disclosures.)

3.10 Informed Consent

(a) When psychologists conduct research or provide assessment, therapy, counseling, or consulting services in person or via electronic transmission or other forms of communication, they obtain the informed consent of the individual or individuals using language that is reasonably understandable to that person or persons except when conducting such activities without consent is mandated by law or governmental regulation or as otherwise provided in this Ethics Code. (See also Standards 8.02, Informed Consent to Research; 9.03, Informed Consent in Assessments; and 10.01, Informed Consent to Therapy.)

(b) For persons who are legally incapable of giving informed consent, psychologists nevertheless (1) provide an appropriate explanation, (2) seek the individual's assent, (3) consider such persons' preferences and best interests, and (4) obtain appropriate permission from a legally authorized person, if such substitute consent is permitted or required by law. When consent by a legally authorized person is not permitted or required by law, psychologists take reasonable steps to protect the individual's rights and welfare.

(c) When psychological services are court ordered or otherwise mandated, psychologists inform the individual of the nature of the anticipated services, including whether the services are court ordered or mandated and any limits of confidentiality, before proceeding.

(d) Psychologists appropriately document written or oral consent, permission, and assent. (See also Standards 8.02, Informed Consent to Research; 9.03, Informed Consent in Assessments; and 10.01, Informed Consent to Therapy.)

3.11 Psychological Services Delivered to or Through Organizations

(a) Psychologists delivering services to or through organizations provide information beforehand to clients and when appropriate those directly affected by the services about (1) the nature and objectives of the services, (2) the intended recipients, (3) which of the individuals are clients, (4) the relationship the psychologist will have with each person and the organization, (5) the probable uses of services provided and information obtained, (6) who will have access to the information, and (7) limits of confidentiality. As soon as feasible, they provide information about the results and conclusions of such services to appropriate persons.

(b) If psychologists will be precluded by law or by organizational roles from providing such information to particular individuals or groups, they so inform those individuals or groups at the outset of the service.

3.12 Interruption of Psychological Services

Unless otherwise covered by contract, psychologists make reasonable efforts to plan for facilitating services in the event that psychological services are interrupted by factors such as the psychologist's illness, death, unavailability, relocation, or retirement or by the client's/patient's relocation or financial limitations. (See also Standard 6.02c, Maintenance, Dissemination, and Disposal of Confidential Records of Professional and Scientific Work.)

4. Privacy and Confidentiality

4.01 Maintaining Confidentiality

Psychologists have a primary obligation and take reasonable precautions to protect confidential information obtained through or stored in any medium, recognizing that the extent and limits of confidentiality may be regulated by law or established by institutional rules or professional or scientific relationship. (See also Standard 2.05, Delegation of Work to Others.)

4.02 Discussing the Limits of Confidentiality

(a) Psychologists discuss with persons (including, to the extent feasible, persons who are legally incapable of giving informed consent and their legal representatives) and organizations with whom they establish a scientific or professional relationship (1) the relevant limits of confidentiality and (2) the foreseeable uses of the information generated through their psychological activities. (See also Standard 3.10, Informed Consent.)

(b) Unless it is not feasible or is contraindicated, the discussion of confidentiality occurs at the outset of the relationship and thereafter as new circumstances may warrant.

(c) Psychologists who offer services, products, or information via electronic transmission inform clients/patients of the risks to privacy and limits of confidentiality.

4.03 Recording

Before recording the voices or images of individuals to whom they provide services, psychologists obtain permission from all such persons or their legal representatives. (See also Standards 8.03, Informed Consent for Recording Voices and Images in Research; 8.05, Dispensing With Informed Consent for Research; and 8.07, Deception in Research.)

4.04 Minimizing Intrusions on Privacy

(a) Psychologists include in written and oral reports and consultations, only information germane to the purpose for which the communication is made.

(b) Psychologists discuss confidential information obtained in their work only for appropriate scientific or professional purposes and only with persons clearly concerned with such matters.

4.05 Disclosures

(a) Psychologists may disclose confidential information with the appropriate consent of the organizational client, the individual client/patient, or another legally authorized person on behalf of the client/patient unless prohibited by law.

(b) Psychologists disclose confidential information without the consent of the individual only as mandated by law, or where permitted by law for a valid purpose such as to (1) provide needed professional services; (2) obtain appropriate professional consultations; (3) protect the client/patient, psychologist, or others from harm; or (4) obtain payment for services from a client/patient, in which instance disclosure is limited to the minimum that is necessary to achieve the purpose. (See also Standard 6.04e, Fees and Financial Arrangements.)

4.06 Consultations

When consulting with colleagues, (1) psychologists do not disclose confidential information that reasonably could lead to the identification of a client/patient, research participant, or other person or organization with whom they have a confidential relationship unless they have obtained the prior consent of the person or organization or the disclosure cannot be avoided, and (2) they disclose information only to the extent necessary to achieve the purposes of the consultation. (See also Standard 4.01, Maintaining Confidentiality.)

4.07 Use of Confidential Information for Didactic or Other Purposes

Psychologists do not disclose in their writings, lectures, or other public media, confidential, personally identifiable information concerning their clients/patients, students, research participants, organizational clients, or other recipients of their services that they obtained during the course of their work, unless (1) they take reasonable steps to disguise the person or organization, (2) the person or organization has consented in writing, or (3) there is legal authorization for doing so.

5. Advertising and Other Public Statements

5.01 Avoidance of False or Deceptive Statements

(a) Public statements include but are not limited to paid or unpaid advertising, product endorsements, grant applications, licensing applications, other credentialing applications, brochures, printed matter, directory listings, personal resumes or curricula vitae, or comments for use in media such as print or electronic transmission, statements in legal proceedings, lectures and public oral presentations, and published materials. Psychologists do not knowingly make public statements that are false, deceptive, or fraudulent concerning their research, practice, or other work activities or those of persons or organizations with which they are affiliated.

(b) Psychologists do not make false, deceptive, or fraudulent statements concerning (1) their training, experience, or competence; (2) their academic degrees; (3) their credentials; (4) their institutional or association affiliations; (5) their services; (6) the scientific or clinical basis for, or results or degree of success of, their services; (7) their fees; or (8) their publications or research findings.

(c) Psychologists claim degrees as credentials for their health services only if those degrees (1) were earned from a regionally accredited educational institution or (2) were the basis for psychology licensure by the state in which they practice.

5.02 Statements by Others

(a) Psychologists who engage others to create or place public statements that promote their professional practice, products, or activities retain professional responsibility for such statements.

(b) Psychologists do not compensate employees of press, radio, television, or other communication media in return for publicity in a news item. (See also Standard 1.01, Misuse of Psychologists' Work.)

(c) A paid advertisement relating to psychologists' activities must be identified or clearly recognizable as such.

5.03 Descriptions of Workshops and Non-Degree-Granting Educational Programs

To the degree to which they exercise control, psychologists responsible for announcements, catalogs, brochures, or advertisements describing workshops, seminars, or other non-degree-granting educational programs ensure that they accurately describe the audience for which the program is intended, the educational objectives, the presenters, and the fees involved.

5.04 Media Presentations

When psychologists provide public advice or comment via print, Internet, or other electronic transmission, they take precautions to ensure that statements (1) are based on their professional knowledge, training, or experience in accord with appropriate psychological literature and practice; (2) are otherwise consistent with this Ethics Code; and (3) do not indicate that a professional relationship has been established with the recipient. (See also Standard 2.04, Bases for Scientific and Professional Judgments.)

5.05 Testimonials

Psychologists do not solicit testimonials from current therapy clients/patients or other persons who because of their particular circumstances are vulnerable to undue influence.

5.06 In-Person Solicitation

Psychologists do not engage, directly or through agents, in uninvited in-person solicitation of business from actual or potential therapy clients/patients or other persons who because of their particular circumstances are vulnerable to undue influence. However, this prohibition does not preclude (1) attempting to implement appropriate collateral contacts for the purpose of benefiting an already engaged therapy client/patient or (2) providing disaster or community outreach services.

6. Record Keeping and Fees

6.01 Documentation of Professional and Scientific Work and Maintenance of Records

Psychologists create, and to the extent the records are under their control, maintain, disseminate, store, retain, and dispose of records and data relating to their professional and scientific work in order to (1) facilitate provision of services later by them or by other professionals, (2) allow for replication of research design and analyses, (3) meet institutional requirements, (4) ensure accuracy of billing and payments, and (5) ensure compliance with law. (See also Standard 4.01, Maintaining Confidentiality.)

6.02 Maintenance, Dissemination, and Disposal of Confidential Records of Professional and Scientific Work

(a) Psychologists maintain confidentiality in creating, storing, accessing, transferring, and disposing of records under their control, whether these are written, automated, or in any other medium. (See also Standards 4.01, Maintaining Confidentiality, and 6.01, Documentation of Professional and Scientific Work and Maintenance of Records.)

(b) If confidential information concerning recipients of psychological services is entered into databases or systems of records available to persons whose access has not been consented to by the recipient, psychologists use coding or other techniques to avoid the inclusion of personal identifiers.

(c) Psychologists make plans in advance to facilitate the appropriate transfer and to protect the confidentiality of records and data in the event of psychologists' withdrawal from positions or practice. (See also Standards 3.12, Interruption of Psychological Services, and 10.09, Interruption of Therapy.)

6.03 Withholding Records for Nonpayment

Psychologists may not withhold records under their control that are requested and needed for a client's/patient's emergency treatment solely because payment has not been received.

6.04 Fees and Financial Arrangements

(a) As early as is feasible in a professional or scientific relationship, psychologists and recipients of psychological services reach an agreement specifying compensation and billing arrangements.

(b) Psychologists' fee practices are consistent with law.

(c) Psychologists do not misrepresent their fees.

(d) If limitations to services can be anticipated because of limitations in financing, this is discussed with the recipient of services as early as is feasible. (See also Standards 10.09, Interruption of Therapy, and 10.10, Terminating Therapy.)

(e) If the recipient of services does not pay for services as agreed, and if psychologists intend to use collection agencies or legal measures to collect the fees, psychologists first inform the person that such measures will be taken and provide that person an opportunity to make prompt payment. (See also Standards 4.05, Disclosures; 6.03, Withholding Records for Nonpayment; and 10.01, Informed Consent to Therapy.)

6.05 Barter With Clients/Patients

Barter is the acceptance of goods, services, or other nonmonetary remuneration from clients/patients in return for psychological services. Psychologists may barter only if (1) it is not clinically contraindicated, and (2) the resulting arrangement is not exploitative. (See also Standards 3.05, Multiple Relationships, and 6.04, Fees and Financial Arrangements.)

6.06 Accuracy in Reports to Payors and Funding Sources

In their reports to payors for services or sources of research funding, psychologists take reasonable steps to ensure the accurate reporting of the nature of the service provided or research conducted, the fees, charges, or payments, and where applicable, the identity of the provider, the findings, and the diagnosis. (See also Standards 4.01, Maintaining Confidentiality; 4.04, Minimizing Intrusions on Privacy; and 4.05, Disclosures.)

6.07 Referrals and Fees

When psychologists pay, receive payment from, or divide fees with another professional, other than in an employer–employee relationship, the payment to each is based on the services provided (clinical, consultative, administrative, or other) and is not based on the referral itself. (See also Standard 3.09, Cooperation With Other Professionals.)

7. Education and Training

7.01 Design of Education and Training Programs

Psychologists responsible for education and training programs take reasonable steps to ensure that the programs are designed to provide the appropriate knowledge and proper experiences, and to meet the requirements for licensure, certification, or other goals for which claims are made by the program. (See also Standard 5.03, Descriptions of Workshops and Non-Degree-Granting Educational Programs.)

7.02 Descriptions of Education and Training Programs

Psychologists responsible for education and training programs take reasonable steps to ensure that there is a current and accurate description of the program content (including participation in required course- or program-related counseling, psychotherapy, experiential groups, consulting projects, or community service), training goals and objectives, stipends and benefits, and requirements that must be met for satisfactory completion of the program. This information must be made readily available to all interested parties.

7.03 Accuracy in Teaching

(a) Psychologists take reasonable steps to ensure that course syllabi are accurate regarding the subject matter to be covered, bases for evaluating progress, and the nature of course experiences. This standard does not preclude an instructor from modifying course content or requirements when the instructor considers it pedagogically necessary or desirable, so long as students are made aware of these modifications in a manner that enables them to fulfill course requirements. (See also Standard 5.01, Avoidance of False or Deceptive Statements.)

(b) When engaged in teaching or training, psychologists present psychological information accurately. (See also Standard 2.03, Maintaining Competence.)

7.04 Student Disclosure of Personal Information

Psychologists do not require students or supervisees to disclose personal information in course- or program-related activities, either orally or in writing, regarding sexual history, history of abuse and neglect, psychological treatment, and relationships with parents, peers, and spouses or significant others except if (1) the program or training facility has clearly identified this requirement in its admissions and program materials or (2) the information is necessary to evaluate or obtain assistance for students whose personal problems could reasonably be judged to be preventing them from performing their training- or professionally related activities in a competent manner or posing a threat to the students or others.

7.05 Mandatory Individual or Group Therapy

(a) When individual or group therapy is a program or course requirement, psychologists responsible for that program allow students in undergraduate and graduate programs the option of selecting such therapy from practitioners unaffiliated with the program. (See also Standard 7.02, Descriptions of Education and Training Programs.)

(b) Faculty who are or are likely to be responsible for evaluating students' academic performance do not themselves provide that therapy. (See also Standard 3.05, Multiple Relationships.)

7.06 Assessing Student and Supervisee Performance

(a) In academic and supervisory relationships, psychologists establish a timely and specific process for providing feedback to students and supervisees. Information regarding the process is provided to the student at the beginning of supervision.

(b) Psychologists evaluate students and supervisees on the basis of their actual performance on relevant and established program requirements.

7.07 Sexual Relationships With Students and Supervisees

Psychologists do not engage in sexual relationships with students or supervisees who are in their department, agency, or training center or over whom psychologists have or are likely to have evaluative authority. (See also Standard 3.05, Multiple Relationships.)

8. Research and Publication

8.01 Institutional Approval

When institutional approval is required, psychologists provide accurate information about their research proposals and obtain approval prior to conducting the research. They conduct the research in accordance with the approved research protocol.

8.02 Informed Consent to Research

(a) When obtaining informed consent as required in Standard 3.10, Informed Consent, psychologists inform participants about (1) the purpose of the research, expected duration, and procedures; (2) their right to decline to participate and to withdraw from the research once participation has begun; (3) the foreseeable consequences of declining or withdrawing; (4) reasonably foreseeable factors that may be expected to influence their willingness to participate such as potential risks, discomfort, or adverse effects; (5) any prospective research benefits; (6) limits of confidentiality; (7) incentives for participation; and (8) whom to contact for questions about the research and research participants' rights. They provide opportunity for the prospective participants to ask questions and receive answers. (See also Standards 8.03, Informed Consent for Recording Voices and Images in Research; 8.05, Dispensing With Informed Consent for Research; and 8.07, Deception in Research.)

(b) Psychologists conducting intervention research involving the use of experimental treatments clarify to participants at the outset of the research (1) the experimental nature of the treatment; (2) the services that will or will not be available to the control group(s) if appropriate; (3) the means by which assignment to treatment and control groups will be made; (4) available treatment alternatives if an individual does not wish to participate in the research or wishes to withdraw once a study has begun; and (5) compensation for or monetary costs of participating including, if appropriate, whether reimbursement from the participant or a third-party payor will be sought. (See also Standard 8.02a, Informed Consent to Research.)

8.03 Informed Consent for Recording Voices and Images in Research

Psychologists obtain informed consent from research participants prior to recording their voices or images for data collection unless (1) the research consists solely of naturalistic observations in public places, and it is not anticipated that the recording will be used in a manner that could cause personal identification or harm, or (2) the research design includes deception, and consent for the use of the recording is obtained during debriefing. (See also Standard 8.07, Deception in Research.)

8.04 Client/Patient, Student, and Subordinate Research Participants

(a) When psychologists conduct research with clients/patients, students, or subordinates as participants, psychologists take steps to protect the prospective participants from adverse consequences of declining or withdrawing from participation.

(b) When research participation is a course requirement or an opportunity for extra credit, the prospective participant is given the choice of equitable alternative activities.

8.05 Dispensing With Informed Consent for Research

Psychologists may dispense with informed consent only (1) where research would not reasonably be assumed to create distress or harm and involves (a) the study of normal educational practices, curricula, or classroom management methods conducted in educational settings; (b) only anonymous questionnaires, naturalistic observations, or archival research for which disclosure of responses would not place participants at risk of criminal or civil liability or damage their financial standing, employability, or reputation, and confidentiality is protected; or (c) the study of factors related to job or organization effectiveness conducted in organizational settings for which there is no risk to participants' employability, and confidentiality is protected or (2) where otherwise permitted by law or federal or institutional regulations.

8.06 Offering Inducements for Research Participation

(a) Psychologists make reasonable efforts to avoid offering excessive or inappropriate financial or other inducements for research participation when such inducements are likely to coerce participation.

(b) When offering professional services as an inducement for research participation, psychologists clarify the nature of the services, as well as the risks, obligations, and limitations. (See also Standard 6.05, Barter With Clients/Patients.)

8.07 Deception in Research

(a) Psychologists do not conduct a study involving deception unless they have determined that the use of deceptive techniques is justified by the study's significant prospective scientific, educational, or applied value and that effective nondeceptive alternative procedures are not feasible.

(b) Psychologists do not deceive prospective participants about research that is reasonably expected to cause physical pain or severe emotional distress.

(c) Psychologists explain any deception that is an integral feature of the design and conduct of an experiment to participants as early as is feasible, preferably at the conclusion of their participation, but no later than at the conclusion of the data collection, and permit participants to withdraw their data. (See also Standard 8.08, Debriefing.)

8.08 Debriefing

(a) Psychologists provide a prompt opportunity for participants to obtain appropriate information about the nature, results, and conclusions of the research, and they take reasonable steps to correct any misconceptions that participants may have of which the psychologists are aware.

(b) If scientific or humane values justify delaying or withholding this information, psychologists take reasonable measures to reduce the risk of harm.

(c) When psychologists become aware that research procedures have harmed a participant, they take reasonable steps to minimize the harm.

8.09 Humane Care and Use of Animals in Research

(a) Psychologists acquire, care for, use, and dispose of animals in compliance with current federal, state, and local laws and regulations, and with professional standards.

(b) Psychologists trained in research methods and experienced in the care of laboratory animals supervise all procedures involving animals and are responsible for ensuring appropriate consideration of their comfort, health, and humane treatment.

(c) Psychologists ensure that all individuals under their supervision who are using animals have received instruction in research methods and in the care, maintenance, and handling of the species being used, to the extent appropriate to their role. (See also Standard 2.05, Delegation of Work to Others.)

(d) Psychologists make reasonable efforts to minimize the discomfort, infection, illness, and pain of animal subjects.

(e) Psychologists use a procedure subjecting animals to pain, stress, or privation only when an alternative procedure is unavailable and the goal is justified by its prospective scientific, educational, or applied value.

(f) Psychologists perform surgical procedures under appropriate anesthesia and follow techniques to avoid infection and minimize pain during and after surgery.

(g) When it is appropriate that an animal's life be terminated, psychologists proceed rapidly, with an effort to minimize pain and in accordance with accepted procedures.

8.10 Reporting Research Results

(a) Psychologists do not fabricate data. (See also Standard 5.01a, Avoidance of False or Deceptive Statements.)

(b) If psychologists discover significant errors in their published data, they take reasonable steps to correct such errors in a correction, retraction, erratum, or other appropriate publication means.

8.11 Plagiarism

Psychologists do not present portions of another's work or data as their own, even if the other work or data source is cited occasionally.

8.12 Publication Credit

(a) Psychologists take responsibility and credit, including authorship credit, only for work they have actually performed or to which they have substantially contributed. (See also Standard 8.12b, Publication Credit.)

(b) Principal authorship and other publication credits accurately reflect the relative scientific or professional contributions of the individuals involved, regardless of their relative status. Mere possession of an institutional position, such as department chair, does not justify authorship credit. Minor contributions to the research or to the writing for publications are acknowledged appropriately, such as in footnotes or in an introductory statement.

(c) Except under exceptional circumstances, a student is listed as principal author on any multiple-authored article that is substantially based on the student's doctoral dissertation. Faculty advisors discuss publication credit with students as early as feasible and throughout the research and publication process as appropriate. (See also Standard 8.12b, Publication Credit.)

8.13 Duplicate Publication of Data

Psychologists do not publish, as original data, data that have been previously published. This does not preclude republishing data when they are accompanied by proper acknowledgment.

8.14 Sharing Research Data for Verification

(a) After research results are published, psychologists do not withhold the data on which their conclusions are based from other competent professionals who seek to verify the substantive claims through reanalysis and who intend to use such data only for that purpose, provided that the confidentiality of the participants can be protected and unless legal rights concerning proprietary data preclude their release. This does not preclude psychologists from requiring that such individuals or groups be responsible for costs associated with the provision of such information.

(b) Psychologists who request data from other psychologists to verify the substantive claims through reanalysis may use shared data only for the declared purpose. Requesting psychologists obtain prior written agreement for all other uses of the data.

8.15 Reviewers

Psychologists who review material submitted for presentation, publication, grant, or research proposal review respect the confidentiality of and the proprietary rights in such information of those who submitted it.

9. Assessment

9.01 Bases for Assessments

(a) Psychologists base the opinions contained in their recommendations, reports, and diagnostic or evaluative statements, including forensic testimony, on information and techniques sufficient to substantiate their findings. (See also Standard 2.04, Bases for Scientific and Professional Judgments.)

(b) Except as noted in 9.01c, psychologists provide opinions of the psychological characteristics of individuals only after they have conducted an examination of the individuals adequate to support their statements or conclusions. When, despite reasonable efforts, such an examination is not practical, psychologists document the efforts they made and the result of those efforts, clarify the probable impact of their limited information on the reliability and validity of their opinions, and appropriately limit the nature and extent of their conclusions or recommendations. (See also Standards 2.01, Boundaries of Competence, and 9.06, Interpreting Assessment Results.)

(c) When psychologists conduct a record review or provide consultation or supervision and an individual examination is not warranted or necessary for the opinion, psychologists explain this and the sources of information on which they based their conclusions and recommendations.

9.02 Use of Assessments

(a) Psychologists administer, adapt, score, interpret, or use assessment techniques, interviews, tests, or instruments in a manner and for purposes that are appropriate in light of the research on or evidence of the usefulness and proper application of the techniques.

(b) Psychologists use assessment instruments whose validity and reliability have been established for use with members of the population tested. When such validity or reliability has not been established, psychologists describe the strengths and limitations of test results and interpretation.

(c) Psychologists use assessment methods that are appropriate to an individual's language preference and competence, unless the use of an alternative language is relevant to the assessment issues.

9.03 Informed Consent in Assessments

(a) Psychologists obtain informed consent for assessments, evaluations, or diagnostic services, as described in Standard 3.10, Informed Consent, except when (1) testing is mandated by law or governmental regulations; (2) informed consent is implied because testing is conducted as a routine educational, institutional, or organizational activity (e.g., when participants voluntarily agree to assessment when applying for a job); or (3) one purpose of the testing is to evaluate decisional capacity. Informed consent includes an explanation of the nature and purpose of the assessment, fees, involvement of third parties, and limits of confidentiality and sufficient opportunity for the client/patient to ask questions and receive answers.

(b) Psychologists inform persons with questionable capacity to consent or for whom testing is mandated by law or governmental regulations about the nature and purpose of the proposed assessment services, using language that is reasonably understandable to the person being assessed.

(c) Psychologists using the services of an interpreter obtain informed consent from the client/patient to use that interpreter, ensure that confidentiality of test results and test security are maintained, and include in their recommendations, reports, and diagnostic or evaluative statements, including forensic testimony, discussion of any limitations on the data obtained. (See also Standards 2.05, Delegation of Work to Others; 4.01, Maintaining Confidentiality; 9.01, Bases for Assessments; 9.06, Interpreting Assessment Results; and 9.07, Assessment by Unqualified Persons.)

9.04 Release of Test Data

(a) The term *test data* refers to raw and scaled scores, client/patient responses to test questions or stimuli, and psychologists' notes and recordings concerning client/patient statements and behavior during an examination. Those portions of test materials that include client/patient responses are included in the definition of *test data*. Pursuant to a client/patient release, psychologists provide test data to the client/patient or other persons identified in the release. Psychologists may refrain from releasing test data to protect a client/patient or others from substantial harm or misuse or misrepresentation of the data or the test, recognizing that in many instances release of confidential information under these circumstances is regulated by law. (See also Standard 9.11, Maintaining Test Security.)

(b) In the absence of a client/patient release, psychologists provide test data only as required by law or court order.

9.05 Test Construction

Psychologists who develop tests and other assessment techniques use appropriate psychometric procedures and current scientific or professional knowledge for test design, standardization, validation, reduction or elimination of bias, and recommendations for use.

9.06 Interpreting Assessment Results

When interpreting assessment results, including automated interpretations, psychologists take into account the purpose of the assessment as well as the various test factors, test-taking abilities, and other characteristics of the person being assessed, such as situational, personal, linguistic, and cultural differences, that might affect psychologists' judgments or reduce the accuracy of their interpretations. They indicate any significant limitations of their interpretations. (See also Standards 2.01b and c, Boundaries of Competence, and 3.01, Unfair Discrimination.)

9.07 Assessment by Unqualified Persons

Psychologists do not promote the use of psychological assessment techniques by unqualified persons, except when such use is conducted for training purposes with appropriate supervision. (See also Standard 2.05, Delegation of Work to Others.)

9.08 Obsolete Tests and Outdated Test Results

(a) Psychologists do not base their assessment or intervention decisions or recommendations on data or test results that are outdated for the current purpose.

(b) Psychologists do not base such decisions or recommendations on tests and measures that are obsolete and not useful for the current purpose.

9.09 Test Scoring and Interpretation Services

(a) Psychologists who offer assessment or scoring services to other professionals accurately describe the purpose, norms, validity, reliability, and applications of the procedures and any special qualifications applicable to their use.

(b) Psychologists select scoring and interpretation services (including automated services) on the basis of evidence of the validity of the program and procedures as well as on other appropriate considerations. (See also Standard 2.01b and c, Boundaries of Competence.)

(c) Psychologists retain responsibility for the appropriate application, interpretation, and use of assessment instruments, whether they score and interpret such tests themselves or use automated or other services.

9.10 Explaining Assessment Results

Regardless of whether the scoring and interpretation are done by psychologists, by employees or assistants, or by automated or other outside services, psychologists take reasonable steps to ensure that explanations of results are given to the individual or designated representative unless the nature of the relationship precludes provision of an explanation of results (such as in some organizational consulting, preemployment or security screenings, and forensic evaluations), and this fact has been clearly explained to the person being assessed in advance.

9.11 Maintaining Test Security

The term *test materials* refers to manuals, instruments, protocols, and test questions or stimuli and does not include *test data* as defined in Standard 9.04, Release of Test Data. Psychologists make reasonable efforts to maintain the integrity and security of test materials and other assessment techniques consistent with law and contractual obligations, and in a manner that permits adherence to this Ethics Code.

10. <u>Therapy</u>

10.01 Informed Consent to Therapy

(a) When obtaining informed consent to therapy as required in Standard 3.10, Informed Consent, psychologists inform clients/patients as early as is feasible in the therapeutic relationship about the nature and anticipated course of therapy, fees, involvement of third parties, and limits of confidentiality and provide sufficient opportunity for the client/patient to ask questions and receive answers. (See also Standards 4.02, Discussing the Limits of Confidentiality, and 6.04, Fees and Financial Arrangements.)

(b) When obtaining informed consent for treatment for which generally recognized techniques and procedures have not been established, psychologists inform their clients/patients of the developing nature of the treatment, the potential risks involved, alternative treatments that may be available, and the voluntary nature of their participation. (See also Standards 2.01e, Boundaries of Competence, and 3.10, Informed Consent.)

(c) When the therapist is a trainee and the legal responsibility for the treatment provided resides with the supervisor, the client/patient, as part of the informed consent procedure, is informed that the therapist is in training and is being supervised and is given the name of the supervisor.

10.02 Therapy Involving Couples or Families

(a) When psychologists agree to provide services to several persons who have a relationship (such as spouses, significant others, or parents and children), they take reasonable steps to clarify at the outset (1) which of the individuals are clients/patients and (2) the relationship the psychologist will have with each person. This clarification includes the psychologist's role and the probable uses of the services provided or the information obtained. (See also Standard 4.02, Discussing the Limits of Confidentiality.)

(b) If it becomes apparent that psychologists may be called on to perform potentially conflicting roles (such as family therapist and then witness for one party in divorce proceedings), psychologists take reasonable steps to clarify and modify, or withdraw from, roles appropriately. (See also Standard 3.05c, Multiple Relationships.)

10.03 Group Therapy

When psychologists provide services to several persons in a group setting, they describe at the outset the roles and responsibilities of all parties and the limits of confidentiality.

10.04 Providing Therapy to Those Served by Others

In deciding whether to offer or provide services to those already receiving mental health services elsewhere, psychologists carefully consider the treatment issues and the potential client's/patient's welfare. Psychologists discuss these issues with the client/patient or another legally authorized person on behalf of the client/patient in order to minimize the risk of confusion and conflict, consult with the other service providers when appropriate, and proceed with caution and sensitivity to the therapeutic issues.

10.05 Sexual Intimacies With Current Therapy Clients/Patients

Psychologists do not engage in sexual intimacies with current therapy clients/patients.

10.06 Sexual Intimacies With Relatives or Significant Others of Current Therapy Clients/Patients

Psychologists do not engage in sexual intimacies with individuals they know to be close relatives, guardians, or significant others of current clients/patients. Psychologists do not terminate therapy to circumvent this standard.

10.07 Therapy With Former Sexual Partners

Psychologists do not accept as therapy clients/patients persons with whom they have engaged in sexual intimacies.

10.08 Sexual Intimacies With Former Therapy Clients/Patients

(a) Psychologists do not engage in sexual intimacies with former clients/patients for at least two years after cessation or termination of therapy.

(b) Psychologists do not engage in sexual intimacies with former clients/patients even after a two-year interval except in the most unusual circumstances. Psychologists who engage in such activity after the two years following cessation or termination of therapy and of having no sexual contact with the former client/patient bear the burden of demonstrating that there has been no exploitation, in light of all relevant factors, including (1) the amount of time that has passed since therapy terminated; (2) the nature, duration, and intensity of the therapy; (3) the circumstances of termination; (4) the client's/patient's personal history; (5) the client's/patient's current mental status; (6) the likelihood of adverse impact on the client/patient; and (7) any statements or actions made by the therapist during the course of therapy suggesting or inviting the possibility of a posttermination sexual or romantic relationship with the client/patient. (See also Standard 3.05, Multiple Relationships.)

10.09 Interruption of Therapy

When entering into employment or contractual relationships, psychologists make reasonable efforts to provide for orderly and appropriate resolution of responsibility for client/patient care in the event that the employment or contractual relationship ends, with paramount consideration given to the welfare of the client/patient. (See also Standard 3.12, Interruption of Psychological Services.)

10.10 Terminating Therapy

(a) Psychologists terminate therapy when it becomes reasonably clear that the client/patient no longer needs the service, is not likely to benefit, or is being harmed by continued service.

(b) Psychologists may terminate therapy when threatened or otherwise endangered by the client/patient or another person with whom the client/patient has a relationship.

(c) Except where precluded by the actions of clients/patients or third-party payors, prior to termination psychologists provide pretermination counseling and suggest alternative service providers as appropriate.

APPENDIX Q

THE AMERICAN ASSOCIATION FOR MARRIAGE AND FAMILY THERAPY (AAMFT) NEW CODE OF ETHICS (NEW)

AAMFT CODE OF ETHICS

Effective July 1, 2001

Preamble

The Board of Directors of the American Association for Marriage and Family Therapy (AAMFT) hereby promulgates, pursuant to Article 2, Section 2.013 of the Association's Bylaws, the Revised AAMFT Code of Ethics, effective July 1, 2001.

The AAMFT strives to honor the public trust in marriage and family therapists by setting standards for ethical practice as described in this Code. The ethical standards define professional expectations and are enforced by the AAMFT Ethics Committee. The absence of an explicit reference to a specific behavior or situation in the Code does not mean that the behavior is ethical or unethical. The standards are not exhaustive. Marriage and family therapists who are uncertain about the ethics of a particular course of action are encouraged to seek counsel from consultants, attorneys, supervisors, colleagues, or other appropriate authorities.

Both law and ethics govern the practice of marriage and family therapy. When making decisions regarding professional behavior, marriage and family therapists must consider the AAMFT Code of Ethics and applicable laws and regulations. If the AAMFT Code of Ethics prescribes a standard higher than that required by law, marriage and family therapists must meet the higher standard of the AAMFT Code of Ethics. Marriage and family therapists comply with the mandates of law, but make known their commitment to the AAMFT Code of Ethics and take steps to resolve the conflict in a responsible manner. The AAMFT supports legal mandates for reporting of alleged unethical conduct.

The AAMFT Code of Ethics is binding on Members of AAMFT in all membership categories, AAMFT-Approved Supervisors, and applicants for membership and the Approved Supervisor designation (hereafter, AAMFT Member). AAMFT members have an obligation to be familiar with the AAMFT Code of Ethics and its application to their professional services. Lack of awareness or misunderstanding of an ethical standard is not a defense to a charge of unethical conduct.

The process for filing, investigating, and resolving complaints of unethical conduct is described in the current Procedures for Handling Ethical Matters of the AAMFT Ethics Committee. Persons accused are considered innocent by the Ethics Committee until proven guilty, except as otherwise provided, and are entitled to due process. If an AAMFT Member resigns in anticipation of, or during the course of, an ethics investigation, the Ethics Committee will complete its investigation. Any publication of action taken by the Association will include the fact that the Member attempted to resign during the investigation.

Principle I
Responsibility to Clients

Marriage and family therapists advance the welfare of families and individuals. They respect the rights of those persons seeking their assistance, and make reasonable efforts to ensure that their services are used appropriately.

1.1. Marriage and family therapists provide professional assistance to persons without discrimination on the basis of race, age, ethnicity, socioeconomic status, disability, gender, health status, religion, national origin, or sexual orientation.

1.2 Marriage and family therapists obtain appropriate informed consent to therapy or related procedures as early as feasible in the therapeutic relationship, and use language that is reasonably understandable to clients. The content of informed consent may vary depending upon the client and treatment plan; however, informed consent generally necessitates that the client: (a) has the capacity to consent; (b) has been adequately informed of significant information concerning treatment processes and procedures; (c) has been adequately informed of potential risks and benefits of treatments for which generally recognized standards do not yet exist; (d) has freely and without undue influence expressed consent; and (e) has provided consent that is appropriately documented. When persons, due to age or mental status, are legally incapable of giving informed consent, marriage and family therapists obtain informed permission from a legally authorized person, if such substitute consent is legally permissible.

1.3 Marriage and family therapists are aware of their influential positions with respect to clients, and they avoid exploiting the trust and dependency of such persons. Therapists, therefore, make every effort to avoid conditions and multiple relationships with clients that could impair professional judgment or increase the risk of exploitation. Such relationships include, but are not limited to, business or close personal relationships with a client or the client's immediate family. When the risk of impairment or exploitation exists due to conditions or multiple roles, therapists take appropriate precautions.

1.4 Sexual intimacy with clients is prohibited.

1.5 Sexual intimacy with former clients is likely to be harmful and is therefore prohibited for two years following the termination of therapy or last professional contact. In an effort to avoid exploiting the trust and dependency of clients, marriage and family therapists should not engage in sexual intimacy with former clients after the two years following termination or last professional contact. Should therapists engage in sexual intimacy with former clients following two years after termination or last professional contact, the burden shifts to the therapist to demonstrate that there has been no exploitation or injury to the former client or to the client's immediate family.

1.6 Marriage and family therapists comply with applicable laws regarding the reporting of alleged unethical conduct.

1.7 Marriage and family therapists do not use their professional relationships with clients to further their own interests.

1.8 Marriage and family therapists respect the rights of clients to make decisions and help them to understand the consequences of these decisions. Therapists clearly advise the clients that they have the responsibility to make decisions regarding relationships such as cohabitation, marriage, divorce, separation, reconciliation, custody, and visitation.

1.9 Marriage and family therapists continue therapeutic relationships only so long as it is reasonably clear that clients are benefiting from the relationship.

1.10 Marriage and family therapists assist persons in obtaining other therapeutic services if the therapist is unable or unwilling, for appropriate reasons, to provide professional help.

1.11 Marriage and family therapists do not abandon or neglect clients in treatment without making reasonable arrangements for the continuation of such treatment.

1.12 Marriage and family therapists obtain written informed consent from clients before videotaping, audio recording, or permitting third-party observation.

1.13 Marriage and family therapists, upon agreeing to provide services to a person or entity at the request of a third party, clarify, to the extent feasible and at the outset of the service, the nature of the relationship with each party and the limits of confidentiality.

Principle II
Confidentiality

Marriage and family therapists have unique confidentiality concerns because the client in a therapeutic relationship may be more than one person. Therapists respect and guard the confidences of each individual client.

2.1 Marriage and family therapists disclose to clients and other interested parties, as early as feasible in their professional contacts, the nature of confidentiality and possible limitations of the clients' right to confidentiality. Therapists review with clients the circumstances where confidential information may be requested and where disclosure of confidential information may be legally required. Circumstances may necessitate repeated disclosures.

2.2 Marriage and family therapists do not disclose client confidences except by written authorization or waiver, or where mandated or permitted by law. Verbal authorization will not be sufficient except in emergency situations, unless prohibited by law. When providing couple, family or group treatment, the therapist does not disclose information outside the treatment context without a written authorization from each individual competent to execute a waiver. In the context of couple, family or group treatment, the therapist may not reveal any individual's confidences to others in the client unit without the prior written permission of that individual.

2.3 Marriage and family therapists use client and/or clinical materials in teaching, writing, consulting, research, and public presentations only if a written waiver has been obtained in accordance with Subprinciple 2.2, or when appropriate steps have been taken to protect client identity and confidentiality.

2.4 Marriage and family therapists store, safeguard, and dispose of client records in ways that maintain confidentiality and in accord with applicable laws and professional standards.

2.5 Subsequent to the therapist moving from the area, closing the practice, or upon the death of the therapist, a marriage and family therapist arranges for the storage, transfer, or disposal of client records in ways that maintain confidentiality and safeguard the welfare of clients.

2.6 Marriage and family therapists, when consulting with colleagues or referral sources, do not share confidential information that could reasonably lead to the identification of a client, research participant, supervisee, or other person with whom they have a confidential relationship unless they have obtained the prior written consent of the client, research participant, supervisee, or other person with whom they have a confidential relationship. Information may be shared only to the extent necessary to achieve the purposes of the consultation.

Principle III
Professional Competence and Integrity

Marriage and family therapists maintain high standards of professional competence and integrity.

3.1 Marriage and family therapists pursue knowledge of new developments and maintain competence in marriage and family therapy through education, training, or supervised experience.

3.2 Marriage and family therapists maintain adequate knowledge of and adhere to applicable laws, ethics, and professional standards.

3.3 Marriage and family therapists seek appropriate professional assistance for their personal problems or conflicts that may impair work performance or clinical judgment.

3.4 Marriage and family therapists do not provide services that create a conflict of interest that may impair work performance or clinical judgment.

3.5 Marriage and family therapists, as presenters, teachers, supervisors, consultants and researchers, are dedicated to high standards of scholarship, present accurate information, and disclose potential conflicts of interest.

3.6 Marriage and family therapists maintain accurate and adequate clinical and financial records.

3.7 While developing new skills in specialty areas, marriage and family therapists take steps to ensure the competence of their work and to protect clients from possible harm. Marriage and family therapists practice in specialty areas new to them only after appropriate education, training, or supervised experience.

3.8 Marriage and family therapists do not engage in sexual or other forms of harassment of clients, students, trainees, supervisees, employees, colleagues, or research subjects.

3.9 Marriage and family therapists do not engage in the exploitation of clients, students, trainees, supervisees, employees, colleagues, or research subjects.

3.10 Marriage and family therapists do not give to or receive from clients (a) gifts of substantial value or (b) gifts that impair the integrity or efficacy of the therapeutic relationship.

3.11 Marriage and family therapists do not diagnose, treat, or advise on problems outside the recognized boundaries of their competencies.

3.12 Marriage and family therapists make efforts to prevent the distortion or misuse of their clinical and research findings.

3.13 Marriage and family therapists, because of their ability to influence and alter the lives of others, exercise special care when making public their professional recommendations and opinions through testimony or other public statements.

3.14 To avoid a conflict of interests, marriage and family therapists who treat minors or adults involved in custody or visitation actions may not also perform forensic evaluations for custody, residence, or visitation of the minor. The marriage and family therapist who treats the minor may provide the court or mental health professional performing the evaluation with information about the minor from the marriage and family therapist's perspective as a treating marriage and family therapist, so long as the marriage and family therapist does not violate confidentiality.

3.15 Marriage and family therapists are in violation of this Code and subject to termination of membership or other appropriate action if they: (a) are convicted of any felony; (b) are convicted of a misdemeanor related to their qualifications or functions; (c) engage in conduct which could lead to conviction of a felony, or a misdemeanor related to their qualifications or functions; (d) are expelled from or disciplined by other professional organizations; (e) have their licenses or certificates suspended or revoked or are otherwise disciplined by regulatory bodies; (f) continue to practice marriage and family therapy while no longer competent to do so because they are impaired by physical or mental causes or the abuse of alcohol or other substances; or (g) fail to cooperate with the Association at any point from the inception of an ethical complaint through the completion of all proceedings regarding that complaint.

Principle IV
Responsibility to Students and Supervisees

Marriage and family therapists do not exploit the trust and dependency of students and supervisees.

4.1 Marriage and family therapists are aware of their influential positions with respect to students and supervisees, and they avoid exploiting the trust and dependency of such persons. Therapists, therefore, make every effort to avoid conditions and multiple relationships that could impair professional objectivity or increase the risk of exploitation. When the risk of impairment or exploitation exists due to conditions or multiple roles, therapists take appropriate precautions.

4.2 Marriage and family therapists do not provide therapy to current students or supervisees.

4.3 Marriage and family therapists do not engage in sexual intimacy with students or supervisees during the evaluative or training relationship between the therapist and student or supervisee. Should a supervisor engage in sexual activity with a former supervisee, the burden of proof shifts to the supervisor to demonstrate that there has been no exploitation or injury to the supervisee.

4.4 Marriage and family therapists do not permit students or supervisees to perform or to hold themselves out as competent to perform professional services beyond their training, level of experience, and competence.

4.5 Marriage and family therapists take reasonable measures to ensure that services provided by supervisees are professional.

4.6 Marriage and family therapists avoid accepting as supervisees or students those individuals with whom a prior or existing relationship could compromise the therapist's objectivity. When such situations cannot be avoided, therapists take appropriate precautions to maintain objectivity. Examples of such relationships include, but are not limited to, those individuals with whom the therapist has a current or prior sexual, close personal, immediate familial, or therapeutic relationship.

4.7 Marriage and family therapists do not disclose supervisee confidences except by written authorization or waiver, or when mandated or permitted by law. In educational or training settings where there are multiple supervisors, disclosures are permitted only to other professional colleagues, administrators, or employers who share responsibility for training of the supervisee. Verbal authorization will not be sufficient except in emergency situations, unless prohibited by law.

Principle V
Responsibility to Research Participants

Investigators respect the dignity and protect the welfare of research participants, and are aware of applicable laws and regulations and professional standards governing the conduct of research.

5. 1 Investigators are responsible for making careful examinations of ethical acceptability in planning studies. To the extent that services to research participants may be compromised by participation in research, investigators seek the ethical advice of qualified professionals not directly involved in the investigation and observe safeguards to protect the rights of research participants.

5. 2 Investigators requesting participant involvement in research inform participants of the aspects of the research that might reasonably be expected to influence willingness to participate. Investigators are especially sensitive to the possibility of diminished consent when participants are also receiving clinical services, or have impairments which limit understanding and/or communication, or when participants are children.

5.3 Investigators respect each participant's freedom to decline participation in or to withdraw from a research study at any time. This obligation requires special thought and consideration when investigators or other members of the research team are in positions of authority or influence over participants. Marriage and family therapists, therefore, make every effort to avoid multiple relationships with research participants that could impair professional judgment or increase the risk of exploitation.

5.4 Information obtained about a research participant during the course of an investigation is confidential unless there is a waiver previously obtained in writing. When the possibility exists that others, including family members, may obtain access to such information, this possibility, together with the plan for protecting confidentiality, is explained as part of the procedure for obtaining informed consent.

Principle VI
Responsibility to the Profession

Marriage and family therapists respect the rights and responsibilities of professional colleagues and participate in activities that advance the goals of the profession.

6.1 Marriage and family therapists remain accountable to the standards of the profession when acting as members or employees of organizations. If the mandates of an organization with which a marriage and family therapist is affiliated, through employment, contract or otherwise, conflict with the AAMFT Code of Ethics, marriage and family therapists make known to the organization their commitment to the AAMFT Code of Ethics and attempt to resolve the conflict in a way that allows the fullest adherence to the Code of Ethics.

6.2 Marriage and family therapists assign publication credit to those who have contributed to a publication in proportion to their contributions and in accordance with customary professional publication practices.

6.3 Marriage and family therapists do not accept or require authorship credit for a publication based on research from a student's program, unless the therapist made a substantial contribution beyond being a faculty advisor or research committee member. Coauthorship on a student thesis, dissertation, or project should be determined in accordance with principles of fairness and justice.

6.4 Marriage and family therapists who are the authors of books or other materials that are published or distributed do not plagiarize or fail to cite persons to whom credit for original ideas or work is due.

6.5 Marriage and family therapists who are the authors of books or other materials published or distributed by an organization take reasonable precautions to ensure that the organization promotes and advertises the materials accurately and factually.

6.6 Marriage and family therapists participate in activities that contribute to a better community and society, including devoting a portion of their professional activity to services for which there is little or no financial return.

6.7 Marriage and family therapists are concerned with developing laws and regulations pertaining to marriage and family therapy that serve the public interest, and with altering such laws and regulations that are not in the public interest.

6.8 Marriage and family therapists encourage public participation in the design and delivery of professional services and in the regulation of practitioners.

Principle VII
Financial Arrangements

Marriage and family therapists make financial arrangements with clients, third-party payors, and supervisees that are reasonably understandable and conform to accepted professional practices.

7.1 Marriage and family therapists do not offer or accept kickbacks, rebates, bonuses, or other remuneration for referrals; fee-for-service arrangements are not prohibited.

7.2 Prior to entering into the therapeutic or supervisory relationship, marriage and family therapists clearly disclose and explain to clients and supervisees: (a) all financial arrangements and fees related to professional services, including charges for canceled or missed appointments; (b) the use of collection agencies or legal measures for nonpayment; and (c) the procedure for obtaining payment from the client, to the extent allowed by law, if payment is denied by the third-party payor. Once services have begun, therapists provide reasonable notice of any changes in fees or other charges.

7.3 Marriage and family therapists give reasonable notice to clients with unpaid balances of their intent to seek collection by agency or legal recourse. When such action is taken, therapists will not disclose clinical information.

7.4 Marriage and family therapists represent facts truthfully to clients, third-party payors, and supervisees regarding services rendered.

7.5 Marriage and family therapists ordinarily refrain from accepting goods and services from clients in return for services rendered. Bartering for professional services may be conducted only if: (a) the supervisee or client requests it, (b) the relationship is not exploitative, (c) the professional relationship is not distorted, and (d) a clear written contract is established.

7.6 Marriage and family therapists may not withhold records under their immediate control that are requested and needed for a client's treatment solely because payment has not been received for past services, except as otherwise provided by law.

Principle VIII
Advertising

Marriage and family therapists engage in appropriate informational activities, including those that enable the public, referral sources, or others to choose professional services on an informed basis.

8.1 Marriage and family therapists accurately represent their competencies, education, training, and experience relevant to their practice of marriage and family therapy.

8.2 Marriage and family therapists ensure that advertisements and publications in any media (such as directories, announcements, business cards, newspapers, radio, television, Internet, and facsimiles) convey information that is necessary for the public to make an appropriate selection of professional services. Information could include: (a) office information, such as name, address, telephone number, credit card acceptability, fees, languages spoken, and office hours; (b) qualifying clinical degree (see subprinciple 8.5); (c) other earned degrees (see subprinciple 8.5) and state or provincial licensures and/or certifications; (d) AAMFT clinical member status; and (e) description of practice.

8.3 Marriage and family therapists do not use names that could mislead the public concerning the identity, responsibility, source, and status of those practicing under that name, and do not hold themselves out as being partners or associates of a firm if they are not.

8.4 Marriage and family therapists do not use any professional identification (such as a business card, office sign, letterhead, Internet, or telephone or association directory listing) if it includes a statement or claim that is false, fraudulent, misleading, or deceptive.

8.5 In representing their educational qualifications, marriage and family therapists list and claim as evidence only those earned degrees: (a) from institutions accredited by regional accreditation sources recognized by the United States Department of Education, (b) from institutions recognized by states or provinces that license or certify marriage and family therapists, or (c) from equivalent foreign institutions.

8.6 Marriage and family therapists correct, wherever possible, false, misleading, or inaccurate information and representations made by others concerning the therapist's qualifications, services, or products.

8.7 Marriage and family therapists make certain that the qualifications of their employees or supervisees are represented in a manner that is not false, misleading, or deceptive.

8.8 Marriage and family therapists do not represent themselves as providing specialized services unless they have the appropriate education, training, or supervised experience.

This Code is published by:
American Association for Marriage and Family Therapy
1133 15th Street, NW Suite 300
Washington, DC 20005-2710
(202) 452-0109
(202) 223-2329 FAX
www.aamft.org

Violations of this Code should be brought in writing to the attention of:
AAMFT Ethics Committee
1133 15th Street, NW, Suite 300
Washington, DC 20005-2710
telephone 202/452-0109 - email: ethics@aamft.org

LIST OF REFERENCES

Ackerman, Marc J. & L.J. Steffen. "Child Custody Evaluation Practices: A Survey of Experienced Judges." In preparation.

Ackerman, Marc J. & Melissa Ackerman. "Child Custody Evaluation Practices: A 1996 Survey of Psychologists." *Family Law Quarterly* 30 (1996): 565–86.

Ackerman, Marc J. & Melissa Ackerman. "Custody Evaluation Practices: A Survey of Experienced Professionals (Revisited)." *Professional Psychology: Research and Practice* 28 (1997): 137–45.

Ackerman, Marc J. & S. Kelley. "Child Custody Evaluation Practices: A Survey of Experienced Attorneys." In preparation.

Ackerman, Marc J. & Andrew W. Kane. *Psychological Experts in Divorce Actions*. 3rd ed. New York: Aspen Law and Business, 1998.

Ackerman, Marc. J. *The Essentials of Forensic Psychological Assessment.* New York: John Wiley & Sons, 1999.

Allnutt, S.H., J. M.W. Bradford, D.M. Greenburg, & S. Curry. "Comorbidity of Alcoholism and the Paraphilias."*Journal of Forensic Sciences* 41 (1996): 234–39.

American Bar Association Commission on Mental and Physical Disability Law. *National Benchbook on Psychiatric and Psychological Evidence and Testimony*. Washington, D.C.: American Bar Association, 1998.

American Psychiatric Association. *Diagnostic and Statistical Manual of Mental Disorders, Fourth Edition, Text Revision (DSM-IV-TR).* Washington D.C.: American Psychiatric Association, 2000.

Association of State and Provincial Psychology Boards. Personal communication, April 20, 2000.

Azar, Beth. "Changes Will Improve Quality of Tests." *American Psychological Association Monitor* 30 (1999): 30.

Barnett, D., J. Ganiban & D. Cicchetti. "Maltreatment, Negative Expressivity, and the Development of Type D Attachments from 12 to 24 Months of Age." *Monographs of the Society for Research in Child Development* 64(3) (1999): 97–118.

LIST OF REFERENCES

Bartoi, M.G. & B.N. Kinder. "Effects of Child and Adult Sexual Abuse on Adult Sexuality." *Journal of Sex and Marital Therapy* 24 (1998): 75–90.

Behnke, Stephen. "Release of Test Data and APA's New Ethics Code." *Monitor on Psychology* 34 (2003): 70–72.

Berliner, L. & B.E. Saunders. "Treating Fear and Anxiety in Sexually Abused Children: Results of a Controlled 2-Year Follow-up Study." *Child Maltreatment* 1 (1996): 294–309.

Blanchard et al. "Pedophiles: Mental Retardation, Maternal Age, and Sexual Orientation." *Archives of Sexual Behavior* 28 (1999): 111–27.

Blanchard, E., E. Hickling, A. Taylor, W. Loos, C. Forneris & J. Jaccardi. "Who Develops PTSD from Motor Vehicle Accidents?" *Behavioral Research and Therapy* 34 (1996).

Boney-McCoy, S. & D. Finklehor. "Psychosocial Sequelae of Violent Victimization in a National Youth Sample." *Journal of Consulting and Clinical Psychology* 63(5) (1995): 726–36.

Bow J.N. & F.A. Quinnell. "Child Custody Practices—Five Years Post APA Guidelines." Symposium presented at the Annual Convention of the American Psychological Association, Washington, D.C., August, 2000.

Bow, James N. & Francella A. Quinnell. "Psychologists' Current Practices and Procedures in Child Custody Evaluations: Five Years After American Psychological Association Guidelines." *Professional Psychology: Research and Practice* 32 (2001): 261–68.

Braver, M., J. Bumberry, K. Green & R. Rawson. "Childhood Abuse and Current Psychological Functioning in a University Counseling Center Population." *Journal of Counseling Psychology* 39(2) (1992): 252–57.

Briere, J. "A Self-Trauma Model for Treating Adult Survivors of Severe Child Abuse." In J. Briere, L. Berliner, J. Bulkley, C. Jenny & T. Reid (eds.), *APSAC Handbook on Child Maltreatment,* pp. 140–57. Thousand Oaks, CA: Sage, 1996.

Briere, J. *Therapy for Adults Molested as Children* (2d ed.). New York: Springer, 1996.

Briere, J. & E. Gil. "Self-Mutilation in Clinical and General Population Samples: Prevalence, Correlates, and Functions." *American Journal of Orthopsychiatry* 68 (1998): 609–20.

Briere, J. & M. Runtz. "Child Sexual Abuse: Long-Term Sequelae and Implications for Assessment." *Journal of Interpersonal Violence* 8 (1993): 312–30.

LIST OF REFERENCES

Bumby, K. M. & D. J. Hansen. "Intimacy Deficits, Fear of Intimacy, and Loneliness among Sexual Offenders." *Criminal Justice and Behavior* 24 (1997): 315–31.

Chester, B., R.W. Robin, M.P. Koss, T. Lopez & D. Goldman. "Grandmother Dishonored: Violence Against Women by Male Partners in American Indian Communities." *Violence & Victims* 9 (1994): 249–58.

Chu, J. A. & D. L. Dill. "Dissociative Symptoms in Relation to Childhood Physical and Sexual Abuse." *American Journal of Psychiatry* 147 (1990): 887–92.

Cicchetti, D. & S. Toth. "A Developmental Psychopathology Perspective on Child Abuse and Neglect." *Journal of American Academy of Child and Adolescent Psychiatry*, 34(5) (1995): 541–65.

Connell, Mary & Gerald P. Koocher. "Expert Opinion: HIPAA and Forensic Practice." *American Psychology-Law Society News* 23 (2003): 18–19.

Craig, Robert J. "Testimony Based on the Millon Clinical Multiaxial Inventory: Review, Commentary, and Guidelines." *Journal of Personality Assessment* 73 (1999): 290–304.

Crosby-Currie, C.A. "Children's Involvement in Contested Custody Cases: Practices and Experiences of Legal and Mental Health Professionals." *Law and Human Behavior* 20 (1996): 289–311.

Draucker, Claire. "Family-Of-Origin Variables and Adult Female Survivors of Childhood Sexual Abuse: A Review of the Research." *Journal of Child Sexual Abuse* 5 (1996): 35–63.

Drogin, Eric Y. "Prophets in Another Land: Utilizing Psychological Expertise from Foreign Jurisdictions." *Mental and Physical Disability Law Reporter* 23 (1999): 767–71.

Dubner, A.E. & R.W. Motta. "Sexually and Physically Abused Foster Care Children and Posttraumatic Stress Disorder." *Journal of Consulting and Physical Psychology* 67 (1999): 367–73.

Duncan, L.E. & L.M. Williams. "Gender Role Socialization and Male-on-Male vs. Female-on-Male Child Sexual Abuse." *Sex Roles* 39 (1998): 765–85.

Dyer, Frank J. & Joseph T. McCann. "The Millon Clinical Inventories, Research Critical of Their Forensic Application, and Daubert Criteria." *Law and Human Behavior* 24 (2000): 487–97.

Eddelson, J.L. "Problems with Children's Witnessing of Domestic Violence." *National Resource Center on Domestic Violence,* 1997. Available at *http://www.vaw.umn.edu.*

LIST OF REFERENCES

Elliott, D.M. "Impaired Object Relations in Professional Women Molested as Children." *Psychotherapy* 21 (1994): 79–86.

Elliott, D.M. & J. Breire. "Sexual Abuse Trauma among Professional Women: Validating the Trauma Symptom Checklist-40 (TSC-40)." *Child Abuse & Neglect* 16 (1992): 391–98.

Faller, Kathleen Coulborn. "The Parental Alienation Syndrome: What Is It and What Data Support It?" *Child Maltreatment* 3 (1998): 100.

Famulario, R., R. Kinschereff & T. Fenton. "Posttraumatic Stress Disorder among Children Clinically Diagnosed as Borderline Personality Disorder." *Journal of Nervous and Mental Diseases* 170 (1991): 428–31.

Famulario, R., T. Fenton, M. Augustyn & B. Zukerman. "Persistence of Pediatric Post Traumatic Stress Disorder After 2 Years." *Child Abuse & Neglect* 20(12) (1996): 1245–48.

Fantuzzo, J., W. DelGaudio, M. Atkins, R. Meyers & M. Noone. "A Contextually Relevant Assessment of the Impact of Child Maltreatment on the Social Competencies of Low-Income Urban Children." *Journal of American Academy of Child and Adolescent Psychiatry* 37(11) (1998): 1201–08.

Fantuzzo, J. & W. Mohr. "Prevalence and Effects of Child Exposure to Domestic Violence: The Future of Children." *Domestic Violence and Children* 9 (1999).

Fisher, Celia B. *Decoding the Ethics Code: A Practical Guide for Psychologists.* Thousand Oaks, CA: Sage, 2003: 29.

Gardner, Richard. "Recommendations for Dealing with Parents Who Induce a Parent Alienation Syndrome in Their Children." *Journal of Divorce and Remarriage* 28 (1998): 1–23.

Garlic, Y., W.L. Marshall & D. Thornton. "Intimacy Deficits and Attribution of Blame among Sexual Offenders." *Legal and Criminological Psychology* 1 (1996): 251–58.

Georgia Psychological Association. *Recommendations for Psychologists' Involvement in Child Custody Cases.* Atlanta, Ga.: Georgia Psychological Association, 1990.

Goldberg, R., W. Pachas & D. Keith. "Relationship Between Traumatic Events in Childhood and Chronic Pain." *Disability and Rehabilitation: An International Multidisciplinary Journal* 21(1) (1999): 23–30.

Graham-Bermann, S.A. "Family Worries: The Assessment of Interpersonal Anxiety in Children from Violent and Nonviolent Families." *Journal of Clinical Child Psychology* 25(3) (1996): 280–87.

LIST OF REFERENCES

Graham-Bermann, S.A. & A.A. Levendosky. "The Social Functioning of Preschool-Age Children Whose Mothers are Emotionally and Physically Abused." *Journal of Emotional Abuse* 1 (1998): 59–84.

Greenberg, S. "Liability and Immunity of the Expert Witness." Symposium presented at the Annual Convention of the American Psychological Association, San Francisco, CA, August, 2001.

Gronnerod, Cato. "Temporal Stability in the Rorschach Method: A Meta-Analytic Review." *Journal of Personality Assessment* 80 (2003): 287.

Hagen, Margaret A. & Castagna, Nicole. "The Real Numbers: Psychological Testing in Custody Evaluations." *Professional Psychology: Research and Practice* 32 (2001): 269–71.

Hampton, R.L. & R.J. Gelles. "Violence toward Black Women in a Nationally Representative Sample of Black Families." *Journal of Comparative Family Studies* 25 (1994): 105–19.

Healy, K. & C. Smith. "Batterer Programs: What Criminal Justice Agencies Need to Know." *Research in Action,* July. Washington, DC: National Institute of Justice (NCJ171683), 1998.

Hellman, J. "A Survey of Judges, School Psychologists, Private Psychologists and Attorneys Regarding the Child Custody Determination Process." University of Northern Colorado.

Hess, Allen. "Millon Clinical Multiaxial Inventory-III." In James C. Impara and Barbara S. Plake, *The Thirteenth Mental Measurements Yearbook.* Lincoln, Nebraska: University of Nebraska-Lincoln (1998): at 665–67.

Hibbard, Stephen. "A Critique of Lilienfeld *et al.'s* 'The Scientific Status of Projective Techniques.'" *Journal of Personal Assessment* 80 (2003): 260–71.

Higgins, J., R. Gore, D. Gutkind. "Effects of Child-rearing by Schizophrenic Mothers: A 25-Year Follow-up." Acta Psychiatrica Scandinavica 96 (1997): 402–04.

Ho, C.K. "An Analysis of Domestic Violence in Asian American Communities: A Multicultural Approach to Counseling." In K.P. Monteiro (ed.), *Ethnicity and Psychology,* pp. 138–51. Dubuque, IA: Kendall-Hunt, 1996.

Ho, M.K. *Minority Children and Adolescents in Therapy.* Newbury Park, CA: Sage, 1992.

Hughes, H.M. "Impact of Spouse Abuse on Children of Battered Women." *Violence Update* 2 (1992): 8–11.

LIST OF REFERENCES

Hughes, H.M., & Graham-Bermann, S.A. "Children of Battered Women: Impact of Emotional Abuse on Adjustment and Development." *Journal of Emotional Abuse,* 1(2) (1998): 23–50.

Jackson, A.M., N.S. Warner, R. Hornbein, N. Nelson & E. Fortescue. "Beyond the Best Interests of the Child Revisited: An Approach to Custody Evaluations." *Journal of Divorce* 3 (1980): 207–22.

Johnson, Jeanne J. & Jeffrey L. Helms. "Test Security in the Twenty-First Century." *American Journal of Forensic Psychology* 21 (2003): 24 and 27–28.

Joint Committee on Standards for Educational and Psychological Testing of the American Education Research Association, the American Psychological Association, and the National Council on Measurement in Education. *Standards for Educational and Psychological Testing.* Washington, D.C.: American Educational Research Association, 1999.

Joint Committee on Testing Practices. *Rights and Responsibilities of Test Takers: Guidelines and Expectations.* Washington D.C.: JCTP Publications, 2000.

Jones, Ann. *Next Time, She'll Be Dead: Battering & How To Stop It,* Boston: Beacon Press, 1994.

Jouriles, E.N. & W.D. Norwood. "Physical Aggression toward Boys and Girls in Families Characterized by the Battering of Women." *Journal of Family Psychology* 9 (1995): 69–78.

Kantor, G.K., J.L. Jasinski & E. Aldarondo. "Socioeconomic Status and Incidence of Marital Violence in Hispanic Families." *Violence & Victims* 9 (1994): 207–22.

Keilitz, S., P. Hannaford & H. Efkman. "The Effectiveness of Civil Protection Orders." In *Legal Interventions in Family Violence: Research Findings and Policy Implications,* a project of the American Bar Association's Criminal Justice Section, Commission on Domestic Violence, Center on Children and the Law and Commission on Legal Problems of the Elderly presented to the National Institute of Justice. July, 1998 NCJ 171666, 47–48.

Kilpatrick, D.G. & B.E. Saunders. *Prevalence and Consequences of Child Victimization: Results from the National Survey of Adolescents* (No. 93-IJ-CX-0023). Charleston: National Crime Victims Research & Treatment Center, Department of Psychiatry & Behavioral Sciences, Medical University of South Carolina, 1999.

Kirkland, Karl & Kristen L. Kirkland. "Frequency of Child Custody Evaluation Complaints and Related Disciplinary Action: A Survey of the

Association of State and Provincial Psychology Boards." *Professional Psychology: Research and Practice* 32 (2001): 171–74.

Koopman, E.J., E.J. Hunt, F.G. Favretto, L.S. Coltri, & T. Britten. "Professional Perspectives on Court-Connected Custody Mediation." *Family and Conciliation Courts Review* 29 (1991): 304–17.

Krugman, R.D., & M.K. Krugman. "Emotional Abuse in the Classroom." *American Journal of Diseases of Children* 138 (1984): 284–86.

LaFortune, K. & B. Carpenter. "Child Custody Evaluation Practices: A Survey of Mental Health Professionals." *Behavioral Sciences and the Law* 16 (1998): 207–24.

LaFortune, K.A. & B.N. Carpenter. "Custody Evaluations: A Survey of Mental Health Professionals." *Behavioral Sciences and the Law* 16 (1998): 207–24.

Lampel, Anita. "Use of the Millon Clinical Multiaxial Inventory-III in Evaluating Child Custody Litigants." *American Journal of Forensic Psychology* 17 (1999): 19–31.

Landberg, G. "Proposed Model for the Intervention of the Mental Health Specialist in the Resolution of Difficult Child Custody Disputes." *Journal of Preventive Psychiatry* 1(3) (1982): 309–18.

Lee, C.M., C.P.M. Beauregard & J. Hunsley. "Lawyers' Opinions Regarding Child Custody Mediation and Assessment Services: Implications for Psychological Practice." *Professional Psychology* 29(2) (1998): 120–55.

Lee, M.Y. & P. Au. "Chinese Battered Women in North America: Their Experience and Treatment." In A.R. Roberts (ed.), *Battered Women and Their Families,* 2d ed., pp. 448–82. New York: Springer, 1998.

Lenihan, Jenie. "Childhood Sexual Abuse: Gender Differences in Prevalence, Experience and Outcomes." Paper presented at the 104th Annual Convention of the American Psychological Association, Toronto, Canada, August 1996.

Lesserman, J., Z. Li, D. Drossman, T.C. Toomey, G. Nachman & L. Glogau. "Impact of Sexual and Physical Abuse Dimensions on Health Status: Development of an Abuse Severity Measure." *Psychomatic Medicine* 59(2) (1997): 152–60.

Leviatian, R. D., S.V. Parikh, A.D. Lesage, K.M. Hegadoren & M. Adams. "Major Depression in Individuals with a History of Child Physical or Sexual Abuse: Relationship to Neurovegetative Features, Mania, and Gender." *American Journal of Psychiatry* 155 (1998): 1746–52.

LIST OF REFERENCES

Lilienfeld, Scott O., James M. Wood & Howard N. Garb. "The Scientific Status of Projective Techniques." *Psychological Science in the Public Interest* 1 (2000): 27–66.

Lohr, Jeffrey M., Katherine A. Fowler & Scott O. Lilienfeld. "The Dissemination and Promotion of Pseudoscience in Clinical Psychology: The Challenge to Legitimate Clinical Science." *The Clinical Psychologist* 55(3) (2002): 5.

Lombardo, S. & R. Pohl. "Sexual Abuse History of Women Treated in Psychiatric Outpatient Clinic." *Psychiatric Services* 48 (1997): 534–36.

Lowenstein, L.F. "Parental Alienation Syndrome: A Two-Step Approach Toward a Solution." *Contemporary Family* 20 (1998): 514.

Mannarino, A.P. & J.A. Cohen. "Abuse-Related Attributions and Perceptions, General Attributions, and Locus of Control in Sexually Abused Girls." *Journal of Interpersonal Violence* 11 (1996): 162–80.

Marshall, W.L. *Phallometric Testing with Sexual Offenders: Limits to Its Value*. Submitted for publication, 1997.

Marshall, W.L., D. Anderson & F. Champagne. "The Importance of Self-Esteem in Sexual Offenders." *Psychology, Crime and Law* 3 (1996): 81–106.

Marshall, W.L., S.M. Hudson, R. Jones & Y.M. Fernandez. "Empathy in Sex Offenders." *Clinical Psychology Review* 15 (1995): 99–113.

Maynes, L.C. & L.L. Feinauer. "Acute and Chronic Dissociation and Somatized Anxiety as Related to Childhood Sexual Abuse." *American Journal of Family Therapy* 22 (1994): 265–75.

Millon T., R. Davis & C. Millon. "The Millon Clinical Multiaxial Inventory-III Manual (2d ed.)." Minneapolis, MN: National Computer Systems (1997): 98.

Moenssens, Andre A., ed. *www.forensic-evidence.com*. University of Missouri-Kansas City School of Law.

Mok, Doris & Diana Elliott. "Gender Comparison of Child Sexual Abuse." Paper presented at the Annual Convention of the American Psychological Association, Toronto, Canada, August, 1996.

Nebraska Psychological Association. *Guidelines for Child Custody Evaluations*. Lincoln, Nebr.: Nebraska Psychological Association, 1986.

Neff, J.A., B. Holamon & T.D. Schluter. "Spousal Violence among Anglos, Blacks, and Mexican-Americans: The Role of Demographic Variables, Psychosocial Predictors, and Alcohol Consumption." *Journal of Family Violence* 10 (1995): 1–21.

LIST OF REFERENCES

New Jersey State Board of Psychological Examiners. *Specialty Guidelines for Psychologists in Custody/Visitation Evaluations*. Newark, N.J.: New Jersey State Board of Psychological Examiners, 1993.

Norton, I.M. & S.M. Manson. "A Silent Minority: Battered American Indian Women." *Journal of Family Violence* 10 (1995): 307–17.

Parker, J.G. & C. Herrera. "Interpersonal Processes in Friendship: A Comparison of Abused and Nonabused Children's Experiences." *Developmental Psychology* 32(6) (1996): 1025–38.

Parry, John W. "Admissibility of Expert Evidence." *Mental and Physical Disability Law Reporter* 24 (2000): 10.

Pelcovitz, D., S. Kaplan, B. Goldenberg, F. Mandell, J. Lehane & J. Guarrera. Post-traumatic Stress Disorder in Physically Abused Adolescents. *Journal of American Academy of Child and Adolescent Psychiatry* 33(3) (1996): 305–12.

Peters, Debra & Lillian Range. "Self-Blame and Self-Destruction in Sexually Abused Children." *Journal of Child Sexual Abuse* 5 (1996): 19–33.

Piran, N., P. Lerner, P.E. Garfinkel, S.H. Kennedy & C. Brouillette. "Personality Disorders in Anoretic Patients." *International Journal of Eating Disorders* 7 (1998): 589–99.

Polusny, M.A. & V.M. Follette. Long-Term Correlates of Child Sexual Abuse: Theory and Review of the Empirical Literature. *Applied and Preventive Psychology* 4 (1995): 143–66.

Rand, Deirdre Conway. The Spectrum of Parental Alienation Syndrome. *American Journal of Forensic Psychology* 15 (1997): 23–92.

Raymond, N.C., E. Coleman, F. Ohlerking, G.A. Christenson & M. Miner. "Psychiatric Comorbidity in Pedophilic Sex Offenders." *Americal Journal of Psychiatry* 156 (1999): 786–88.

Retzlaff, Paul D. "Comment on the Validity of the MCMI-III." Law and Human Behavior 24 (2000): 499–500.

Retzlaff, Paul. "Millon Clinical Multiaxial Inventory-III." In James C. Impara and Barbara S. Plake, *The Thirteenth Mental Measurements Yearbook.* Lincoln, Nebraska: University of Nebraska-Lincoln (1998): at 667–68.

Risin, Leslie & J. Regis MacNamara. "Validation of Child Sexual Abuse: The Psychologist's Role." *Journal of Clinical Psychiatry* 45 (1989): 175–84.

Rogers, Richard, Randall T. Salekin, & Kenneth W. Sewell. "The MCMI-III and the *Daubert* Standard: Separating Rhetoric from Reality." *Law and Human Behavior* 24 (2000): 501–06.

LIST OF REFERENCES

Rogers, Richard, Randall T. Salekin, and Kenneth W. Sewell. "Validation of the Millon Clinical Multiaxial Inventory for Axis II Disorders: Does It Meet the *Daubert* Standard?" *Law and Human Behavior* 23 (1999): 425–33.

Rossman, B.B.R., H.M. Hughes & M.S. Rosenberg. *Children and Interpersonal Violence: The Impact of Exposure*. Philadelphia, PA: Brunner/Mazel, 2000.

Roys, Deloris & Robert Timms. "Personality Profile of Adult Males Sexually Molested by Their Maternal Caregivers: Preliminary Findings." *Journal of Child Sexual Abuse* 4 (1995): 63–77.

Salmon, P. & S. Calderbank. The Relationship of Childhood Physical and Sexual Abuse to Adult Illness Behavior. *Journal of Psychosomatic Research* 40(3) (1996): 329–36.

Sanders, M.J. & B. Bursch. "Forensic Assessment of Illness Falsification, Munchausen by Proxy, and Facticious Disorder, NOS." *Child Maltreatment* 7 (2002): 112–24.

Sattler, J. *Clinical and Forensic Interviewing of Children and Families*. San Diego: Jerome M. Sattler Publishing. Inc., 1998.

Saunders et al. "Prevalence, Case Characteristics, and Long-Term Psychological Correlates of Child Rape among Women: A National Survey." *Child Maltreatment: Journal of the American Professional Society in the Abuse of Children* 4 (1999): 187–200.

Schreier, H. & J. Libow. "Munchausen Syndrome by Proxy: Diagnosis and Prevalence." *American Journal of Orthopsychiatry* 63 (1993): 318–29.

Schutte, James W. "Using the MCMI-III in Forensic Evaluations." *American Journal of Forensic Psychology* 19 (2000): 5–20.

Scott, R. I. & H.D. Day. "Association of Abuse-Related Symptoms and Style of Anger Expression for Female Survivors of Childhood Incest." *Journal of Interpersonal Violence* 11 (1996): 207–20.

Sexton, Mark et al. "Sexual Abuse and Body Image: A comparison of Abused and Non-Abused Women." Paper presented at the 98th Annual Meeting of the American Psychological Association, Boston, August 1990.

Shear L.E. "Children's Lawyers in California Family Law Courts: Balancing Competing Policies and Values Regarding Questions of Ethics." *Family and Conciliation Courts Review* 34(2) (1996): 256–302.

Sigmon, Sandra, Melodie Greene, Kelly Rohan, and Jennifer Nichols. "Copies and Adjustment in Male and Female Survivors of Childhood Sexual Abuse." *Journal of Child Sexual Abuse* 5 (1996): 57–75.

LIST OF REFERENCES

Simon, R.I. "The Credible Forensic Psychiatric Evaluation in Sexual Harassment Litigation." *Psychiatric Annuals* 26 (1996): 139–48.

Simon, Robert I. & Daniel W. Shuman. "Conducting Forensic Examinations on the Road: Are You Practicing Your Profession Without a License?" *Journal of the American Academy of Psychiatry & Law* 27 (1999): 75–82.

Smarts, L.S. & C.J. Salts. "Attorney Attitudes Toward Divorce Mediation." *Mediation Quarterly* 6 (1984): 65–72.

Smith, Steven R. "Politics, Disability, Sexual Predators and More: Recent Decisions of the U.S. Supreme Court." *Bulletin of the American Academy of Forensic Psychology* 22 (2001): 1, 6–18 at 15.

Sorenson, S.B., D.M. Upchurch & H. Shen. "Violence and Injury in Marital Arguments: Risk Patterns and Gender Differences." *American Journal of Public Health* 86 (1996): 35–40.

Steiger, H. & M. Zanko. "Sexual Trauma among Eating Disordered, Psychiatric, and Normal Female Groups: Comparison of Prevalences and Defense Styles." *Journal of Interpersonal Violence* 5 (1990): 74–86.

Tang, C.S.-K. "Psychological Impact of Wife Abuse: Experiences of Chinese Women and Their Children." *Journal of Interpersonal Violence* 12 (1997): 466–78.

Thornberry, T. "Violent Families and Youth Violence." *Office of Juvenile Justice and Delinquency Prevention, Fact Sheet #21.* December 1994.

van der Kolk, B.A., J.C. Perry & J.L. Herman. "Childhood Origins of Self-Destructive Behavior." *American Journal of Psychiatry* 148 (1991): 1665–71.

Vissing,Y.M., M.A. Straus, R.J. Gelles & J.W. Harrop. "Verbal Aggression by Parents and Psychosocial Problems of Children." *Child Abuse & Neglect* 15 (1991): 223–38.

Walker, L. *The Battered Woman Syndrome* (2d ed.). New York: Springer Publishing, 2000.

Wallerstein, Judith & Tony J. Tanke. "To Move or Not to Move: Psychological and Legal Considerations in the Relocation of Children Following Divorce." *Family Law Quarterly* 30 (1996): 319.

Walsh, B.W. & P.M. Rosen. *Self-Mutilation: Theory, Research, and Treatment.* New York: Guilford, 1998.

Ward, T., S.M. Hudson & W.L. Marshall. "Attachment Styles in Sex Offenders: A Preliminary Study." *Journal of Sex Research* 33 (1996): 17–26.

LIST OF REFERENCES

Weiner, Irving B., Charles D. Spielberger & Norman Abeles. "Scientific Psychology and the Rorschach Inkblot Method." *The Clinical Psychologist* 55(4) (2002): 7–12.

Weiner, Richard. "Extending *Daubert* Beyond Scientific Expert Testimony." *American Psychological Association Monitor* 30 (1999): 47.

Weston, Drew, Pamella Ludolph, Barbara Misile, Stephen Ruffins & Judith Block. "Physical and Sexual Abuse in Adolescent Girls with Borderline Personality Disorder." *American Journal of Orthopsychiatry* 60 (1990): 55–66.

Wolf, D.A. & P.G. Jaffe. "Prevention of Domestic Violence: Emerging Initiatives." Paper presented at the Asilomar Conference on Children and Intimate Violence. Pacific Grove, CA, 1999.

Yoshihama, M. & S.B. Sorenson. "Physical, Sexual and Emotional Abuse by Male Intimates: Experiences of Women in Japan." *Violence & Victims* 9 (1994): 63–77.

Youngstrom, Eric A. & Christine P. Busch. "Expert Testimony in Psychology: Ramifications of Supreme Court Decision in *Kumho Tire Co., Ltd. v. Carmichael.*" *Ethics & Behavior* 10 (2000): 185–93.

TABLE OF CASES

TABLE OF CASES

Caraballo v. Hernandez, No. 92-3359 (Fla. Dist. Ct. App. 1993) § 4.43

Casby v. Hazlerig, W2001-02073-COA-R3-CV (Tenn. App. July 24, 2002) § 4.43

Colorado ex rel. S.J.C., 776 P.2d 1103 (Colo. Sup. Ct. 1989) § 14.26

Cook v. City of Topeka, 654 P.2d 953 (Kan. 1982) § 1.20

Corbett v. Morgenstern, 934 F. Supp. 680 (E.D. Pa. 1996) § 13.42

Coy v. Iowa, 487 U.S. 1012 (1988) § 6.7

Crafton v. Gibson, No. 40A04-011-CV-490 (Indiana Ct. of App., July 11, 2001) § 4.43

Crum v. Sullivan, 921 F.2d 642 (6th Cir. 1990) § 1.20

Culbertson v. Chapman, 496 N.W.2d 821 (Minn. Ct. App. 1993) § 2.31

Cummings v. Sherman, 132 P.2d 998 (Wash. 1943) § 3.25

Dalton v. Miller, 984 P.2d 666 (Colo. App. Ct. April 29, 1999) § 1.20

Darragh v. Superior Court, 900 P.2d 1215 (Ariz. Ct. App. 1995) § 1.18A

Daubert v. Merrell Dow Pharmaceuticals, Inc., 509 U.S. 579, 113 S. Ct. 2786, 125 L. Ed. 2d 469 (1993) §§ 1.14; 1.20; 2.1A

Daubert v. Merrell Dow Pharmaceuticals, Inc., 43 F.3d 1311 (9th Cir. 1995) §§ 1.20; 2.1A

David M. v. Margaret H., No. 19020 (W. Va. Oct. 19, 1989) § 14.26

Deatherage v. Examining Board of Psychology, 134 Wn. 2d 131, 948 P.2d 828 (Wash. 1997) § 1.18A

Deed v. Condrell, 568 N.Y.S.2d 679 (N.Y. Sup. Ct. 1991) § 1.20

Department of Public Social Services v. Diana G., 270 Cal. Rptr. 534 (Cal. Ct. App. 1990) § 14.26

D.G. v. Alabama Department of Human Resources, 569 So. 2d 400 (Ala. Civ. App. 1990) § 15.10

Dickerson v. Dickerson, 55 S.W.3d 267 (Mo. App. W.D. 2001), § 12.14

Dill v. Colorado, 927 P.2d 1315 (Colo. Sup. Ct. 1996) § 13.42

Doe v. Holt, No. 379PA91 (N.C. Sup. Ct. 1992) § 13.42

D'Onofrio v. D'Onofrio, 365 A.2d 27 (N.J. Sup. Ct. 1976) § 4.43

Duff v. Lewis, 958 P.2d 82 (Nev. 1998) §§ 1.18A; 1.20

Duffy v. Reeves, No. 91-590 (R.I. Sup. Ct. 1993) § 12.14

D.W. v. Alabama Deparatment of Human Resources, 595 So. 2d 502 (Ala. Civ. App. 1992), § 14.26

TABLE OF CASES

E.C. v. District of Columbia, 589 A.2d 1245 (D.C. 1991) § 14.26

Egly v. Blackford County (Indiana) Department of Public Welfare, No. 05A02-9003-CV-174 (Ind. Ct. App. 2d Dist. July 23, 1991) § 8.29

Elling v. Graves, 640 N.E.2d 1156 (Ohio Ct. App. 1994) § 1.20

Ellison (Eldridge) v. Ellison, No. 86696 (Okla. May 21, 1996) § 2.31

Estelle v. Smith, 451 U.S. 454 (1980) § 2.12

Fenwick v. Fenwick, No. 1999-SC-1055-DG (Ky. Sept. 18, 2003) § 4.43

Forrester v. White, 484 U.S. 219 (1988) § 1.20

Frasser v. United States, 83 F.3d 591 (2d Cir. 1996) § 2.31

Frasser v. United States, 236 Conn. 625 (Conn. 1996) § 2.31

Frye v. United States, 293 F. Supp. 1013 (D.C. Cir. 1923) § 1.14

General Electric Co. v. Joiner, 522 U.S. 136 (1997) §§ 1.20; 2.1A

Goodson v. Goodson, 816 So. 2d 420 (Miss. App. 2002) § 4.43

Gootee v. Lightner, 224 Cal. App. 3d 587 (1990) § 1.20

Green v. Ross, 691 So. 2d 542 (Fla. Dist. Ct. App. 1997) § 2.31

Guity v. Kandilakis, 821 S.W.2d 595 (Tenn. Ct. App. 1991) § 1.20

Gustafson v. Mazer, 54 P.3d 743, 113 Wash. App. 770 (Wash. Ct. App. 2002) § 1.20

Hadden v. Florida, No. 87,574 (Fla. 1997) § 13.42

Hadden v. State, 670 So. 2d 77 (Fla. App. 1st Dist. 1996) § 13.42

Hall v. Sykes, 164 F.R.D. 46, 33 Fed. R. Serv. 3d 428 (Va. 1996) § 1.20

Hartford Insurance Co. v. Manor Inn, 617 A.2d 590 (Md. Ct. Spec. App. 1992) § 2.31

Hayes v. Indiana, 667 N.E.2d 222 (Ind. Ct. App. 1996) § 2.31

Hartog v. Hartog, 535 N.E.2d 239 (Mass. App. Ct. 1989) § 1.20

Herndon v. Tuhey, No. 75184 (Mo. 1993) § 4.43

H.F. v. T.F., 168 Wis. 2d 62, 483 N.W.2d 803 (Wis. 1992) § 4.43

Hill v. Divecchio, No. 522 Pitt. 1991 (Pa. Super. Ct. 1993) § 4.43

Hodson v. Moore, 464 N.W.2d 699 (Iowa Ct. App. 1990) § 4.43

Hollandsworth v. Knyzewski, Case No. 02-720 (Ark. June 5, 2003) § 4.43

Holtzman v. Knott (In re H.S.H.-K), 533 N.W.2d 419 (Wis. Sup. Ct. 1995) § 4.43

Howard v. Drapkin, 271 Cal. Rptr. 893 (Cal. Ct. App. 1990) §§ 1.16; 1.20

TABLE OF CASES

TABLE OF CASES

Richard D. v. Rebecca G. 228 Wis. 2d 658, 599 N.W.2d 90 (Wis. Ct. App. 1999) § 4.43

R.J.M. v. State of Alaska, Dep't of Health and Soc. Servs., 1999 WL 35765 (Alaska, Jan 29, 1999) § 14.26

R.M. v. Tippecanoe County Department of Public Welfare, 582 N.E.2d 417 (Ind. Ct. App. 1991) § 14.26

Roe v. Superior Court, 280 Cal. Rptr. 380 (Ct. App. 1991) § 1.20

Rosenberg v. Helinski, 616 A.2d 866 (Md. 1992) § 1.20

Roth v. Bookert (In re Adoption of J.J.B.), 868 P.2d 1256 (N.M. Ct. App. 1993) § 4.43

Rowles v. Rowles, No. 73 W.D. 1994 (Pa., Nov. 29, 1995) § 4.43

Rubano v. DiCenzo, 759 A.2d 959 (R.I. 2000) § 4.43

Runyan v. Smith, 730 A.2d 881 (N.J. Super. Ct. App. Div. 1999) § 1.20

San Diego Department of Social Services v. Nita M., 268 Cal. Rptr. 214 (Cal. Ct. App. 1990) § 14.26

San Francisco Department of Social Services v. Joan R., 276 Cal. Rptr. 183 (Cal. Ct. App. 1990) § 15.10

Schever v. Rhodes, 416 U.S. 232 (1974) § 1.16

Schuster v. Altenberg, 144 Wis. 2d 223, 424 N.W.2d 159 (1988) § 2.22

Schwarcz v. Schwarcz, 548 A.2d 556 (Pa. Super. Ct. 1988) § 14.26

Sears v. Rutishauser, 466 N.E.2d 210 (Ill. 1984) § 1.16

Seider v. Board of Exam'rs of Psychologists, 762 A.2d 551 (Me. Sup. Jud. Ct. 2000) § 1.20

Seigneur v. Olson (In re Guardianship of Nelson), 519 N.W.2d 15 (N.D. 1994) § 4.43

S.E.S. v. Grant County Department of Welfare, 582 N.E.2d 886 (Ind. Ct. App. 1991) § 15.10

Sigg v. Sigg, No. 940650 (Utah Ct. App. Oct. 26, 1995) § 4.43

Silva v. Lori S1, 270 Cal. Rptr. 411 (Cal. Ct. App. 1990) § 14.26

S.J. v. Alabama Department of Human Resources, 579 So. 2d 640 (Ala. Civ. App. 1991) § 8.29

Smith v. Smith, 869 S.W.2d 55 (Ky. Ct. App. 1994) § 16.12

Snow v. Koeppl, 159 Wis. 2d 77, 464 N.W.2d 215 (Ct. App. 1990) § 1.20

Snyder v. Scheerer, 436 S.E.2d 299 (W. Va. 1993) § 14.26

Spaulding v. Butler, 782 A.2d 1167 (Vt. Sup. Ct. 2001) § 4.43

TABLE OF CASES

West Virginia Department of Human Services v. Peggy F., 399 S.E.2d 460 (W. Va. 1990) § 14.26

White v. Illinois, 502 U.S. 346, 112 S. Ct. 736, 116 L.Ed.2d 848 (1992) § 6.17

Whiteman v. Whiteman, No. CA94-12-229 (Ohio Ct. App. June 26, 1995) § 2.31

Wilde v. Wilde, No. A-618-00T5 (N.J. Super. Ct. App., June 22, 2001) § 4.43

Wilkenson v. Balsam, No. 2:94-CV-175 (D. Vt. Apr. 17, 1995) § 13.42

Williams v. Rappeport, 699 F. Supp. 501 (D. Md. 1988) § 1.20

Wilson v. Messinger, 840 S.W.2d 203 (Ky. 1992) § 4.43

Wisconsin v. Locke, 502 N.W.2d 891 (Wis. Ct. App. 1993) § 13.42

Wisconsin v. Maday, 507 N.W.2d 365 (Wis. Ct. App. 1993) § 13.42

Wisconsin v. S.H., No. 90-0766-CR (Wis. Ct. App. Dec. 18, 1990) § 13.42

Zamstein v. Marvasti, 692 A.2d 781 (Conn. 1997) §§ 1.18A; 13.42

Zarrett v. Zarrett, 1998 N.D. 49, 574 N.W.2d 855 (N.D. 1998) § 4.43

Zeller v. Zeller, 640 N.W.2d 53 (N.D. 2002) § 4.43

INDEX

INDEX

INDEX